ACTA UNIVERSITATIS STOCKHOLMIENSIS
Stockholm Studies in Modern Philology
New Series 16

Stockholm University

Computer mediated discourse across languages

Laura Álvarez López, Charlotta Seiler Brylla & Philip Shaw (eds.)

Stockholm Studies in Modern Philology, New Series, appears every third or fourth year and contains articles on linguistics, philological and literary subjects in modern languages.

©The authors and Acta Universitatis Stockholmiensis 2013
ISSN 0585-3583
ISBN (electronic) 978-91-87235-39-9
ISBN (print) 978-91-87235-40-5
Printed in Sweden by USAB, Stockholm 2013
Distributor: Stockholm University Library

This book was published with the financial support from The Lars Hierta Memorial Foundation.

Talks given at the meetings of Språkvetenskapliga föreningen vid Stockholms universitet 2010-2013

November 25th, 2010	Elisabeth Löfstrand. *Ockupationsarkivet från Novgorod - människor och språk i kontakt.*
May 18th, 2011	Camilla Bardel. *Variation och homogenitet i tredjespråksinlärning.*
November 9th, 2011	Jarmo Lainio. *Från svinalängornas skulor till finrummen i Strasbourg – Från invandrarspråk till europeiskt minoritetsspråk.*
May 16th, 2012	Mattias Heldner. *Interaktivt beteende – om samtal, men inte om orden.*
November 21st, 2012	Olle Josephson. *Svenska, engelska och språkpolitik.*
May 29th, 2013	Philip Shaw. *Crores of rupees on Bonfire Night: the structure of the global English vocabulary.*

Editorial board

Laura Álvarez López Associate Professor (Portuguese)
Anders Bengtsson Associate Professor (French)
Victorine Hancock Associate Professor (French)
Tora Hedin Assistant Professor (Czech)
Jenny Larsson Associate Professor (Baltic Linguistics)
Charlotta Seiler Brylla Associate Professor (German)
Philip Shaw Professor (English)

All at Stockholm University

Contents

Introduction 11

Sharing. Zum Teilen von Erzählungen in Onlineforen
Susanne Tienken 17

Compounding in a Swedish Blog Corpus
Robert Östling & Mats Wirén 45

De l'influence de la langue parlée dans les forums Internet:
aspects linguistiques et variation diastratique
Per Förnegård & Françoise Sullet-Nylander 65

Spelling and identity in Scottish internet discourse
Philip Shaw 97

Imagearbeit mit *missverstehen* in Diskussionsforen
Johanna Salomonsson 115

The role of blogs and forums in the linguistic expectations of
pilgrims on the Camino to Santiago
Una Cunningham 137

Zitate in Blogs und Tagebüchern – ein Vergleich
Sara Eriksson 155

Introduction
Laura Álvarez López, Charlotta Seiler Brylla & Philip Shaw
Stockholm University

At the end of the last century the web was conceived of as a library where information could be posted and retrieved, so that there was a fairly clear distinction between the roles of producers and consumers of information. Since then what is called Web 2.0 has emerged as a highly interactive space where all participants are both producers and consumers. Intensive users of the virtual space find that it has changed the nature of their existence in the 'non-virtual' world. In this volume we look at the linguistic and discoursal complexities of interaction in the virtual space in relation to events and discourses outside it.

The words 'linguistic and discoursal' reflect the expansion of an earlier interest in the common features of what has been called internet language (Crystal 2001 is often cited) to a wider concern with the variety of spaces opened up by the internet and their discoursal, pragmatic, and sociolinguistic characteristics. Androutsopoulos (2006: 421) refers to "a shift of focus from medium-related to user-related patterns of language use, which brings the 'variety of group practices' to the center of attention." As Herring (2008: 613) says "subsequent research has revealed computer mediated language and interaction to be sensitive to a variety of technical and situational factors, making it far more complex and variable than envisioned by early descriptions".

Internet channels are not genres, but enable the development of textual practices that draw on earlier genres and may create stable genres in the virtual space. 'Remediation' (Bolter & Grusin 1999) is the transfer of a text-type familiar in an older medium to an electronic medium, and it is a pervasive feature of internet discourse. In bereavement chatrooms (Tienken this volume), for example, narrative is used to share one's grief with a large and indeterminate audience. This could be regarded as a remediation both of the non-narrative sharing of one's grief with a similar audience afforded by wearing mourning garments and of the practice of narrative presentation of ones' problems to a more restricted audience in a self-help group. But this internet sharing is not particularly like either of these foregoing forms, and that is because the internet facilitates a number of social and discursive practices that were quite difficult in the past.

The term *affordances* has been used for these practices that the internet makes possible. Gaver defines the term as follows:

> [...] affordances are the fundamental objects of perception. People perceive the environment directly in terms of its potentials for action, without significant intermediate stages involving memory or inferences. For instance, we perceive stairways in terms of their "climbability," a measurable property of the relationship between people and stairs. (Gaver 1991: 79)

Androutsopoulos (2006) warns against too great a focus on the technical aspects of internet communication and discourse, and it is clear that the existence of an affordance does not deterministically require its use. Nevertheless, where the affordances have the potential to satisfy social needs, 'remediated' forms change quite rapidly to take advantage of them. Some affordances are at the institutional level (who can communicate and how), and others at the levels of discourse structure and content.

Institutionally, the web allows publishing without editing or at least allows the establishment of fora in which this can be done. Anyone with access can publish what they like in whatever language or language variety they like. One consequence of this is at least a potential for users of minority languages to publish more and more widely: Wikipedia versions with more than ten thousand entries exist, for example, in Neapolitan, Occitan, Low German, and Gaelic and many other occluded languages. This is an affordance that this volume particularly aims to attend to. It accommodates not only the multiple approaches to analysis called for by Herring (2008) but also discourse in a variety of languages. However our impression from the discussion of discourse in French, German, Swedish and English is that very similar features can be seen across languages. This underlines both the globalized nature of twenty-first century discourses and the role of the shared electronic environment in forming the discourses and roles available.

Another affordance at this level is the removal of geographical restriction. In principle it is as easy to listen to New Zealand radio in Sweden as to Swedish, and in a chatroom participants can interact across continents, if they want to. In particular, the nature of emigration and diaspora has been radically changed by the availability of electronic channels, and the virtual community they afford (Issa-Salwe 2006). This opportunity is, however, restricted by language barriers, particularly where local forms obscure to outsiders are used to index local identity. One might argue that English was the lingua franca of the web but this is a truth with modifications; not everyone knows English and by no means everyone wants to use it (Cunningham, this volume). The chapters in this volume show interaction in a variety of languages, and while English phrases are used and English texts quoted by users of other languages, the forums described are impenetrable to those who do not know the language in question. Language remains a barrier when distance itself has been eliminated.

A third affordance, also one with limitations, is a changed relation to time. Old texts in paper media can be destroyed and if they persist can be hard to locate; web material is hard to delete and is quite easily retrievable by search engines (and state or commercial spies) indefinitely. However, expressions of emotion or opinion in Web 2.0 rapidly lose prominence as they are pushed down the Facebook or chatroom page. A fourth affordance of the internet as institution is access to vast quantities of text, affording alarming possibilities of search by state or commercial bodies, but also an advantage specifically for linguists: the web provides a huge corpus of texts of various types, most of them quite spontaneous and unedited, which is available for corpus study (Östling and Wirén, this volume).

On the discourse level, an affordance of Web 2.0 is that it allows spontaneous sharing of experiences with a wide and indeterminate audience (Herring 2008) rather than the publication of predetermined texts so that quite private feelings and experiences can be shared in detail. In this way channels like chatrooms and Facebook blur the public and the private. Related to this is the affordance of synchronous dialogic interaction in writing, which is actually a new form of discourse, as well as the great facilitation of asynchronous interaction in writing, a remediation of exchanges of letters or notes. In this intensive interaction old strategies of politeness and face-management appear in new forms (Salomonsson, this volume).

Another discourse-level affordance is an increased and different potential for intertextuality; the copy-and-paste function and the ability to create hyperlinks to other documents change the nature of texts and authorship (Eriksson, this volume). The dialogic and mutually illuminating aspects of texts become much more explicit. The potential of earlier forms like the commonplace book and the 'album' is magnified because the production of links and citations is so simple, and in fact expected. The convergence of media in Web 2.0, the affordance to include pictures and sound means that the discourse is often, perhaps usually, multimodal. In more or less web-native genres like Facebook pages, pictures and sounds are very often inherent features.

These institutional and discoursal affordances lead to web pages which include much material which is either not text or not text written by the 'author'. But amongst these other elements there is a considerable proportion of original rapidly written, unedited, personal, often dialogic text and this in turn has resulted in the development of informal and slangy versions of the written language with many features of speech. These are non-standard in the sense that they are unlike standard written language, and also in the sense that they may represent features of non-standard, and therefore often identity-indexing, speech (Förnegård and Sullet-Nylander, this volume). Sociolinguistic analyses of this discourse show that there is language variation based on age, gender and region (Shaw, this volume).

The chapters in this volume examine internet discourse in the light of these specific affordances. A key practice afforded by the virtual world is that of 'sharing' one's experiences, opinions, listening, reading or viewing. Tienken examines the activity of 'sharing' by means of narratives of personal experience. She shows how the tools of 'non-virtual' narrative analysis can be used to distinguish narratives with new functions in new media, but also how the remediation of narratives of personal experience has transformed them, in the context of an ethic of 'sharing'. A distinction she makes which is useful for several of the chapters is that between the relatively short narratives necessary for exchanging practical advice, and the longer accounts of personal experiences where 'sharing' has a larger affective element.

In Tienken's analysis one of the key issues is who benefits from the 'sharing' of the narratives. Cunningham also looks at the sharing of experiences, but in a context which is even more clearly one where inexperienced participants can profit from the advice of the more experienced. She looks at comments and advice around walking the pilgrimage route to Santiago de Compostela and focuses particularly on the topic of language. Just like the internet, the pilgrimage route is a globalized forum and Cunningham observes the ambiguous role of 'lingua-franca' English in the globalized environment that characterizes not only the internet, but also this volume as a whole.

Eriksson looks at the effect of the discourse affordances of the internet on diary blogs, viewed as remediated versions of paper diaries. She focuses on the vastly increased potential for intertextuality and shows – in a finding that recurs in the volume in several places – that connections can be traced and many functions are retained, but the greater affordance for intertextuality results in greater use and in expansion of the functions of intertextuality.

Cunningham and Tienken look at discourse which is dialogic but fairly asymmetrical in the sense that participants are either in a role as narrator/adviser or as listener/appreciator/ advisee. In Eriksson's diaries the dialogic element is created by a single author drawing on intertextual resources (and one might observe that this surviving monologic element marks them as *early* web 2.0 discourses). Salomonsson, however, looks, using politeness theory, at chatrooms in which discussion and debate are symmetrical – people are arguing about social or political issues. The tone is a little harder and the key lexeme that Salomonsson focuses on – *missverstehen* 'misunderstand' is embedded in issues of face-saving. Misunderstandings are rather likely in the impoverished environment of a chat room (as compared to face-to-face or Skype interaction) and claims of misunderstanding can also be used to mitigate actual disagreement.

Salomonsson uses a word as a way in to examining discourse issues, but the remaining three contributions actually focus on language itself rather than discourse. As a consequence of this focus, a corpus approach and a certain amount of quantification are possible for all three. As noted above, a variety of features of the virtual environment combine to encourage a style of language quite remote from the written standard with a number of features more or less restricted to 'netspeak' (Crystal 2001) and many others that resemble spoken dialogue.

Förnegård and Sullet-Nylander examine these features of the French of the net, showing that orality is resource that can be drawn on for stylistic effect. As in Tienken's narratives, linguistic resources are used to index the persona and role that the producer wishes to establish. Nonetheless French 'netspeak' is not merely written speech. Causal conjunctions are important in 'sharing' and other dialogic interactions, and very common in speech. But while speech shows an overwhelming predominance of *parce que* 'because' over *car* 'since, for', this corpus actually contains more instances of *car*. Förnegård and Sullet-Nylander speculate that this is due to a desire for economy (*car* has fewer than half the keystrokes of *parce que)*, and this suggests another effect of remediating discourse from speech to writing: what is easy to say may be tiresome to write.

Just as internet users can index identity and style by varying the mix of 'oral' and standard written features, those who control two varieties of a language can index their identity or the social context they wish to evoke by choosing more or less locally marked forms. Shaw examines a corpus of social media pages from Scotland and shows how Scots features occur sporadically throughout, but with very little writing in consistent Scots. Standard English forms predominate; some features that are common in English 'netspeak' (Crystal 2001) are absent here because they do not sound like things Scots people would say.

Finally Östling and Wirén make use of the affordance of the web to examine very large quantities of authentic language to answer some general questions about the frequency and functions of compounds in Swedish: how frequent are novel compounds, for example? (surprisingly frequent, it turns out). More specifically: what are the associations of words which could be translated *fag, fan, freak, nerd,* and *dork* as final elements of compounds? As well as showing how examination of words can lead back to discourse and reveal subtle semantic effects that are unclear without huge corpora, the article exemplifies the use of corpus methods on internet material, and the pitfalls that have to be avoided.

The internet has become the locus of a wide variety of discourses and genres which have superficially little in common. What they do have in common is, however, their formation at the meeting point of permanent human needs and rapidly changing affordances, which lead to the transformation of old codes and genres. The articles in this volume respond to the complexity and multiplicity of internet discourse by adopting a variety of analytic approaches which we hope collectively do justice to the variety of interactions it embodies.

References

Androutsopoulos J. (2006), Introduction: Sociolinguistics and computer-mediated communication, *Journal of Sociolinguistics* 10(4), pp. 419–438.

Bolter, J. D & Grusin, R. (1999), *Remediation: Understanding New Media,* Cambridge, MA: MIT Press.

Crystal, D. (2001), *Language and the Internet.* Cambridge, U.K.: Cambridge University Press.

Issa-Salwe, A. M. (2006), The internet and the Somali diaspora: The web as a new means of expression, *Bildhaan: An International Journal of Somali Studies* 6, pp. 54-67.

Gaver, W.W. (1991), Technology Affordances, in Robertson, S. P., Olson, G. M. & Olson, J. S. (eds.), *Proceedings of the ACM CHI 91 Human Factors in Computing Systems Conference April 28 - June 5*, New Orleans, Louisiana. pp. 79-84.

Herring S. (2008), Computer-Mediated Discourse, in Tannen, D., Schiffrin, D. & Hamilton, H. (eds.), *Handbook of Discourse Analysis*, Oxford: Blackwell, pp. 618-634.

Sharing. Zum Teilen von Erzählungen in Onlineforen

Susanne Tienken

Universität Stockholm

1. Einleitung

Der Forschungsschwerpunkt im Bereich zur Sprache des Internets hat sich in den letzten Jahren grundlegend verschoben. Die „erste Welle" linguistischer CMC-Forschung[1] (Androutsopoulos 2006a: 420) zeichnete sich im Wesentlichen durch den Fokus auf die Kartierung und Typologisierung von sprachlichen Formen aus, die als neu und spezifisch für das Internet gelten. Als charakteristisch kann hier das von David Crystal (2004) geprägte Konzept des *Netspeak* angeführt werden, das sowohl eine neue Varietät als auch ein neues Medium erfassen sollte. Bereits Dürscheid (2004) reagiert darauf und stellt in ihrer Problematisierung des „Mythos Netzsprache" fest, dass auch Sprache im Internet äußerst heterogen ist und ihre Ausdrucksformen sich eben je nach Anwendungsbereich auch unterscheiden können. Es geht nunmehr weniger um die systematische Erfassung typischer Strukturmerkmale als darum, *computer-mediated discourse* und die damit einhergehenden, medial eingebundenen Praktiken zu verstehen (Androutsopoulos 2006a: 421) und als Formen von Interaktion zu untersuchen (Herring 2011). Mittlerweile sind zudem die meisten Bereiche des öffentlichen und des privaten Lebens vom Gebrauch neuer Medien durchzogen und es lässt sich deshalb wohl weniger denn je von einer homogenen Netzsprache sprechen, sondern immer nur von ihrem lokalen Gebrauch, der in einen direkten Bezug zur nicht-virtuellen Lebenswelt zu setzen ist.

Dies lässt sich recht eindrucksvoll zum Beispiel an „Peggy" illustrieren, bei welcher Micro-Blogging und Status-Updates auf Facebook als Praktiken ausgewiesen werden können (Lee 2011). An den Online-Aktivitäten von „Peggy", einer jungen, mediengewohnten Frau in Hongkong, kann Lee zeigen, dass die einzelnen neuen Medien wie *Blog*, *Facebook*, *MSN* etc. je nach kommunikativem Bedarf eingesetzt und miteinander vernetzt werden und auf konkrete Ereignisse außerhalb des WWW Bezug nehmen. Peggy doku-

---

[1] Computer-mediated communication.

mentiert nämlich unter anderem ihre gesamte Schwangerschaft in einem Portfolio verschiedener sozialer Medien, wobei sie auch während der Geburt keine Ausnahme macht. Über ihr Smartphone beschreibt sie den Wehenverlauf und teilt ihre jeweilige Befindlichkeit auf Facebook mit, was jeweils von ihren Freunden *kommentiert* wird. Das Durchleben körperlicher Erfahrung ist unauflöslich mit dem Schreiben von Status Updates verbunden. Daraus lässt sich schließen, dass die neuen Medien neue Kommunikationsformen hervorbringen, die wiederum neue Arten von *Dasein in der Welt* konstituieren.

In ähnlicher Weise wie in der Internetlinguistik hat sich in der linguistischen Erzählforschung ein Paradigmenwechsel vollzogen, nämlich der Wandel der Analyse von *Erzählungen als Text/Struktur* hin zu einer Analyse von *Erzählungen als Praxis* (vgl. De Fina & Georgakopoulou 2012). Der Begriff der Praxis zielt dabei auf die Routinen und Aktivitäten ab, die mit einem Genre und dessen zugrundeliegendem sozialen Bedürfnis verbunden sind (vgl. Fairclough 1995: 8-15). Grundlage dieser veränderten Sichtweise in der Erzählforschung ist eine dialogistische Perspektive auf Erzählen und Erzählungen (vgl. De Fina & Georgakopoulou 2008), bei der es weniger um Sprache als System geht als um *languaging*, den Sprachgebrauch. In diesem Verständnis ist die narrative Darstellung von Ereignissen weniger als statisches Endprodukt, sondern eher als dynamische Konstruktion zu verstehen, die ständiger Kalibrierung unterliegt (vgl. Linell 2009: 252). Erzählungen werden folglich nicht mehr nur im Sinne von Labov und Waletzky als eine verbale Technik betrachtet, um Geschehnisse zu rekapitulieren und einen Verlauf zu rekonstruieren (1967: 13) sondern sie werden als wechselseitiger Ausdruck kommunikativer Bedürfnisse untersucht. Das analytische Ziel ist folglich, Erzählen als Element menschlicher „Alltags- bzw. Sprachpraxis" (Tophinke 2009: 246) in der Interaktion zu verstehen (Georgakopoulou 2011). Der Gewinn einer solch veränderten Sichtweise liegt dabei vor allem darin, dass Erzählungen weniger als Artefakte betrachtet werden, die aus unterschiedlichen Komponenten bestehen, sondern eher als Werkzeuge, die von Sprachbenutzenden in Gebrauch genommen werden (Georgakopoulou 2011). Von Interesse ist, was Menschen eigentlich *tun*, wenn sie *einem anderen* etwas erzählen und sich in der Interaktion konventionalisierter Formen bedienen.

Im vorliegenden Beitrag sollen Ansätze aus der CMC-Forschung und aus der linguistischen Erzählforschung zusammengeführt werden: Anhand der Analyse von *geteilten* Erzählungen und Kommentaren in einem Onlineforum über Schwangerschaft und Geburt soll eine Praxis der Neuen Medien erschlossen werden, die fortan im Anschluss an Wee (2011) als *Sharing* bezeichnet wird.

2. Formen von *Sharing*

Das *Teilen* von Texten und Bildern mit anderen Nutzern ist aus pragmatischer Perspektive ohne Zweifel eines der deutlichsten Charakteristika sprachlicher Aktivitäten im Internet, wie sie uns heute in der partizipatorischen Form des Web 2.0 begegnen und kann als eine wesentliche Neuerung im kommunikativen Haushalt der Gesellschaft (vgl. Luckmann 1988; Luckmann 2003) angesehen werden. Eine solche Neuerung ist nicht als Zufallserscheinung zu betrachten, sondern vor allem als Effekt der Wechselwirkung von medialer Affordanz und sozialem Motiv von Sprachbenutzern (Miller & Shepherd 2004). Das bedeutet, dass mediale Neuerungen allein keine neuen Formen generieren, sondern dass die Hervorbringung in soziale Prozesse innerhalb einer Gesellschaft eingebettet ist.

Aus lexikologischer Perspektive ist vor allem die Allgegenwart des Lexems *Teilen* im Kontext Neuer und Sozialer Medien auffällig. *Geteilt* oder zum *Teilen* aufgefordert wird quasi überall. Diese Ubiquität bestärkt die Annahme, es mit einem soziokulturell relevanten Phänomen zu tun zu haben, wenn auch mit einem, das alles andere als eindeutig bestimmbar ist.

Im vorliegenden Beitrag soll es um eine Form des Teilens gehen, die zwar nicht exklusiv auf die neuen Medien beschränkt ist, die aber gerade in sozialen Medien wie Onlineforen eine zentrale Rolle spielt: nämlich um *erzählendes Teilen*.

Zum besseren Verständnis der Wechselwirkung von medialer Affordanz und sprachlich-sozialer Aktivität ist es jedoch sinnvoll, zunächst auf eine „grundlegende Form" von Sharing einzugehen. Mit einer solchen grundlegenden Form ist die Nutzung der technischen Möglichkeit zu verstehen, digitale Texte, Photos oder Filme Anderen online zugänglich zu machen. *Sharing* ist dabei vor allem als direkte Reaktion auf die mediale Affordanz des Web 2.0 aufzufassen und deshalb auch ausschließlich an das Medium gebunden. Diese Form des *Teilens vorproduzierter Inhalte* ist sowohl in den privaten wie auch in den institutionellen Domänen des Webs zu finden. So bieten z. B. Online-Versionen von Fernsehsendern, Tageszeitungen und Zeitschriften die Möglichkeit an, durch schlichtes Anklicken eines entsprechenden Buttons redaktionelle Inhalte in sozialen Medien zu veröffentlichen – eben zu *teilen*. Auch auf medialen Plattformen wie *YouTube* und *Flickr* oder, wie im Beispiel unten, auf der Social Network Site *Facebook* sind Funktionen für das Teilen von Inhalten explizit ausgewiesen und als *Teilen* benannt (siehe Abb. 1).

Bei dieser Aktivität fällt auf, dass es sich nicht nur um eine einfache Wiedergabe handelt, sondern dass ich mich jeweils bereits im Akt des Teilens als jemand positioniere, der den veröffentlichten Inhalt als relevant ansieht. *Sharing* geht also auch immer mit der Indexikalisierung von Identität einher (vgl. Bucholtz & Hall 2005). Wenn ich zum Beispiel die Botschaft der Facebookgruppe *La Révolution Syrienne en Français* (siehe Abb. 2) teile, indiziere ich durch das Teilen an sich, dass ich die Situation in Syrien 2012 für Völkermord halte und dass ich als jemand aufzufassen bin, der über einen solchen Zustand besorgt ist.

Abbildung 1: Teilen und Kommentieren redaktioneller Inhalte.

Abbildung 2: Moralische Verpflichtung als Aspekt von Sharing.

Slogans dieser Art erinnern zweifelsohne an Buttons mit politischen Botschaften, die gut sichtbar an Jacken oder Taschen getragen werden (und vor allem: wurden). Der Unterschied dieses politischen *Sharings* zum Tragen von Buttons mit politischen Slogans wie *Atomkraft – Nein danke* ist jedoch nicht unwesentlich: Bei beiden geht es zwar um den Ausdruck von Solidaritätserklärungen mit vorgeformten politischen Botschaften und beides trägt zur Konstruktion von Identität bei. Der Unterschied liegt jedoch auf der zeitlichen, räumlichen und soziopragmatischen Ebene: Im Gegensatz zum Tragen von Buttons ist das Teilen politischer Botschaften auf Facebook nämlich eine ausgesprochen kurzfristige Angelegenheit und verschwindet durch die Begrenzung des Bildschirms recht zügig aus dem Blickfeld aktueller Ereignisse, sobald neuere Status Updates Platz beanspruchen.[2] Zudem lässt sich auf Facebook als medialem Raum – im Gegensatz zum Tragen von Buttons an z. B. Bushaltestellen, Schulen etc. – über die Kontoeinstellungen beeinflussen, wer die Botschaft überhaupt empfängt. Ein weiterer Unterschied besteht darin, dass sich beim Teilen in den sozialen Medien eine Art pragmatischer Zugzwang für die Lesenden ergibt – *Share it if you care*. Dies ist in der Praxis des Teilens angelegt, was sich Interesseorganisationen wie z. B. der Naturschutzbund durch das explizite Auffordern *Bitte teilen* dem Kontext entsprechend zunutze machen:

Abbildung 3: Explizite Aufforderung zum Teilen.

---

[2] Wobei sich diese Flüchtigkeit nur auf die Sichtbarkeit des aktuellen Zeitfensters bezieht: Der Beitrag an sich bleibt auf der sogenannten Timeline der teilenden Person weiterhin recherchierbar.

Weitere, wenn auch weniger politisch funktionalisierte Varianten des *Teilens* ergeben sich aus der mobilen Technologie von Smartphone-Applikationen, bei denen zum Beispiel Zeit- und Streckenangaben der täglichen Joggingrunde als Status Update – wiederum in sozialen Medien wie z. B. Facebook oder Twitter – veröffentlicht werden können. Auch hier ist aber das *Teilen* als Reaktion auf die mediale Affordanz und als Teil der Identitätskonstruktion *sportlicher Mensch* zu verstehen.

Im Unterschied zum Erzählen in Webforen handelt es sich bei den bisher genannten Formen von *Sharing* um das Teilen vorproduzierter Texte und Bilder. Beiden Formen gemeinsam ist jedoch, dass der geteilte Inhalt im diskursiven Raum sozialer Medien als relevant hervorgehoben wird. Ebenso wie bei dem Teilen vorproduzierter Formate ist es der medialen Affordanz des partizipatorischen Webs zuzuschreiben, dass persönliche Erzählungen mehr oder weniger unaufgefordert in narrativer Form öffentlich dargeboten werden. Menschen teilen Erlebnisse nämlich unter anderem aus dem einfachen Grund, dass ihnen im partizipatorischen Web die Möglichkeit dazu gegeben wird. So wird etwa der Besucher auf der Startseite der Online-Fotoplattform *Flickr* ebenso konkret zum Teilen aufgefordert[3] wie die Trauernden auf dem Nachruf-Portal *Gedenkseiten.de*.

Bezeichnenderweise wird der Zweck von *Gedenkseiten.de* damit erklärt, dass man mit Familie und Freunden gemeinsame Erinnerungen an Verstorbene *teilen* kann. Trotz der Öffentlichkeit des Portals wird durch die Nennung von *Familie* und *Freunden* sowie durch die Darstellung vertrauter Nähe des abgebildeten Paares ein Kontext von Privatheit hergestellt.

Abbilddung 4: Gemeinsam Trauern im Web.

Anders als bei Face-to-Face-Begegnungen sind Online-Erzählungen mediatisiert und unterschiedliche semiotische Ressourcen werden zur Sinnbildung

---

[3] Nämlich durch die Aufforderung *Share your life in photos*.

herangezogen. Bei der Gestaltung einer *Gedenkseite* werden etwa sowohl visuelle als auch textuelle Gestaltungsmittel verwendet. Neben der Möglichkeit, einen Text einzustellen, können die Nutzer von *Gedenkseiten.de* Fotos hinzufügen und virtuelle Kerzen „anzünden". Mit diesen Kerzen wird Erinnern symbolhaft dargestellt und Beileid öffentlich bezeugt – Trauer wird somit *geteilt*. Dies ist wiederum konstitutiv für die Website, die folgerichtig die Anzahl der „Kerzen" auf der Startseite angibt: *196.422 brennende Kerzen*. Narrative Elemente der Gedenkseiten können mit Fotos illustriert oder mit Videoclips auf z. B. YouTube verlinkt werden. Dies entspricht zwar der medialen Konvergenz, also der grenzüberschreitenden Verwendung verschiedener vormals getrennt gehaltener semiotischer Modi im sogenannten Web 2.0 überhaupt (vgl. Androutsopoulos 2006b: 281) und ist nicht allein charakteristisch für *Sharing*. Es wird allerdings deutlich, inwiefern das Medium die Ausformung sozialer Praktiken, hier des Trauerns, beeinflusst und dazu beiträgt, die Grenzen zwischen Leben offline und Leben online sowie zwischen öffentlich und privat zunehmend zu verwischen. Hastings et al. (2007) kommen in ihrer Studie über ein Webforum für trauernde Eltern zu dem Schluss, dass die Teilnehmenden durch ihre Beiträge aktiv und gemeinsam ein Gegennarrativ zur herrschenden gesellschaftlichen Norm des – äußerst begrenzten – Redens über den Verlust eines Kindes herstellen. Anders als in anderen sozialen Zusammenhängen sei es ihnen im Forum möglich, die Erinnerung an das verstorbene Kind zu pflegen. Die Erfahrung des Verlusts eines Kindes werde durch die Kommunikation im Forum aus ihrer Individualität gelöst, wobei die Erkenntnis, dass Andere eine ähnliche Erfahrung gemacht haben, eine zentrale Rolle im Heilungsprozess trauernder Eltern spiele. Erst durch die Schilderung der eigenen Erlebnisse und Gefühle sowie durch die Rezeption der Erzählungen Anderer wird Gemeinschaft erzeugt. Teilendes Erzählen ist also ein *gemeinschaftliches kommunikatives Projekt*, was durch gegenseitige Bezugnahme ständig angezeigt wird (vgl. Arminen 1998).

Die sprachliche Gestaltungsfreiheit ist beim teilenden Erzählen bedeutend größer als beim Teilen vorproduzierter Inhalte und dementsprechend weit gestreut lassen sich persönliche Erzählungen in zahlreichen Webforen und Blogs finden (vgl. Tophinke 2009; Page 2012). Dabei kann es sich um Krankengeschichten, Jagderlebnisse oder die narrative Darbietung von Kochrezepten handeln, die einem bestimmten Lebensstil oder einer besonderen Diät verpflichtet sind. Oder eben um die Erzählung über eine Geburt. Erzählende *teilen* eine Erfahrung, indem man eine Geschichte im Web im Rahmen eines Blogs oder eines Webforums anderen zugänglich macht.

Eingewandt werden muss an dieser Stelle, dass das Phänomen des *Teilens von persönlichen Erzählungen* mit anderen keineswegs auf die Neuen Medien beschränkt ist. Auch das institutionalisierte Erzählen der eigenen Leidensgeschichte in Selbsthilfegruppen (Arminen 2004) kann als eine Form von *Sharing* verstanden werden. Besonders Krankheitsberichte in Webforen ähneln der Erzählpraxis, wie sie bei Treffen von Mitgliedern von Selbsthilfegruppen, z. B. den Anonymen Alkoholikern vorzufinden ist (Arminen 1998, 2001, 2004; Page 2012). In beiden Zusammenhängen, online und offline, ist die Selbstoffenbarung gleichermaßen relevant (vgl. Page 2012) wie die Metakommentare zur vollzogenen Praxis des Typs *Thank you for Sharing*. Gleichfalls bedeutsam ist, dass die Form des Erzählens den jeweils spezifischen Kontext, eben den des *Teilens* hervorbringt. Dass Erfahrungen qua Teilen durch Erzählen kollektiviert werden (vgl. Georgakopoulou 2005), gehört zu den Grundannahmen linguistischer Erzählforschung:

> Telling a story in a conversation can be considered as a prototypical form of human communication: In this activity language is used to [...] - share emotions and attitudes with respect to this past event and its participants. (Becker & Quasthoff 2005:1)

Bei dieser grundlegenden Annahme stellt sich allerdings die Frage, inwiefern ein *Teilen* quasi „automatisch" im Erzählvorgang enthalten ist oder ob *Teilendes Erzählen* als Kontext eben interaktiv herzustellen ist (vgl. Auer 1986; Gumperz 1992; Quasthoff 2001; Becker & Quasthoff 2005; Kern, Morek & Ohlhus 2012). *Teilen* „passiert" nicht einfach irgendwie durch die Einbettung in einen bestimmten Kontext, sondern es wird vielmehr von den Interagierenden aktiv gestaltet. Das teilende Erzählen in einem Webforum an sich definiert die Situation, in der sich das Erzählen ereignet, unvermeidlicherweise als Situation *von Sharing*. Erzählungen können daher mit Quasthoff (1980: 180-182) als „rahmenrelevante Diskurseinheiten" betrachtet werden, bei denen die *Art und Weise der Erfahrungsrepräsentation* den Kontext, unter anderem die soziale Beziehung zwischen den Interagierenden, konstituiert. Dabei ist die Orientierung am Anderen, an erwarteten Reaktionen sowie an vorherigen Beiträgen von zentraler Bedeutung. Um *Sharing* als sinngebende Praxis von Interagierenden im kommunikativen Haushalt einer Gesellschaft zu verstehen, bedarf es also einer dialogistischen Perspektive. Die Frage ist deshalb: Was macht Erzählen zu *Sharing*?

3. Material und Methode: Ethische Stellungnahme

Das hauptsächliche Datenset dieser Untersuchung besteht aus 54 Threads zum Thema Geburt, d. h. sämtlichen Threads, die in Rahmen eines gewählten Webforums für werdende Eltern unter der Sparte *Geburtsberichte* innerhalb eines Jahres (November 2011-November 2012) angelegt wurden. Hinzu kommen 50 Threads aus der Sparte *Hurra, endlich schwanger (1.-5. Monat)* aus der gleichen abgegrenzten Zeitspanne.

Forum für werdende Eltern		
Hurra, endlich schwanger (1.-5. Monat) Alles was die ersten Monate einer Schwangerschaft betrifft	77641 Beiträge	1785 Themen
Endspurt - gemeinsam Kugeln (6.-10. Monat) Alle Themen rund um die letzten Monate der Schwangerschaft...	366158 Beiträge	1450 Themen
Sternenkinder für alle Mütter und Väter, die ihr Kind durch eine Fehl- oder Totgeburt verloren haben.	3319 Beiträge	199 Themen
Geburtsberichte Erzählt eure spannenden Geburtserlebnisse	2427 Beiträge	306 Themen

Abbildung 5: Spartenangebot des gewählten Forums.

Bei den *Geburtsberichten* der gewählten Zeitspanne handelt es sich in 53 Fällen um kontextuell elizitierte, forschungsunabhängig entstandene persönliche Erzählungen, sowie um die jeweils folgenden veröffentlichten Kommentare. Die Bezeichnung *Geburtsbericht* entspricht nicht der sprachwissenschaftlichen Auffassung von *Bericht* (vgl. z. B. Quasthoff 1980), sondern ist eher als eine Art Ethnokategorie, also Selbstdefinition der Sprachbenutzenden zu verstehen. Aus linguistischer Sicht sind sie als *persönliche Erzählungen* zu kategorisieren. Die Teilnehmenden selbst gebrauchen durchgehend *Bericht*, wenn sie sich explizit auf den veröffentlichten Text beziehen. *Erzählen* und *berichten* wird von den Teilnehmenden synonym gebraucht. Mit kontextuell elizitiert ist hier gemeint, dass die Erzählenden zwar der Aufforderung der Website nachkommen, *spannende Geburtserlebnisse* zu *erzählen*, eine Aufforderung durch die forschende Person jedoch unterbleibt. Hinzu kommt aus dieser Sparte ein nicht-elizitierter Thread mit dem Angebot, Fragen zu einer Hausgeburt zu beantworten. Bei den Threads aus der Sparte *Hurra, endlich schwanger* sind 50 zur näheren Durchsicht ausgewählt worden. Nach einem seriellen und kontrastierenden Lesen ist aus dem Datenset jeweils ein Thread zur näheren Analyse ausgewählt worden, der als typisch identifiziert werden konnte. Sowohl der initiierende Beitrag als auch die Kommentare werden im Rückgriff auf Fragestellungen der linguistischen Erzähltheorie mit Hilfe eines Close Reading Verfahrens auf Aspekte sozialer Interaktion und sozialer Sinnerzeugung hin untersucht.

Da es sich beim gewählten Material um persönliche Erzählungen und Kommentare von Individuen handelt, möchte ich im Folgenden ethische Betrachtungen und Vorbehalte bei der Verwendung von Material aus dem Internet darlegen.

Ethische Stellungnahmen sind im Bereich der Forschung zum Sprachgebrauch im Internet verhältnismäßig rar gesät und Richtlinien verbleiben auf dem Stand des Empfehlenswerten. Anders als bei narrativen Interviews, Observationen oder Versuchsanordnungen fehlen bisher eindeutige Richtlinien, inwiefern die Zustimmung von Usern bei der Verwendung ihrer im

Internet veröffentlichten Texte zu wissenschaftlichen Zwecken erforderlich ist. Stommel und Koole (2010: 362) geben in diesem Zusammenhang zu bedenken, dass die Kontaktaufnahme mit Forumsteilnehmerinnen und -teilnehmern von der Community als störend empfunden werden sowie mitunter wegen fehlender Kontaktangaben unmöglich sein kann.

Bei Untersuchungen zum Sprachgebrauch im Internet sind weiterhin Aspekte des Datenschutzes zu beachten. Für die vorliegende Studie sind keine Daten zu Personen erhoben oder gespeichert worden. In der Analyse wird lediglich auf Informationen zurückgegriffen, die explizit oder implizit in den Beiträgen im Forum enthalten sind, aber z. B. keine, die im Profil der Erzählenden angegeben werden, wie z. B. der Wohnort. Neben ethischen hat dies auch forschungsstrategische Gründe, da lediglich aufgegriffen wird, was von den Erzählenden selber relevant gemacht wird. Dazu gehört zum Beispiel das Geschlecht der Erzählenden.

Um die Integrität der User zu schützen, sind die Nicknames und der Name des Forums in der Untersuchung anonymisiert worden. Da jedoch über die Volltextsuche Beiträge in öffentlichen Internetforen ausfindig gemacht werden können, gilt es bei jedem wörtlichen Zitat, das Forschungsinteresse mit der Wahrung persönlicher Integrität abzuwägen. Ethische Vorbehalte stehen deshalb hinter der Entscheidung, Erzählungen aus der Sparte *Sternenkinder* (vgl. Abb. 5) sowie Erzählungen Minderjähriger und Erzählungen, die Rückschlüsse auf gesundheitliche Probleme zulassen, nicht zur Analyse heranzuziehen.

Neben der persönlichen Integrität von Usern ist das Urheberrecht zu berücksichtigen (z.B. Crystal 2011: 14). Bei der Wahl des Forums für diese Studie wurde dementsprechend auf solche Foren verzichtet, bei denen die Betreiber in den Forenregeln urheberrechtliche Ansprüche auf den Inhalt der Website stellen und die weitere Verwendung von Texten aus dem Forum in anderen Kontexten explizit untersagen. Es wurden zudem diejenigen Foren ausgeschlossen, bei denen der Zugang ein Passwort erfordert, da in diesem Fall davon auszugehen ist, dass sich die User bewusst einer vollständigen Öffentlichkeit entziehen. Gewählt wurde ein uneingeschränkt öffentliches Forum, das die Benutzer ausdrücklich zum verantwortungsvollen Umgang mit den eigenen Beiträgen auffordert.

Trotz der offensichtlichen Problematik bietet die Beschäftigung mit Erzählungen und Diskussionsbeiträgen aus dem Internet einen spezifischen heuristischen Wert (Rutter & Smith 2005): Die unterschiedlichen Formate der Neuen Medien ermöglichen die Analyse spontaner persönlicher Erzählungen in einem nie zuvor gewesenen Ausmaß (vgl. Page 2012). Es handelt sich bei Forumsbeiträgen um ein Material, das forschungsunabhängig entstanden ist und das zudem in eine Interaktionsform eingebunden ist. Anders als bei elizitierten Erzählungen können bei der Analyse der Beiträge aus den Webforen zu Schwangerschaft und Geburt auch interaktionale Aspekte beachtet werden, und Schlüsse für die Bedeutung medialer Affordanzen bei Prozessen sozialer Sinnbildung in der Interaktion gezogen werden.

4. *Sharing* als das Teilen von Ressourcen

Wie oben diskutiert, *teilen* Erzählende in Webforen ihre Erlebnisse und Erfahrungen mit anderen Teilnehmenden im Forum, im untersuchten Fall Erfahrungen mit Schwangerschaft und Geburt. Die Teilnehmenden werden im Forum als *werdende Eltern* kategorisiert (siehe Abb. 5), was nahelegt, dass es sich bei den Teilnehmenden um Personen handelt, die sich zwar nicht in identischen aber doch ähnlichen Lebenssituationen befinden, befinden werden oder befunden haben, ohne einander jedoch persönlich zu kennen oder eine familiäre Bindung aufzuweisen.[4] Wee (2011) schlägt vor, *Sharing* im übertragenen Sinne als das Teilen von Ressourcen zu verstehen. Bei *Sharing* als Aktivität geht es dann um die Darstellung einer Erfahrung, die eine Person entweder bereits gemacht hat oder die zum Zeitpunkt des Erzählens noch andauert (vgl. Wee 2011). Das wäre im Kontext eines Webforums zu Schwangerschaft und Geburt das abgeschlossene Erlebnis der Geburt eines Kindes gegenüber der noch andauernden Schwangerschaft.

Gemäß Wee (2011) beeinflusst diese Art von Aspektualität, wer den „Nutzen" aus der Situation des *Sharing* ziehen kann: Teile die erzählende Person eine bereits abgeschlossene Erfahrung, sei zu erwarten, dass die Schilderung den Adressaten bei der zukünftigen Bewältigung einer ähnlichen Situation – hier dem Bewältigen von Schwangerschaft und Geburt – dienlich sein könne. Dauere die Erfahrung hingegen noch an, liege der Nutzen des Teilens eher bei der erzählenden Person. Beide Konstellationen – andauernde bzw. abgeschlossene Erfahrung – lassen sich im Webforum finden und sollen im Folgenden anhand der Beispiele *Schwangerschaftsübelkeit* und *Der krönende Abschluss* diskutiert werden.

4.1 Schwangerschaftsübelkeit

Die „Aspektualität" tritt im Falle des Threads *Schwangerschaftsübelkeit* deutlich hervor: Nach der Eröffnung der Interaktionssituation durch den informellen Gruß *Hallo* schildert die Threadstarterin (TS1) eine noch andauernde Erfahrung, nämlich die von Übelkeit aufgrund von Schwangerschaft

---

[4] Es ist möglich, dass sich auch Personen im Forum bewegen, die weder schwanger noch Eltern sind. Diese treten allerdings nicht in Erscheinung und können deshalb nicht erfasst werden.

und eines Dilemmas nach der Befragung ärztlicher Expertise. Diese Erfahrung an sich ist anderen Schwangeren, denen übel ist, jedoch kaum dienlich. Auch ist von einem Katharsis-Effekt für TS1 im Sinne eines sich-von-der-Seele-Schreibens nichts zu bemerken. Bisher „profitiert" also keine der Teilnehmenden von der Darstellung allein. Vielmehr skizziert TS1 ein Problem, bei dessen Lösung sie auf Hilfe hofft: Sie leidet unter ihrer Schwangerschaftsübelkeit, besonders da sie am (auf das Posting) folgenden Tag an einem Betriebsausflug teilnehmen möchte. Die zu behandelnde Erfahrung wird auch in der gewählten Überschrift des Threads relevant gemacht, was den Lesenden eine rasche Identifizierung des zentralen Problems ermöglicht. Den von der Frauenärztin vorgeschlagenen medizinischen Präparaten gegen die Übelkeit begegnet sie nach weiterer Informationssuche im Internet offenbar mit Misstrauen (siehe Abb. 6).

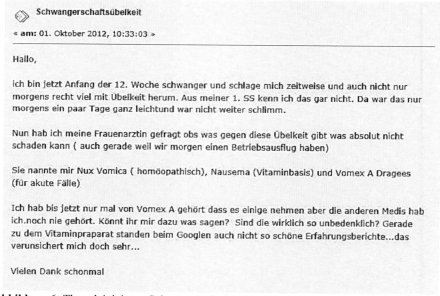

Abbildung 6: Threadeinleitung Schwangerschaftsübelkeit.

TS1 bittet aufgrund ihrer Sorge explizit durch die Fragen *Könnt ihr mir dazu was sagen? Sind die wirklich so unbedenklich?* um Orientierungshilfe von Seiten derer, die bereits Erfahrung mit den aufgeführten Medikamenten gemacht haben. Die Annahme sozialer Verbindlichkeit wird durch den im Voraus formulierten *Dank* indiziert und entspricht den Interaktionsnormen, wie sie in hauptsächlich von Frauen besuchten Webumgebungen vorzufinden sind (vgl. Herring 1994; Ley 2007).

Bereits Minuten nach ihrem Posting erhält TS1 die erste, augenscheinlich hastig verfasste Antwort, bei der zwar ihr informelles *Hallo* mit einem ebenso informellen *hi* erwidert wird, die allerdings nur als teilresponsiv angesehen werden kann, da sie zum einen nur eines der angesprochenen Präparate behandelt, zum anderen nichts über Unbedenklichkeit der Medikamente aussagt:

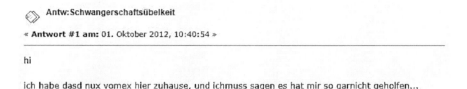

Abbildung 7: Teilresponsivität in Antwort #1.

Diese Antwort wird offensichtlich als nicht ausreichend nützlich bewertet, denn nach einigen Stunden ohne weitere Reaktion auf die Anfrage der Threadstarterin wird der Bedeutsamkeit des Problems durch ein Posting einer weiteren Teilnehmerin im Thread beigepflichtet:

Abbildung 8: Affiliation und Anspruch überindividueller Relevanz in Antwort #2.

Interessanterweise wird zum einen durch *Das würde mich auch interessieren* sowie durch die wörtliche Wiederholung des im Voraus ausgesprochenen *Danke schonmal* die affiliierende Haltung zum Posting von TS1 signalisiert, zum anderen aber auch durch den Gebrauch des Indefinitpronomens *man* die überindividuelle Relevanz des aufgegriffenen Dilemmas indiziert. Der „Nutzen" des Sharing im Sinne von Wee (2011) liegt also nicht nur bei TS1, sondern durch die Öffentlichkeit der Interaktion auch bei anderen Mitgliedern des Forums, die von den explizit angeforderten Erfahrungsberichten profitieren können. Die kommunikative Konstellation ist also von der medialen Affordanz, den strukturell vorgegebenen Möglichkeiten des Forums zur Partizipation geprägt.

Was hier inhaltlich zu beobachten ist – die Äußerung von Misstrauen gegenüber der Unbedenklichkeit der von der Frauenärztin empfohlenen Medikamente und die Anforderung von Erfahrungsberichten – lässt sich im Anschluss an Anthony Giddens Reflexivitätstheorie deuten, nämlich, dass sich Individuen der Postmoderne in verstärktem Ausmaß an den Erfahrungen von Peers und weniger an Autoritäten bzw. Experten orientieren (Giddens 1991; vgl. Wee 2011). Die Beobachtung von Interaktionen in Webforen wie der hier angeführten kann darüber hinaus verdeutlichen, dass es sich bei dieser

Umorientierung nicht um einen bloßen Austausch der wissenstragenden Bezugsperson geht, sondern vor allem um den Einbezug von subjektiven Empfindungen der Antwortgebenden sowie um eine veränderte Position der Hilfesuchenden. Bedeutsam ist nämlich, dass *Antworten* im Plural erwünscht sind, was der Hilfesuchenden eine größere Bandbreite an wählbaren Handlungsalternativen eröffnet.

Im Laufe des Nachmittags gehen dann auch auf wesentlich verschiedenen Erfahrungen basierende Antworten ein, was die beiden nachfolgenden Beispiele demonstrieren. In *Antwort #3* wird die Wirksamkeit eines Präparats bestätigt, in *Antwort #5* dahingegen die erfahrene Wirkungslosigkeit:

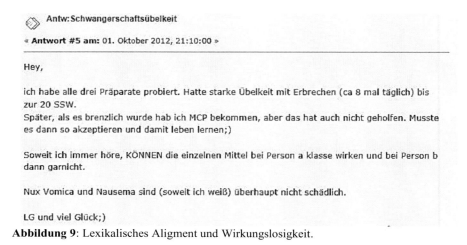

Abbildung 9: Lexikalisches Aligment und Wirkungslosigkeit.

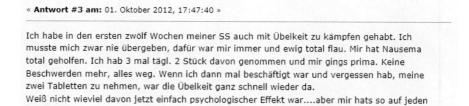

Abbildung 10: Lexikalisches Alignment und Wirksamkeit.

Beide Teilnehmerinnen vollziehen durch die Wiederholung von *Übelkeit* ein lexikalisches *Alignment* (vgl. Pickering & Harrod 2006) und signalisieren somit ihr *Einverständnis mit der interaktiven Situation*, nämlich des Erfahrungsaustausches über Schwangerschaftsübelkeit. Gleichzeitig bezeugen Sie durch diese Wiederholung auch ihre *Identifikation mit der Situation von TS1*, was als eine *Affiliation* zu deuten ist (Stivers 2008; Chen 2012): Die eigene, bereits durchlebte Situation wird mit der gegenwärtig andauernden von TS1 gleichgesetzt.

Bedeutsam ist aber darüber hinaus, dass sich die Teilnehmerinnen durch das Beschreiben der eigenen Symptome sowie durch die Bestätigung der Einnahme der bereits genannten Medikamente aber auch als qualifiziert Antwortende darstellen. Erst nach diesem Vorlauf wird der Aufforderung von TS1 nachgekommen, eine Einschätzung der Medikamente abzugeben. Auffällig ist dabei vor allem, dass die dargestellte Erfahrung nicht als unumstößliche Wahrheit oder eben als anzunehmender *Ratschlag* konstruiert wird, sondern durch die Darstellung in der ersten Person Singular als subjektiv erfahren: *Mir hat Nausema total geholfen* bzw. *Später als es brenzlich wurde hab ich MCP bekommen, aber das hat auch nicht geholfen. Musste es dann so akzeptieren und damit leben lernen.*

Beide Teilnehmerinnen verstärken zudem die Subjektivität ihrer Aussage, indem sie die medizinisch feststellbare Allgemeingültigkeit der eigenen Erfahrung verringern: *Weiß nicht wieviel davon jetzt einfach ein psychologischer Effekt war.* Bei Antwort #5 kommt die Relativität der Aussage durch die Polarisierung von *Person a* und *Person b* sowie durch die typografisch markierte Verwendung des Modalverbs *können* zum Ausdruck: *Soweit ich immer höre, KÖNNEN die einzelnen Mittel bei Person a klasse wirken und bei Person b dann garnicht.* Es wird folglich nicht einmal der Versuch unternommen, eine Art Expertenstatus zu beanspruchen. *Sharing* unterscheidet sich somit eindeutig von der Aktivität des *Beratens* (vgl. Locher 2006) oder anderen Formen der Wissensvermittlung online, die eine Vereindeutigung von Wissen anstreben, „Wahrheit" beanspruchen und ein geringes Maß an Selbstoffenbarung aufweisen (vgl. Wee 2011: 360).

Erzählen persönlicher Erfahrungen bedeutet immer auch die Evaluierung eines Geschehnisses aus der Perspektive der erzählenden Person. Beim *Sharing* geht es darüber hinaus gerade nicht um die Vermittlung einer Perspektive, sondern um eine soziale Praxis, um den *Austausch* von Erfahrungen, der einer gegenseitigen Rückversicherung gewählter Handlungsalternativen dient. In „Schwangerschaftsübelkeit" zeigt sich dies darin, dass TS1 früh am Morgen, nicht einmal 24 Stunden nach dem Anlegen des Threads berichtet, für welche Behandlung sie sich entschieden hat, nämlich *die Globulis* und *die Vomex* und welche Maßnahmen sie eventuell ergreifen wird, nämlich *evtl zu Nausema wechseln, wenns nix bringt* (vgl. Abb. 11). Es gibt zwar keinen konkreten Hinweis darauf, inwiefern die vorhergehenden Antworten sie bei ihrer Entscheidung beeinflusst haben, aber es wird deutlich, dass TS1 keine Handlungsalternativen äußert, die die im Thread diskutierten in Frage stellen könnten.

Obwohl also die Aspektualität in *Schwangerschaftsübelkeit* ausgesprochen deutlich ist, tritt weniger deutlich hervor, wer in der gegebenen Situation eigentlich profitiert. TS1 *weiß* am Ende des Threads konkret vermutlich nicht mehr als am Anfang, nur hat sie offensichtlich ihre eingangs offenbarte *Unsicherheit* überwinden können. Insofern lässt sich zwar von einem Nutzen

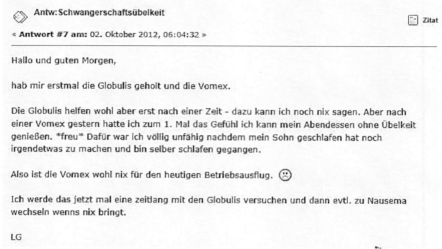

Abbildung 11: Abschließender Beitrag von TS1.

für TS1 sprechen, der jedoch nicht folgenlos für die anderen Teilnehmenden bleibt. Dass TS1 ihre Entscheidung den anderen Teilnehmenden offenbart, kann möglicherweise weniger als ein Teilen von Ressourcen als vielmehr eine Form von *Commitment* gegenüber dem Forum und der dort ausgeübten Praxis aufgefasst werden (Ley 2007).

4.2 Der krönende Abschluss

Während es sich beim Sharing in *Schwangerschaftsübelkeit* um verschriftlichtes konversationelles Erzählen handelt, um eine Art *Small Stories* (Georgakopoulou 2007), ist *Der krönende Abschluss* als eine persönliche Erzählung im klassischen Sinne zu betrachten, die den strukturellen Kriterien im Sinne von Labov/Waletzky (1997 [1967]) durchaus entspricht. Dies ist insofern wenig erstaunlich, da es sich um vom Forum elizitierte Erzählungen handelt, auch wenn dies auf munterere Weise geschieht als dies bei Labov/Waletzky der Fall war[5]. Allerdings liegt anders als bei forschungselizitierten Erzählungen keine Asymmetrie vor. Die Erzählenden folgen der Aufforderung, *spannende Geburtserlebnisse* zu liefern (siehe Abb. 5). Entsprechend sind in der Sparte Geburtsberichte durchgängig wesentlich längere Schilderungen über die Geburt eines Kindes zu verzeichnen, wobei es sich bei der erzählenden Person in sämtlichen Fällen um die Mutter des neugeborenen

---

[5]Dort wurden Situationsschilderungen ernsthafter Lebensgefahr angefordert.

Kindes handelt.[6] Sowohl Erstgebärende als auch Mehrfachgebärende veröffentlichen Geburtserzählungen in dem untersuchten Webforum. Die Aspektualität des Teilens von Erfahrungsressourcen ist eindeutig: Die im Kontext relevante Erfahrung, die Geburt, ist bereits durchlebt. Inwiefern der Nutzen deshalb bei den Lesenden liegt, bleibt allerdings zu diskutieren. Als Teilnehmende in der Interaktion treten nämlich sowohl Frauen in Erscheinung, die eine Geburt noch vor sich haben, als auch Frauen, die bereits eine oder auch schon mehrere Geburten hinter sich haben.

Erzählungen in Gesprächen haben oftmals eine Art zweistufiges Präludium, *story preface* (Ochs & Capps 2001), in dem die/der Erzählende zunächst den Anspruch auf einen längeren Turn, nämlich die Erzählung, ankündigt (z. B.: *Also, weisst Du, was mir gestern passiert ist?*) und der/die Interaktionspartner/in diesen Anspruch akzeptiert (z.B.: *Nee, was denn?*). Im Webforum dürfte diese Funktion eine untergeordnete Rolle spielen, da in der Sparte *Geburtsberichte* explizit zum Erzählen aufgefordert wird und somit um den Redeanspruch an sich nicht mehr verhandelt werden muss. Auch die Konkurrenz zu anderen Interaktionsteilnehmern entfällt: Im Webforum kann niemand unterbrochen werden. Sacks (1992: 226) gibt dem *story preface* einen erweiterten Sinn: [...] it is an utterance that asks for the right to produce extended talk, and says that the talk will be interesting, as well as doing other things.

Die Erzählenden müssen also nicht nur einen Turn rechtfertigen, sondern, quasi als Nebeneffekt, einleitend einer anderen Erwartung gerecht werden, nämlich der, ein relevantes Erlebnis als *interessant* anzukündigen. Verblüffenderweise wird im Forum denn auch explizit zum *spannenden* Erzählen aufgefordert, was nicht nur die Erzählung inhaltlich und stilistisch vorstrukturiert, sondern eben auch die Interaktionsrollen prägt und somit auch die Gestaltung *zur* Situation beeinflusst. Dies ist grundlegend für das Verständnis vom erzählenden Teilen als Praxis.

Zur Ankündigung einer lesenswerten Erzählung stellt das Webforum den Erzählenden die Affordanz der *Überschrift* bereit, die aber von den Erzählenden noch mit Inhalt gefüllt werden muss. Was erwartungsgemäß auch geschieht. Erzählen impliziert immer die interaktionale Relevantsetzung einer bestimmten Erfahrung und die Annahme, dass die Erfahrung auch für das Lesepublikum oder die Zuhörerschaft von Bedeutung ist. *Spannendes* Erzählen ist dahingegen als Zugeständnis an die Anderen zu verstehen. Beim Sharing soll sich niemand langweilen. Was anscheinend auch nicht geschieht. Anders als bei dem kurz gefassten teilenden Erzählen in *Schwangerschaftsübelkeit*, bei dem die Überschrift die zentrale Problematik nüchtern zusammenfasst, handelt es sich bei der Überschrift *Der krönende Abschluss oder So einfach kann gebären sein* um ein Spiel mit der Kollokation *krönender Abschluss* sowie mit dem idiomatischen Muster *X oder So einfach kann*

---

[6] Erzählungen von Vätern fehlen im untersuchten Dataset gänzlich.

Y sein (vgl. Abb. 12). Zudem handelt es sich um ein Spiel mit den Erwartungen darüber, wie eine Geburt zu bewältigen ist. *So einfach kann Gebären sein* signalisiert somit ein hohes Maß an *reportability* (vgl. Labov 2010), oder eben ein hohes Maß an *shareability*. Das Wissen darüber, wie eine Geburt einfach und handlungsmächtig zu bemeistern ist, muss zweifelsohne als Ressource gedeutet werden, die zumindest denen etwas nutzen kann, die noch mindestens eine Geburt vor sich haben. Die Threadstarterin (TS2) beginnt ihre Erzählung mit einer Frage, die im mündlichen Erzählen häufig erscheint und die auch nur von der erzählenden Person selber beantwortet werden kann, nämlich *Wo fange ich jetzt am besten an* (vgl. Labov 2010). Labov (2010) geht davon aus, dass die grundlegende Dynamik von Erzählungen auf die wechselseitige Beziehung von Erzähl- und Glaubwürdigkeit zurückzuführen ist. Das Vorkommen von *Where should I begin?* Einheiten sieht er als erstes Element einer narrativen Präkonstruktion, die temporal und kausal auf die Schilderung des *most reportable events* hinführt:

> Before beginning a narrative, a narrator must construct a chain of events, each the cause of its successor, that links the most reportable event of the narrative to an initiating event set in an initial matrix that needs no further accounting and is not in itself reportable. (Labov 2010: 21).

Auch in „Der krönende Abschluss" (vgl. Abb. 12) lässt sich ohne Zweifel eine Ereigniskette rekonstruieren, bei der die gelungene Hausgeburt des vierten Kindes der Erzählerin das Kernereignis ausmacht, worauf die Überschrift ja auch schon hinweist. Zudem kündigt TS2 sogar selbst die *Vorgeschichte* an, *die für einiges ausschlaggebend war*. Sicherlich lässt sich diese Einheit so deuten, dass die Erzählerin auf diese Weise die Kausalität der Erzählung indiziert und die nachfolgenden Darlegungen rechtfertigt. Bei einer solchen Sichtweise, die sich im Prinzip ausschließlich für die Strukturierung von Erzählungen interessiert und auch die Vorgeschichte als „not in itself reportable" betrachtet, geraten allerdings pragmatische Aspekte aus dem Blickfeld, die für das teilende Erzählen[7] von zentraler Bedeutung sind. *Wo fange ich jetzt am besten an?* leitet nämlich nicht nur die Erzählung ein, sondern eben immer gleichzeitig auch die Beziehung zwischen erzählender und lesender bzw. zuhörender Person, was für Sharing als Praxis von Bedeutung ist. Es handelt sich um eine Situationseröffnung (vgl. Mondada & Schmitt 2010), bei der sich eine erzählende Person Anderen zuwendet und die Bereitschaft signalisiert, ihnen auf bestmögliche Weise eine Geschichte zu erzählen. Dies ist das kontextuelle Wesen von *Sharing*.

---

[7] Und vermutlich beim Erzählen überhaupt.

Der krönende Abschluss oder So einfach kann gebären sein
« am: 17. September 2012, 19:14:17 »

Wo fange ich jetzt am besten an....

Ich glaube bei meiner Vorgeschichte,die für einiges ausschlaggebend war:

Meine erste Tochter kam per Not KS in Vollnarkose nach 21. Std Wehen und PDA.

Die Herztöne gingen durch den Stress irgendwann in den Keller und es wurde vermutet,dass mein Becken zu klein ist (Töchterchen mal mit 50cm,3470g und 34 cm KU).

Bei meinem Sohn hiess es dann irgendwann,dass er ziehmlich gross und schwer wird,dass er garantiert nicht durchs Becken passt und deswegen am besten ein geplanter KS besser ist....erst wehrte ich mich wehement,dann liess ich mich überreden,nachdem der Chefarzt (und die müssen es ja wissen) meinte,dass er def. nicht ins Becken passt,weil er ja 10 Tage vor ET noch nicht mal annähernd reingerutscht ist.
Mein "Riesenkind" kam dann mit 52 cm,3790g und 36 cm KU per prim. KS (wo ich mir noch im OP liegend hätte in den Hintern beissen können,dass ich dem Mist zugestimmt habe).

Mir ging es nach den KS gut (körperlich),aber innerlich wusste ich,dass es das nicht gewesen sein kann.

Mein Gefühl sagte mir immer,dass ich dazu imstande bin ein Kind normal zur Welt zu bringen.

Als ich dann mit Zwerg Nummer 3 schwanger wurde begann ich mich zu informieren......und ja,es war möglich nach 2 KS es spontan zu versuchen,wenn man gewisse Dinge beachtet.

Ich fand ein KKH welches mir die spontane Geburt ermöglichen sollte......

Es klappte....unter grossen Stress,weil der liebe Oberarzt entweder einen mega Zeitdruck hatte oder immense Angst vor einer Ruptur...ich weiss es nicht.

Unter Hektik und Kristellern (absolutes No Go nach KS) wurde meine 3. Maus spontan geboren.

Zuerst happy,dass es geklappt hat,ihm nachhinein traurig,dass ich so eingeschränkt entbinden musste (durfte weder baden,noch laufen,Dauer CTG,Wehenhemmer,weil denen die Wehen zu schnell kamen,Dammschnitt ohne gefragt zu werden,Kristellern,Powerpressen etc.).

Nummer 4 schlich sich unbemerkt ein.....mein Mann wollte sich sterilisieren lassen,Termin stand schon fast,dann das.....trotz Kondom und Kontrolle danach schwanger.

Nach langem hin und her wurd entschieden...das Kind bleibt!

Abbildung 12: Preface von Der krönende Abschluss.

Die Gestaltung der *Vorgeschichte* geschieht schließlich immer im Hinblick darauf, dem Anderen Zugang zum eigenen Empfinden und zur gewählten Handlungsalternative (hier *das einfache Gebären*) zu ermöglichen, was im vorliegenden Fall durch den expliziten Ausdruck der eigenen, inneren *Stimme* geschieht (vgl. Wortham 2001): *[...] aber innerlich wusste ich, dass es das nicht gewesen sein kann. Mein Gefühl sagte mir immer, dass ich dazu imstande bin ein Kind normal zur Welt zu bringen.* Diese Äußerung impliziert zudem, dass der medizinische Eingriff des Kaiserschnitts als *unnormal* kategorisiert wird.

Die eigene Stimme wird der zunächst unpersönlich gehaltenen medizinischen Expertise gegenübergestellt […] *es wurde vermutet, dass mein Becken zu klein ist, Bei meinem Sohn hiess es dann irgendwann, dass er ziemlich gross und schwer wird.* Auch medizinische Berufskategorien wie der *Chefarzt* sowie der *Oberarzt* werden genannt, wobei deren Kompetenz aufgrund falscher Beurteilung (*Riesenkind*) und mangelnden Einfühlungsvermögens (*unter grossen Stress*) stark in Frage gestellt wird. Im Laufe der Vorgeschichte positioniert sich TS2 als eine, deren Handlungsmächtigkeit bei der Geburt ungerechtfertigterweise durch medizinische Experten stark eingeschränkt wurde (*dann liess ich mich überreden, Dammschnitt, ohne gefragt zu werden*) und die vollzogene Prozedur eines geplanten Kaiserschnitts als *Mist* verurteilt (vgl. Nentwich 2009). Es lässt sich also ebenso wie bei „Schwangerschaftsübelkeit" ein grundlegendes Misstrauen gegenüber Experten feststellen, wobei die Threadstarterin in „Der krönende Abschluss" eine Handlungsalternative nicht mehr diskutieren muss, sondern ihre Erfahrung bereits als Ressource einbringen kann.

Sämtliche geschilderten Ereignisse der Vorgeschichte wären sicherlich in sich reportable gewesen, ein Ausbau zu einer eigenständigen persönlichen Erzählung wäre aber dem Anliegen von TS2 nicht dienlich. Stattdessen wird die Vorgeschichte Bestandteil eines Shareable, nämlich der alternativen, selbstbestimmten Geburt. Das Verhalten der Hebamme steht dem der eingangs genannten Ärzte konträr gegenüber, sie tut nämlich das, was TS2 ihr sagt:

> Sie fragte mich, was ich denn machen möchte, ich sagte ihr dann, dass sie bitte einmal nachschauen soll, wie weit sich untenherum schon was getan hat und ich danach wieder in die Wanne möchte.
>
> Sie untersuchte mich schnell, MuMu 3-4 cm offen, Kind tief im Becken.
>
> Also ich wieder in die Wanne gehuscht und da erstmal noch eine halbe Stunde alleine gedöst, geatmet, getönt und über Whatsapp die Septembärmädels auf den neusten Stand gehalten.
>
> Gegen 8.40 Uhr wollte ich dann gerne die Hebamme und meinen Mann bei mir haben.

Abbildung 13: Inszenierung der Hebamme.

Die Hebamme erhält dementsprechend auch keine eigene Stimme wie die Ärzte, sondern das Ergebnis ihrer medizinischen Untersuchung *MuMu 3-4 cm, Kind tief im Becken* wird in den Erzählfluss von TS2 völlig unmarkiert integriert. Die Hebamme wird als eine erwünschte Figur inszeniert, deren Expertentum die eigene Handlungsmächtigkeit nicht bedroht.

> Irgendwann ging ich ins Bett und schlief ein.
>
> Der Samstag war ruhig,der Sonntag auch....
>
> Montag früh wieder Wehen...Mist...gerade heute,wo sich Besuch angesagt hat.
>
> Ich warnte Menne vor erreichbar zu sein,backte schnell den Kuchen und genoss dann doch den Tag mit meinen Mädels (Danke an Carina,Hanne und Tine!!!)
>
> Den ganzen Tag über kamen die Wehen in Abständen zwischen 25 und 5 min.....ich war genervt,hatte keine Lust mehr,wollte nur noch schlafen.
>
> Bin dann um 21.20 Uhr ins Bett.....und schlief die Nacht durch.
>
> Am Dienstag ging der Spass von vorne wieder los...Wehen zwischen 25 und 2 Minuten...mein Mann kam nach Hause,ich war nur noch am heulen,habe den Kopf einfach nicht für die Geburt freibekommen.
>
> Sah mich schon die Woche später mit einem KS im KKH liegen.
>
> Abends redete ich dann noch mit Menne,dass ich mich nicht fallen lassen kann,den Kopf nicht frei bekomme,Zuneigung brauche.
>
> Die gab er mir....danach waren die Wehen weg,es war,als wäre eine Last abgefallen,ich fühlte mich gut,locker und schlief bis 4.15 durch,dann musste ich aufs Klo.
>
> Als ich wieder im Bett lag fing es auf einmal an zu ziehen....anders als vorher...nicht über den Bauch,eher innerlich....

Abbildung 14: Details des Geburtsbeginns.

Im Vergleich zu Problemschilderungen wie im Falle von „Schwangerschaftsübelkeit" zeichnen sich Geburtserzählungen wie „Der krönende Abschluss" durch die Schilderung zahlreicher Details aus, die nicht unmittelbar mit dem Geburtsverlauf in Verbindung stehen. Dies kann die Information sein, dass TS2 die *Septembärmädels* über die Smartphoneapplikation WhatsApp auf dem Laufenden hielt (siehe Abb. 13) oder die detaillierte Beschreibung von Ereignislosigkeit (wobei der Tag wiederum mit *Mädels* verbracht wurde) oder die Wiedergabe eines Gesprächs mit ihrem Mann (vgl. Abb. 14). Auch wird die Beschreibung des körperlichen Zustandes beständig mit dem seelischen Empfinden vermischt: *Den ganzen Tag über kamen die Wehen in Abständen zwischen 25 und 5 min .....ich war genervt, hatte keine Lust mehr [...]*.

Der Text von TS2 weist also ein hohes Maß an Selbstoffenbarung (self-disclosure) auf (vgl. Chen 2012: 173), was aber – dialogistisch verstanden – eben nicht als ein Zeichen von Egozentriertheit oder reinem Self-Display zu verstehen ist, sondern als Gewährleistung eines Zugangs zum eigenen Empfinden. Die Erzeugung *narrativer Anteilnahme* durch detaillierte Schilderungen (vgl. Tannen 1989) ist somit konstitutiv für teilendes Erzählen.

Diese Hinwendung zum Lesepublikum wird in den nachfolgenden Kommentaren honoriert. Nur zehn Minuten nach ihrem Posting erhält TS2 den ersten Kommentar, offensichtlich von einer derjenigen Teilnehmerinnen des Forums aus der gleichen „Monatsgruppe" wie TS2, die von TS2 während der Geburt über WhatsApp auf dem Laufenden gehalten wurde:

Antw:Der krönende Abschluss oder So einfach kann gebären sein
« Antwort #3 am: 17. September 2012, 19:24:53 »

Jetzt weiß ich endlich die Details und weiß auch, warum uns keiner direkt sagen konnte, was es ist

Danke für den schönen Bericht. Ich freue mich, dass Du endlich die Geburt hattest, die Du Dir gewünscht hast :)

Und der Rest - der wird schon :)

Hier auch nochmal Herzlichen Glückwunsch zur kleinen süßen Maus!

:) :) :)

Gespeichert

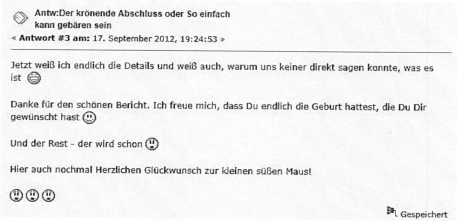

Abbildung 15: Danke für den schönen Bericht.

In Antwort#3 sind es gerade die *Details*, die als erstes relevant gemacht werden. Die Leistung von TS2 als Erzählerin wird ferner gewürdigt, indem ein *Dank* ausgesprochen wird *für den schönen Bericht*. Der Ausdruck von Freude, *dass Du endlich die Geburt hattest, die Du Dir gewünscht hast* ist ebenso als eine Form von Affiliation zu deuten wie der stärker konventionalisierte *Glückwunsch*.

In den Kommentaren zu den Geburtserzählungen fällt ferner auf, dass die Evaluierung des geschilderten Erlebnisses in direkter Verbindung mit der Bewertung der Art und Weise des Schreibens steht, was Erzählungen in Online-Foren vom Erzählen in mündlicher Konversation unterscheiden dürfte:

Antw:Der krönende Abschluss oder So einfach kann gebären sein
Zitat
« Antwort #10 am: 19. September 2012, 10:33:09 »

wooooooooow ich bin hin und weg von deinem Bericht.

Wirklich eine wundervolle Geburt...

Und ihr habt so eine hübsche Tochter :)

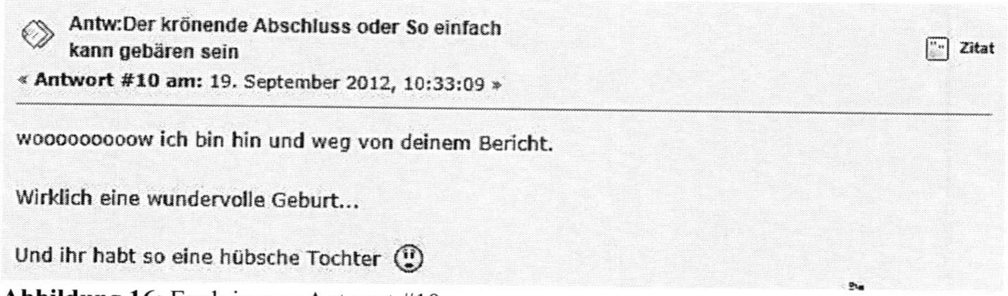

Abbildung 16: Evaluierung Antwort #10.

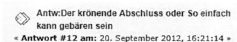

Abbildung 17: Evaluierung Antwort #12.

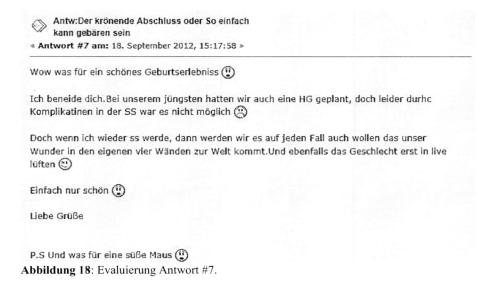

Abbildung 18: Evaluierung Antwort #7.

Ein spannend geschriebener Bericht bedeutet also auch ein gelungenes Geburtserlebnis. Es ist gerade die Nachempfindbarkeit des Erlebnisses, die in Kommentaren als Ressource für bevorstehende Geburten relevant gemacht wird. Kritische Anmerkungen, Lob von Hebamme oder Mann fehlen gänzlich. Bemerkenswerterweise wird die Vorgeschichte oder das Agieren der Ärzte bei den vorhergehenden Geburten in keinem Kommentar genannt, es wird aber deutlich, dass die Vorgeschichte für den Zugang zum Empfinden des Erlebnisses von TS2 von entscheidender Bedeutung ist:

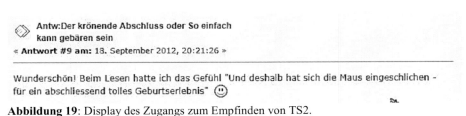

Abbildung 19: Display des Zugangs zum Empfinden von TS2.

Die Frage, wer von der Erzählung „profitiert" (Wee 2011), ist nicht ganz einfach zu beantworten. Dies liegt daran, dass es nicht um konkrete Ratschläge geht, sondern um die subjektive Darlegung einer Erfahrung. Diese ist für andere Teilnehmende im Forum relevant, da sie sich in einer ähnlichen Lebenssituation befinden und ihre Erfahrung mit der von TS2 in Beziehung setzen können. Es tritt jedoch deutlich hervor, dass der Prozess der Affiliation sehr eng mit dem Prozess der Selbstoffenbarung verbunden ist. Wenn TS2 nicht so detailliert ihre Erfahrung geschildert hätte, hätten die anderen Teilnehmenden auch keinen Zugang zum Empfinden von TS2.

5. Fazit

Das partizipatorische Web bietet eine Struktur, die subjektiver Erfahrung wesentlich mehr Platz bereitet als dies im öffentlichen Raum ansonsten der Fall ist. *Sharing* hat sich mit der Herausbildung technologischer Voraussetzung zu einem wichtigen Bestandteil des interaktionalen Repertoires entwickelt.

Im gewählten Online-Forum zu Schwangerschaft und Geburt lassen sich mit Wee (2011) zwei grundlegende, aspektual verschiedene Gegebenheiten von Sharing feststellen: Andauernde Erfahrung und durchlebte Erfahrung.

Beim Aspekt andauernder Erfahrung wie im Falle von *Schwangerschaftsübelkeit* handelt es sich um Schilderungen von Problemen, bei deren Lösung die Antworten der Anderen eine gewisse Orientierung bieten. Es konnte bestätigt werden, dass medizinischer Expertise mit Misstrauen begegnet wird und dass die subjektiven Erfahrungen von Peers gefragt sind. Allerdings konnte festgestellt werden, dass sich das ratsuchende Subjekt aus einer Vielzahl an Handlungsalternativen eine als für sich selbst passende Alternative aussucht. Nicht gewählte Handlungsalternativen werden jedoch doch auch nicht kritisiert. Vielmehr wird mithilfe lexikalischer Alignments eine Affiliation mit der Teilenden signalisiert und ein Kontext harmonischen Austausches hergestellt.

Erzählendes Teilen durchlebter Erfahrung, wie im Falle von *Der krönende Abschluss*, unterscheidet sich vom gewöhnlichen persönlichen Erzählen vor allem im Aufsuchen der Gleichgesinnten, was durch die Existenz von Webforen erleichtert wird. Der Neuigkeitswert der Erzählung ist von geringerer Bedeutung als das Bestreben, sich im Anderen zu spiegeln. Die soziale Ressource, die Sharing hauptsächlich mit sich bringt, ist die gegenseitige Selbstversicherung. Dabei ist das Detailreichtum der Schilderung von hoher Relevanz. Ohne die Selbstoffenbarung hätten die anderen Individuen nämlich keinen Zugang zum mentalen Zustand oder Wissen der Erzählenden. Ohne Selbstoffenbarung keine Affiliation.

Auch wenn die von Wee (2011) vorgeschlagene Aspektualität durchaus nachzuvollziehen ist, muss die Kategorisierung des *Nutzens* in Frage gestellt werden. Im untersuchten Forum geht es beim Sharing vor allem um die

Hinwendung zu den Anderen, und um die Bestätigung der eigenen Evaluierung von Erfahrung. In der Interaktion werden gemeinsam Bewertungen hergestellt, was sowohl den Effekt eines Empowerments mit sich bringt als auch die Homogenisierung von Erfahrung in sich birgt.

6. Bibliographie

Androutsopoulos, J. (2006a), Introduction: Sociolinguistics and computer-mediated communication, *Journal of Sociolinguistics* 10 (4), pp. 419-438.

Androutsopoulos, J. (2006b), From Variation to Heteroglossia in Computer-Mediated Discourse, in Thurlow, C. & Mroczek, K. (eds.), *Digital Discourse. Language in the New Media*. Oxford: Oxford University Press, pp. 277-298.

Arminen, I. (1998), Sharing Experiences: Doing Therapy with the Help of Mutual References in the Meetings of Alcoholics Anonymous, *The Sociological Quarterly* 39 (3), pp. 491-515.

Arminen, I. (2001), Closing of Turns in the Meetings of Alcoholics Anonymous: Members' Methods for Closing "Sharing Experiences", *Research on Language & Social Interaction* 34 (2), pp. 211-251.

Arminen, I. (2004), Second stories: the salience of interpersonal communication for mutual help in Alcoholics Anonymous, *Journal of Pragmatics* 36 (2), pp. 319-347.

Becker, T. & Quasthoff, U. (2005), Introduction. Different dimensions in the field of narrative interaction, in Quasthoff, U. & Becker (eds.), T., *Narrative Interaction*. Philadelphia: John Benjamins, pp. 1-11.

Bucholtz, M. & Hall, K. (2005), Identity and interaction: a sociocultural linguistic approach, *Discourse Studies* 7 (4-5), pp. 585-614.

Chen, G.M. (2012), Why do women write personal blogs? Satisfying needs for self-disclosure and affiliation tell part of the story, *Computers in Human Behavior* 28, pp. 171-180.

Crystal, D. (2004), *A Glossary of Netspeak and Textspeak*. Edinburgh: Edinburgh University Press.

Crystal, D. (2011), *Internet Linguistics: A Student Guide*. London: Routledge.

De Fina, A. (2008), Who tells which story and why? Micro and macro contexts in narrative, *Text & Talk* 28 (3), pp. 421-442.

De Fina, A. & Georgakopoulou, A. (2008), Analyzing narratives as practices, *Qualitative Research* 8 (3), pp. 379-387.

De Fina, A. & Georgakopoulou, A. (2012), *Analyzing Narrative. Discourse and Sociolinguistic Perspectives*. Cambridge: Cambridge University Press.

Dürscheid, C. (2004), Netzsprache - ein neuer Mythos, in Beißwenger, M., Hoffmann L. & Storrer, A. (eds.), *Internetbasierte Kommunikation, Themenheft Osnabrücker Beiträge zur Sprachtheorie*, pp. 141-157.

Fairclough, N. (1995), *Critical discourse analysis: the critical study of language*. London: Longman.

Georgakopoulou, A. (2004), To tell or not to tell? Email stories between on- and offline interactions. *Language@Internet* 1, article 1, http://www.languageatinternet.org/articles/2004

Georgakopoulou, A. (2005), Same old story? On the interactional dynamics of shared narratives, in Quasthoff, U. & Becker, T. (eds.), *Narrative interaction*. Amsterdam: John Benjamins, pp. 223-241.

Georgakopoulou, A. (2007), *Small Stories, Interaction and Identities*. Amsterdam: John Benjamins.

Georgakopoulou, A. (2011), Narrative, *Handbook of Pragmatics Online*, http://benjamins.com/online/hop/.

Hastings, S., Musambira, G. & Hoover, J. (2007), Community as a key to healing after the death of a child, *Communication & Medicine* 4 (2), pp.153-163.

Herring, S. (1994), Politeness in computer culture: Why women thank and men flame, in Bucholtz, M., Liang, A.C., Sutton, L.A., Hines, C. (eds.), *Cultural Performances: Proceedings of the Third Berkeley Women and Language Conference*, pp. 278-294.

Herring, S. (2011), Computer-mediated conversation, Part II: Introduction and overview, *Language@Internet 8*, article 2, http://www.languageatinternet.org/articles/2011/Herring.

Kern, F., Morek, M. & Ohlhus, S. (2012), *Erzählen als Form – Formen des Erzählens*, Berlin/Boston: de Gruyter, pp. 1-9.

Labov, W. & Waletzky, J. (1997 [1967]), Narrative analysis, *Journal of Narrative and Life History* 7, pp. 3-38. [Original in Helm, J. (ed.), *Essays on the Verbal and Visual Arts*, Seattle: University of Washington Press, pp. 12-44.].

Labov, W. (2010), Where Should I Begin?, in Schiffrin, D., De Fina, A., Nylund, A. (eds.), *Telling Stories. Language, Narrative and Social Life*, Washington: Georgetown University Press, pp. 7-22.

Lee, C. (2011), Texts and Practices of Micro-blogging: Status Updates on Facebook. in Thurlow, C. & Mroczek, K. (eds), *Digital Discourse: Language in New Media, Oxford:* Oxford University Press, pp. 110-128.

Ley, B. (2007, Vive Les Roses!: The Architecture of Commitment in an Online Pregnancy and Mothering Group, *Journal of Computer-Mediated Communication* 12, pp. 1388-1408.

Linell, P. (2009), *Rethinking Language, Mind and World Dialogically. Interactional and Contextual Theories of Human Sense-Making*, Charlotte: IAP.

Locher, M. (2006), *Advice online. Advice-giving in an American Internet health column*, Amsterdam: John Benjamins.

Luckmann, T. (1988), Kommunikative Gattungen im kommunikativen Haushalt einer Gesellschaft, in Smolka-Kordt, G., Spangenberg, P. & Tillmann-Bartylla, D. (eds.), *Der Ursprung der Literatur*. München, pp. 279-288.

Luckmann, T. (2003), Von der alltäglichen Erfahrung zum sozialwissenschaftlichen Datum, in Srubar, I. & Vaitkus, S. (eds.), *Phänomenologie und soziale Wirklichkeit*, Opladen: Leske + Budrich, pp.13-26.

Mondada, L. & Schmitt, R. (2010), Zur Multimodalität von Situationseröffnungen, in Mondada, L. & Schmitt, R. (eds.), *Situationseröffnungen. Zur multimodalen Herstellung fokussierter Interaktion*, Tübingen: Narr, pp. 7-52.

Nentwich, J. (2009), Zwischen Provokation und Anpassung: Handlungsmächtigkeit als diskursive Positionierung, *Forum Qualitative Sozialforschung* 10 (3), art. 8, http://nbn-resolving.de/urn:nbn:de:0114-fqs090381.

Page, R. (2012), *Stories and social media: identities and interaction*, New York: Routledge.

Pickering, M. & Garrod, S. (2006), Alignment as the Basis for Successful Communication. *Research on Language and Computation*. http://www.psy.gla.ac.uk/docs/download.php?type=PUBLS&id=1097

Quasthoff, U. (1980), *Erzählen in Gesprächen. Linguistische Untersuchungen zu Strukturen und Funktionen am Beispiel einer Kommunikationsform des Alltags.* Tübingen: Narr.

Quasthoff, U. (2001), Erzählen als interaktive Gesprächsstruktur, in Brinker, K., Antos, G. & Sager, S. (eds.), *Text- und Gesprächslinguistik. Ein internationales Handbuch zeitgenössischer Forschung*, 2. Halbband, Berlin/New York: de Gruyter, pp.1293-1309.

Rutter, J. & Smith, G.W.H. (2005), Ethnographic Presence in a Nebulous Setting, in Hine, C. *Virtual Methods. Issues in Social Research on the Internet*, Oxford, New York: Berg, pp. 81-92.

Sacks, H. (1992), *Lectures on conversation*, Cambridge: Blackwell.

Stivers, T. (2008), Stance, Alignment, and Affiliation during Storytelling: When Nodding Is a Token of Affiliation, *Research on Language and Social Interaction* 41 (1:1), pp. 31-57.

Stommel, W. & Koole, T. (2010), The online support group as community: A microanalysis of the interaction with a new member, *Discourse Studies* 12 (3), pp. 357-378.

Tophinke, D. (2009), Wirklichkeitserzählungen im Internet, in Klein, C. & Martínez, M. (eds.), *Wirklichkeitserzählungen. Felder, Formen und Funktionen nichtliterarischen Erzählens*, Stuttgart: Metzler, pp. 245-274.

Wee, L. (2011), Sharing as an activity type, *Text & Talk* 31 (3), pp. 355-373.

Wortham, S. (2001), *Narratives in action*, New York: Teachers College Press.

Compounding in a Swedish Blog Corpus
Robert Östling & Mats Wirén

Stockholm University

1. Introduction and background

1.1 The problem

Research in compounding for Swedish has a long tradition at Stockholm University, with Benny Brodda starting already in 1967/68 (Brodda 1982: 102). One of the sources that he used was an electronic version of SAOL 9, the Swedish Academy word list in its 9th edition (1950), with compound borders indicated. However, in later work he also looked solely at the forms of words and syllables without any lexical resource at hand (Brodda 1982).

Good compound analysis is highly needed for unrestricted text, especially for languages whose orthographies concatenate compound components (that is, juxtapose the components without an intervening space). This means that every such concatenation corresponds to a word. This way of forming words is extremely productive in most Germanic languages (including Swedish, but with the exception of English) and, for example, Finnish, Hungarian and Greek. Also, in languages like this an unknown word will most likely be a compound (Stymne and Holmqvist 2008). On a related note, compounding seems to be an area where a lot of the creativeness of language is put to work (Svanlund 2009; De Smedt 2012).

So what new is there to say about Swedish compounding that could not be said one or a couple of decades ago? To begin with, there has been an enormous increase in the amount of electronically available data. At the Department of Linguistics, we have collected corpora from several Internet sources during the last years, including 2.7 billion tokens of Swedish blog text. There are two reasons why we consider working with data from the Internet in general and blogs in particular highly useful. First, the sheer amount of data means that we obtain new ways of systematically studying various marginal and low-frequency phenomena that previously were more or less out of reach. One such example concerns neologisms and creative compounding in Swedish, which we can find by looking among words that are extremely low-frequency in spite of the large data set. Secondly, as has frequently been pointed out, text found on the web often has a colloquial and spontaneous character. The umbrella term here is user-generated content, that is, text published predominantly by non-professionals in media such as blogs, forums, reviews, social networks and wikis. User-generated content, including blogs, can thus provide an effective window into language change and variation.[1]

Another reason for us to look anew at compounding is that there are now good lexical resources with permissive "copyleft" licensing[2] for Swedish, notably SALDO (Borin and Forsberg 2009) which contains about 115 000 entries. Earlier attempts at Swedish morphology and compounding (Karlsson 1992; Sjöbergh and Kann 2004; 2006) have used SAOL (the Swedish Academy word list) as a lexical back-end. While SAOL is a rich source (its 13th edition from 2006 comprises about 125 000 entries), its use is restricted and it is not freely available in any machine-readable format.[3]

The basic approach is thus to use the SALDO lexicon and to test the compound algorithm on our set of blog data. More specifically, the goal of this paper is threefold:

- to provide a downloadable, "free software"[4] tool for splitting Swedish compounds;

- to test the accuracy of this tool on our blog corpus (which is downloadable as a citation corpus called the Swedish Blog Sentences corpus);

- to show some uses of compound splitting with respect to this corpus, including quantifying the use of creative compounding.

The program used for analyzing compounds in this work is Free Software, and can be downloaded as part of the SPyRo package from the website of the Department of Linguistics[5].

---

[1] We have already done preliminary work on dialectal word variation in the blog corpus; see http://www.ling.su.se/english/nlp/tools/dialect-maps

[2] This includes the freedom to use, modify and re-distribute the work. All of these are important in a project such as ours, where one needs to adapt a lexicon to specific purposes and then distribute the final software package.

[3] As far as we know, SAOL is available only through individual licenses with the Swedish Academy. Furthermore, although it is accessible on the Internet (at http://www.svenskaakademien.se/ordlista), the text is only available as images of the print edition.

[4] *Free software* denotes software whose source code is available under a copyleft license. This is not to be confused with software available free of charge but without source code or with restrictions on its use. The software used in this study is available under the GNU GPL license; see http://www.gnu.org/copyleft/gpl.html

[5] http://www.ling.su.se/english/nlp/tools/spyro

1.2 What is a Swedish compound?

According to SAG, the Swedish Academy Grammar (Teleman *et al.* 2000), a Swedish compound is a word form that consists of a first and a last component. These components can be root morphemes, derivations or compounds. The fact that a component can itself be a compound introduces recursiveness into word formation, potentially giving rise to very long compound words. Typically, the last component is the main one, grammatically and semantically, with respect to the whole compound.

The most common types in our data (and also the types mostly discussed in SAG, Volume 2) are compound nouns, adjectives and verbs. By a "compound noun", etc., we mean a compound whose last component is a noun, etc., but whose first component may be another part of speech.

For noun compounds, SAG (Volume 2, Nouns, § 25–27) mentions most other parts of speech as possible first components, namely, nouns (*fågel-bok*, bird book), proper nouns (*Zorn-tavla*, Zorn painting), adjectives (*låg-pris*, low price), verbs (*köp-stopp*, buying stop), participles (*vuxen-gymnasium*, adult high-school), pronouns (*vi-känsla*, we feeling), numerals (*andre-pilot*, second pilot), prepositions (*med-vind*, fair wind), and adverbs (*fram-sida*, front side). All of these cases are present in our data; however, it is difficult to see how populated some of the groups are because of ambiguity. For example, should we regard *köp* in *köp-stopp* (buying stop) as a verb (which SAG suggests) or a noun (which is also possible)?

For adjective compounds, SAG (Volume 2, Adjectives, § 33) mentions nouns (*barn-vänlig*, children friendly), proper nouns (*falu-röd*, Falu red), adjectives (*mörk-grön*, dark green), verbs (*prat-glad*, literally "speak happy", talkative), pronouns (*all-svensk*, pan-Swedish, relating to the Swedish football league), prepositions (*mellan-stor*, middle-sized), and adverbs (*bak-tung*, tail-heavy). Again, all of these cases are present in our data.

For verb compounds, SAG (Volume 2, Verbs, § 19) mentions nouns (*hunger-strejka*, hunger-strike), adjectives (*kal-hugga*, clear-cut, with respect to woods), verbs (*bränn-märka*, brand), prepositions (*till-foga*, append), and adverbs (*ill-vråla*, yell terrifically). Yet again, all of these cases are present in our data.

SAG also mentions compounds belonging to most other parts of speech. However, in quantifying the different types, we shall limit ourselves to the most frequent ones, namely, compound nouns, adjectives and verbs.

1.3 Legal issues

In any corpus project, one would ideally want the consent of all the intellectual property right holders for the texts in the corpus. Unfortunately in our case, the rights to the blog corpus we use is owned by some half a million individual writers, or about seven percent of the entire population of Sweden!

Since reproducibility is a cornerstone of all research, and in addition Swedish universities as branches of the government are mandated by the constitution to share data with anyone requesting it, it is important that we find some way to make our corpus publicly available.

For some uses, it is sufficient to provide a search interface, so that users can search for sentences but not download the entire data set. This avoids the copyright issues, but in general is not useful for research in computational linguistics, where one wants to automatically analyze *all* of the data, preferably using one's own programs and not being limited by a search interface. One example of this is SAOL, whose search interface allows search for particular words, but for which only single book pages are returned as bitmaps, not in a machine-readable format.[6] Another example is Litteraturbanken[7], which only allows reading of (or access to) a single page at a time. Of course, both SAOL and Litteraturbanken are circumscribed by copyright protections.

Some projects, such as the WaCky corpus (Baroni *et al.* 2009), choose an "opt-out" model, where copyright holders are not notified by the project about the existence of the corpus, but can request to be excluded from it if they find out. Although a corpus may contain copyrighted material, it consists of material already published on the Internet for which WaCky's automatic routines cannot detect that the material is copyright-protected. The potential damage of an inclusion in WaCky may therefore not be very high. Also, this model is a very practical way of providing easy access for researchers to a valuable resource. On the other hand, such an approach may require the project to either stay under the radar, or have sufficient financial resources to crush any opposition in a legal process.

Alternatively, if the basic unit of processing is at the sentence level or below, one could distribute a "citation" version of the corpus where the sentences are randomly shuffled around, making it impossible to reconstruct the original texts. This is the way that for instance the Swedish Språkbanken material[8] is distributed, also under Swedish law. This approach has been advocated by e.g. Santos and Rocha (2001).

For the purposes of this study, we do not depend on information above the sentence level. The most practical approach thus appears to be the "citation corpus" approach, which we have adopted.

---

[6] http://www.svenskaakademien.se/ordlista
[7] http://litteraturbanken.se
[8] http://spraakbanken.gu.se/eng/node/1587/

2. Data

The current study is based on two major resources: a large corpus of Swedish blog posts, and the SALDO lexicon of Swedish morphology. In this section we discuss these resources.

2.1 Blog corpus

Our blog corpus consists of Swedish blog posts obtained from Twingly[9] from November 2010 until September of 2012, in total about 2.7 billion tokens, spread over 220 million posts from 660 000 different blogs.

The set of sentences from the blog corpus on which this study was based, is available for download at the Department of Linguistics website.[10]

A smaller amount of blog text has been annotated and published as the Stockholm Internet Corpus (Östling 2013), available from the department website under a permissive copyleft license.[11] Although its annotation quality is higher than the full, automatically processed corpus, the small size (currently about 8 000 words) prevents us from using it in our current study.

Due to the large quantity of text, all processing is done automatically. The material contains some undesirable elements that may be difficult for the computer to detect and filter out accurately, such as:

- duplication, for instance due to quotations
- automatically generated or translated text
- text in foreign languages
- passwords and other random letter sequences

All of these may result in artifacts. For instance, a misspelling in an article quoted by many blogs may show up as a relatively common variant, even though it was only actually written once.

For all its problems we choose to use this corpus because the sheer amount of text, from a wide variety of different sources, puts us in a very good position to investigate uncommon compounds and compounding patterns in general usage.

---

[9] http://www.twingly.com/
[10] http://www.ling.su.se/sbs
[11] http://www.ling.su.se/sic

2.2 Preprocessing

All text has been tokenized, and annotated with parts of speech (POS tagged) and citation forms (lemmatized), using the Stagger POS tagger (Östling 2013). While elaborate algorithms have been developed for tokenizing Internet text, we found that a simple regular expression-based tokenizer provided satisfactory results after it was modified to handle some typical Internet phenomena, such as emoticons (*smileys*).

The automatic annotation process is not perfectly accurate. In a sample of (poorly written) blog posts, about 8% of tokens were analyzed incorrectly. In the more conventional written Swedish of the Stockholm–Umeå Corpus (Gustafson-Capková and Hartmann 2008), this figure is close to 3%. An error analysis shows that most of the difference can be explained by colloquial forms of a small number of highly frequent function words, such as "*o*" (also written "*å*", properly spelled "*och*", "*att*" or "*å*", meaning and/to/on) and "*de*" (properly "*de*", "*dem*" or "*det*", meaning they/them/the/it); compare Table 6 of Östling (2013). More training data in the domain of blog texts should be expected to improve accuracy, and such a project is ongoing.

This preprocessing step provides two important pieces of information for the future analysis: whether a word belongs to the four parts of speech considered for compound analysis (noun, adjective, verb or adverb), and the citation form of the word, on which the compound analysis is based.

In section 3.2, we show that although errors in this step do propagate into the final compound analysis, the impact is relatively minor for noun and adjective compounds. Many non-words are however mistaken for verbs or adverbs during preprocessing, which makes it difficult for us to accurately analyze verb and adverb compounds.

2.3 Lexicon

We use the SALDO lexicon of Swedish morphology (Borin and Forsberg 2009), containing 115 661 words[12] as the basis of our algorithm.

Compounding forms are divided into initial and middle forms, the latter typically end with the linking morpheme -*s*-. While the compounding form of a word is often simply the word's stem, there are exceptions, such as "*gatu-kontor*" (highways department), where "-*a*" in the stem "*gata*" is replaced by "-*u*". Using the SALDO lexicon makes it trivial to include these. The

---

[12] This is the number, at the time of writing, of *lemgrams* in the SALDO morphological lexicon. Each lemgram represents a word, an abbreviation or a multi-word expression, and contains its citation form as well as inflectional and compounding morphological forms.

same applies to the sometimes idiosyncratic behavior of the linking morpheme.

The final segment of a compound is identical to the corresponding word in isolation, and also behaves like it in terms of inflectional morphology. Thus, we can simply use the inflectional forms in SALDO for final compound segments.

3. Methods

3.1 Compound analysis

Our basic approach to analyzing a potential compound which is not in the SALDO lexicon in its entirety is very simple:

> *For a given word of a given part of speech, find the shortest possible sequence of compound segments in the SALDO lexicon, which put together form the word in question with the correct part of speech.*

For instance, given the word *kändisgala* (*celebrity gala*), which we know to be a noun from the preprocessing, a dictionary look-up gives us four initial hypotheses:

1. *kändis-gala* (noun, *celebrity gala*)

2. *kändis-gala* (verb, *to celebrity-crow*)

3. *känd-is-gala* (noun, *famous ice gala*)

4. *känd-is-gala* (verb, *to famous-ice-crow*)

Hypotheses (2) and (4) can be eliminated because the part of speech of the compound as a whole and its final segment do not agree, and hypothesis (3) can be eliminated since it contains three segments whereas (1) only contains two.

There are however several complications to this conceptually simple method, which we will now discuss.

Letter pairs Swedish orthography does not allow more than two identical letters in a row, which means that a letter pair may be split in three different ways. For instance, *glasskål* could be *glass-skål* (icecream bowl), *glas-skål* (glass bowl) or *glass-kål* (icecream cabbage). This special rule generates some more ambiguity, which however does not seem to be a problem in practice. One could also consider introducing a similar rule for s/ss ambiguity, since it is fairly common (although prescriptively frowned upon) to omit the *-s-* linking morpheme when it is followed by another *s*, as in *blåbär(s)soppa* (blueberry soup). Sequences that would consist of more than three letters are very rare (one example is *Råå-å-ål, eel from the Råå river*), and we do not consider these.

Words in SALDO The SALDO lexicon contains non-compounds and highly lexicalized compounds, as well as mostly compositional compounds, but does not provide any information about which category a given word belongs to. In order to avoid the difficult problem of how to demarcate the borders between these categories, we could simply treat all in-lexicon words as atomic and refuse to split them. Unfortunately, this would leave us unable to answer one important question: *how often are compounds used?* For this reason, we do try to split words that occur in SALDO. Since a naive approach results in erroneously splitting many non-compounds, we use a simple semantic filter to extract plausible analyses. An analysis is only accepted if the compound shares an ancestor within two levels in SALDO:s semantic hierarchy, with the proposed segments. For instance, the compound *gastryck* is found in SALDO and has two analyses: *gas-tryck* (*gas pressure*) and the less probable *gast-ryck* (*ghost twitching*). The former analysis is accepted, since the compound is directly related to both *gas* and *tryck* in the semantic hierarchy. Because no such connection exists for the second analysis, it is rejected. If all analyses are rejected, we do not consider the word a compound.

No short segments Many non-compounds may be interpreted as compounds consisting of very short segments, such as the English *hate* which could be interpreted as *ha-te* (*having-tea*). For this reason, unless a hyphen is used, compound segments shorter than three letters are not allowed. This unfortunately means that we will not detect the (relatively few) such compounds that actually exist, and others may want to make a different decision.

No more than four segments Compounds with more than four segments are very rare in practice, Sjöbergh and Kann (2006) found only two cases among 3400 compounds manually checked. Like the previous case with very short segments, allowing very long compounds tends to introduce many errors where non-compounds receive some nonsensical segmentation.

Fewest-segments heuristic Karlsson (1992) uses this highly efficient heuristic, referring to it as the "Compound Elimination Principle", and listing the only six cases he had found which gave possibly unintended results. One such case is "*finskor*" (Finnish women), which is always preferred to "*fin-skor*" (fine shoes). However, all of his six cases involve inflected word forms which our algorithm would circumvent, since it works with citation forms. Still, it is possible to construct cases where our algorithm would also miss a possible compound. For example, *finska* (*Finnish language*) would always be preferred to *fin-ska* (*high-class ska music*), even though the latter might be intended in some cases.

3.2 Accuracy

To be able to say anything about the occurrence of compounds in our corpus, we first need to find out how accurate the algorithm is at identifying and analyzing compounds.

In order to investigate the accuracy of the compound splitting algorithm, we perform a manual inspection of the compound analyses delivered. There are two measures we are interested in: precision, the proportion of compounds identified by the algoritms that are actually Swedish compounds, and recall, the proportion of the total number of compounds in the data that were found by the algorithm.

In total, there were 2 253 395 noun-tagged unique words identified by the algorithm as compounds, and 2 483 827 as non-compounds of which 1 474 were in the SALDO lexicon. We now take a closer look at what the two categories contain.

3.2.1 Precision

Since the total number of compounds is very large, we randomly selected smaller samples of compounds and their analyses by the algorithm.

Generally speaking, rare words are more difficult to analyze, since they are more often misspellings or use non-standard morphology than frequently occurring words. While using frequent words in the evaluation would probably give better-looking accuracy figures, most of the compounds in our corpus are quite rare: the majority (63.3%) of noun compounds occur only once, and another 13.5% just twice.

Unique noun compounds Table 1 summarizes the result of an error analysis of 256 randomly selected nouns that occur only once each in the corpus, and which received at least one analysis as a compound by the algorithm. In 188 cases (73.4%), the system output only one analysis, which turned out to be correct. The second most common case (40, 15.6%) was that the word

Count	Percentage	Result
188	73.4%	Unique correct analysis
5	2.0%	Ambiguous, but at least one correct analysis
14	5.5%	No correct analysis
40	15.6%	Non-compound incorrectly analyzed as compound
9	3.5%	Preprocessing error
256	**100.0%**	**Total**

Table 1: Unique noun-tagged words interpreted as compounds by the algorithm.

was not a Swedish compound at all (but e.g. a misspelling or a foreign word), although the algorithm managed to find some analysis for it. For instance, *trangeldrama* was interpreted as *tran-gel-drama* (whale-oil gel drama), whereas it is most likely a misspelling of *triangel-drama* (triangle drama). Just 14 cases (5.5%) were acceptable Swedish compounds that did not receive any correct analysis. Only in these few cases is the compound splitting algorithm alone responsible for failing to deliver a correct analysis.

In spite of the fact that correct part of speech tagging and lemmatization of blog text is a difficult problem, particularly for words that only occur once and are typically not in the lexicons used by the preprocessing tool, only nine cases (3.5%) among the incorrectly split compounds were due to errors in these preprocessing steps.

It is possible for a compound to have several analyses, which may be more or less probable. For instance, in this sample we observed the compound *flyttemperatur*, which could be interpreted as either *flytt-temperatur* (moving temperature) or as *flyt-temperatur* (floating temperature). In total, five of the correctly analyzed compounds were ambiguous and received at least one correct analysis.

Although the 73.4% precision figure may seem low, the largest share of the errors come from non-compounds (frequently misspellings). If non-compounds and preprocessing errors are excluded, the algorithm finds a unique, correct analysis for 191 of 207 compounds (90.8%).

Count	Percentage	Result
52	52.0%	Unique correct analysis
0	0.0%	Ambiguous, but at least one correct analysis
3	3.0%	No correct analysis
24	24.0%	Non-compound incorrectly analyzed as compound
21	21.0%	Preprocessing error
100	**100.0%**	**Total**

Table 2: Unique adjective-tagged words interpreted as compounds by the algorithm.

Unique adjective compounds Table 2 shows the corresponding precision figures for unique adjectives. The main difference from the nouns is that the number of preprocessing errors is larger, at the expense of the correctly analyzed compounds. In most cases, this is due to the part-of-speech tagger mistaking nouns for adjectives. Excluding non-compounds and preprocessing errors, 52 of 55 (95%) of the proper adjective compounds in the sample receive a unique, correct analysis by the algorithm.

Count	Percentage	Result
32	32.0%	Unique correct analysis
1	1.0%	Ambiguous, but at least one correct analysis
5	5.0%	No correct analysis
35	35.0%	Non-compound incorrectly analyzed as compound
27	27.0%	Preprocessing error
100	**100.0%**	**Total**

Table 3: Unique verb-tagged words interpreted as compounds by the algorithm

Tokens	Percentage	Result
7 293 527	90.7%	Unique correct analysis
9 131	0.1%	Ambiguous, but at least one correct analysis
484	0.0%	No correct analysis
713 747	8.9%	Non-compound incorrectly analyzed as compound
27 384	0.3%	Preprocessing error
8 044 273	**100.0%**	**Total**

Table 4: Noun-tagged words interpreted as compounds by the algorithm.

Unique verb compounds For verbs (table 3), the situation is even worse. 62% of the identified compounds are in fact non-words or mis-tagged words from other parts of speech, frequently nouns ending with the common verb infinitive suffix –a.

Unique adverb compounds Only 10% of unique words identified as adverb compounds are in fact such, since actual adverb compounds seem to be rare, while many non-words and words of other parts of speech are mistaken for adverbs in the preprocessing.

Noun compounds overall We now turn from unique compounds to compounds as they occur in the corpus, with a heavy bias towards a few, common words (see figure 1). For a randomly selected word token in the corpus that the algorithm identifies as a compound, what is the rate of success?

Table 4 shows the result of a manual analysis of the algorithm's performance on 256 randomly chosen such words. Since the analysis is independent of the context in which a word is found, we can simply count a correct analysis of a word occurring 1000 times as that many correct instances, and similarly for incorrect analyses.

While unique compounds are nearly always compositional (for natural reasons), we now run into issues of lexicalization and language change. The word *frukost* (breakfast) makes up 22% of the total instances in this sample, so a great part of the accuracy figure depends on whether or not we accept the analysis *fru-kost*. Historically, this is indeed a compound meaning *early meal*, but in current use the prefix *fru/fro-* (*early*) is obsolete.

In table 4 we have counted the analyses *fru-kost* and *kär-lek* (*love*) as correct for etymological reasons. If one decides to count these two cases as incorrect, the percentage of unique correct analyses immediately drops to 61.9%, so these figures should be interpreted with great care.

The question of when a compound stops being a compound is a matter of definitions, but in practice this is of little consequence since very lexicalized compounds tend to be in the lexicon, and the main purpose of a compound analyzer is to find a way to interpret words *not* in the lexicon.

3.2.2 Recall

Out of 128 randomly selected unique words that were tagged as nouns and were neither in SALDO nor identified as compounds, only 18 (14.1%) were considered to have an analysis as a correctly spelled Swedish compound.

The remaining 85.9% were mainly random letter sequences (e.g. passwords and web addresses), misspellings and parts of sentences written without white space, that the part of speech tagger had (often erroneously) tagged as nouns.

Since about 14.1% of all unique nouns classified as non-compounds are in fact compounds, we see that about 82.5% of all unique noun compounds were correctly identified by the algorithm. Assuming that we really want to discard misspellings, this shows us that our algorithm does not miss very many noun compounds, even for the unique words that are so difficult to analyze.

For adjectives, verbs and adverbs, we also found that few actual compounds are missed by the algorithm.

3.2.3 Discussion

Since very rare words in Swedish are typically compounds, a good compound analyzer would in theory be able to separate "real" words from misspellings, random letter sequences, foreign language words, and similar types of Web Noise.

Misspellings[13] are a fact of life, and of Internet life in particular. By inspecting a random sample of the unique noun-tagged words in the blog corpus, we found that about one fourth of them are misspellings, and quite often misspellings of compounds.

One way to improve the compound analysis algorithm would be to allow for spellings not in the lexicon. However, this has to be done with great care. It is already too easy for a non-word to be interpreted as a (weird) compound, if one also allows *misspelled* compounds, this risk increases further.

3.2.4 Related work

Sjöbergh and Kann (2004) studied algorithms for splitting Swedish compounds, and report that with their best method 99% of compounds were split, and of these 97% were analyzed correctly. This is substantially higher than our figures, but the difference can be explained in part by the following factors:

- They use the Stockholm–Umeå Corpus of published (and presumably proof-read) professional prose (Gustafson-Capková and Hartmann 2008), as opposed to the unedited blog texts by non-professional writers we used. In particular, this means that they did not have to deal with the large amount of non-words observed among the unique letter sequences in the blog corpus. The manual annotation of the Stockholm–Umeå Corpus also means that they did not suffer to the same extent from the preprocessing errors we describe.

- They split word tokens in context, which means that the compound *types* evaluated are biased towards common ones, according to the Zipfian distribution of compounds such as the one shown in figure 1. We draw our evaluation sample from unique or rare word tokens, and as we showed in section 3.2.1, more common words are in general easier to analyze.

As we mentioned towards the end of section 3.2.1, excluding non-compounds and preprocessing errors we also arrive at a figure of 97% precision. This figure is also not directly comparable to that of Sjöbergh and Kann (2004), among other things due to different standards in judging the correctness of analyses, where they are more strict. In short, while a direct

---

[13] Since our software is based on the SALDO lexicon, we define the spelling(s) listed there as "correct", and alternative spelling as misspellings. For words not in the lexicon, the subjective opinions of the authors are used. This is a practical decision to enable automatic analysis, and should not be interpreted as prescriptivist fundamentalism.

comparison with previous work is difficult, it seems that the accuracy of our method is fair.

4. Results

Having established that our methods can be trusted in the majority of cases, at least for some parts of speech, we now turn to look at the overall distributions of compounds. Later, we will also look at how compounding patterns can be used to extract semantic information.

One should keep in mind that the blog corpus contains much noise, which may be misidentified as compounds. This is a particularly large problem for adverb compounds, since actual compounds are quite uncommon and easily disappear in the noise. For this reason we do not consider adverb compounds at all, only briefly discuss adjective and verb compounds, and focus on noun compounds which are the most frequent and where our system produces the most accurate results.

4.1 How common are compounds?

We want to know how common compounds are in the blog corpus. First, we will have a look at compounds that are *not* in the SALDO lexicon, and which are typically quite rare and compositional. Then, we will look at compounds in the SALDO lexicon, which are more common but often highly lexicalized.

Recall from section 3.1 that SALDO does not contain information about which words are compounds, so we are forced to use an imperfect method to attempt to deduce this.

Compounds not in SALDO Table 5 shows the number of different words (types) and the number of instances (tokens) tagged as nouns, adjectives or verbs in the blog corpus. Perhaps the most striking fact is that on the one hand, the vast majority of words in a text are found in the lexicon, but on the other hand, the vast majority of word *types* are not. 7.6% of noun-tagged tokens are interpreted as compounds by our algorithm, compared to 2.6% of adjective-tagged tokens and 0.24% of the verb-tagged.

Figure 1 shows the frequency of words as a function of their rank, that is, how many times we find the most common word, the second most common, the third most common, and so on. Although the total number of compounds varies between different parts of speech, the compound rank/frequency plots all follow *Zipf's law*, according to which the frequency of the n:th word is roughly proportional to $1/n$.

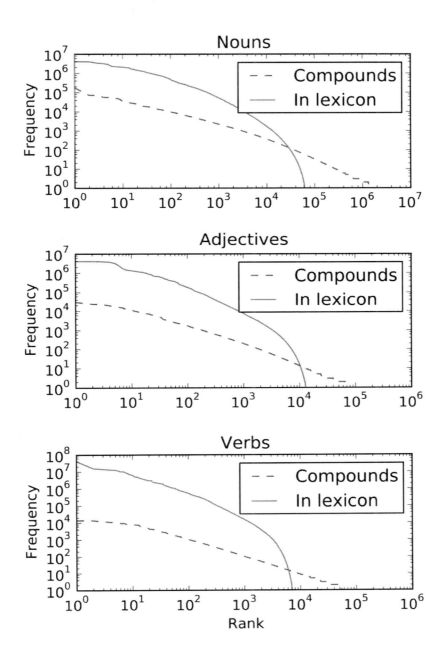

Figure 1: Rank/frequency distribution of different parts of speech.

	Words in SALDO		Compounds not in SALDO	
	Types	Tokens	Types	Tokens
Noun	63 197	334 731 534	3 563 928	30 176 761
Adjective	13 394	111 174 488	206 715	3 429 193
Verb	7 075	426 829 335	187 898	1 082 911

Table 5: Frequencies in the blog corpus of words in SALDO and compounds not in SALDO.

	Non-compounds in SALDO		Compounds	
	Types	Tokens	Types	Tokens
Noun	29 154	295 235 054	3 593 728	67 730 894
Adjective	10 485	106 970 680	209 967	7 581 560
Verb	5 986	422 812 258	189 799	5 104 810

Table 6: Frequencies in the blog corpus of non-compounds in SALDO and compounds.

Compounds in SALDO In table 6, we show how these figures change if one also counts compounds in the SALDO lexicon. As expected, the number of compound types and tokens increases. 17.0% of noun-tagged tokens are now identified as compounds, compared to 5.6% of adjective-tagged tokens and 0.46% of verb-tagged tokens. Comparing table 6 to the number of unique noun compounds (see section 3.2), we find that about 0.6% of all nouns in the blog corpus are *unique* compounds, which demonstrates the level of creativity present in Swedish noun compounding.

4.2 Mapping attitudes through compounds

In order to demonstrate what can be done by computer analysis of our large database of compounds, we will try to create a map of attitudes towards different activities, based on a set of compound constructions with different connotations, denoting different kinds of enthusiasts.

This is an instance of *distributional semantics*, which exploits the correlation between the meaning of a word and its distribution in a language. Often one uses as wide a variety of contexts as possible in order to explore all aspects of a word's meaning, but here we look at compounds with similar denotations, and try to find the connotations associated with each prefix.

We consider five specific compound suffixes: *-bög*, *-fantast*, *-freak*, *-nörd* and *-tönt*. These can all be used to denote an enthusiast of a particular thing or activity, but their connotations are different. *-bög* (a homosexual) conveys a negative judgment of the activity in question, often as being snobbish. *-fantast* (fan) is fairly neutral, while *-freak*, *-nörd* (nerd) and *-tönt* (dork) have the particular (mostly negative) connotations of their English counterparts.

Lexicalized compounds and polysemous suffixes could in theory cause trouble, by breaking our basic assumption that *X-suffix* means exactly "an enthusiast of X" and that the choice of suffix reflects only which attitude towards the activity the writer intends to express. It turns out that most prefixes tend to occur with several different suffixes, and only in exceptional cases are they associated with a single suffix, which is some indication that this is not a problem in practice.

We collect all prefixes that occur at least 25 times in total with the suffixes mentioned, in total 279 prefixes. This is done in order to reduce the high level of noise in the distribution of rare prefixes, and the selected prefixes occur with most of the suffixes. Since the suffixes are not equally frequent, we normalized the distribution of compound frequencies within each suffix. Next, we normalized the frequencies of each *prefix*, in order to obtain a measure of how the suffixes would be distributed for each prefix, if suffixes were equally frequent.

Finally, in order to visualize the result, we used Principal Component Analysis (PCA)[14] to reduce the 5-dimensional vectors of each prefix into two dimensions. The reduced space is shown for the most common prefixes in figure 2. At the bottom, we see typical nerdy activities, such as *data-* (computer) and *språk-* (language). Towards the upper left, there are prefixes associated with *-bög* and *-tönt*, such as *pryl-* (gadget) and *iphone-*. In the upper right, we have prefixes associated with *-fantast*, such as *skräck-* (horror fiction) and *deckar-* (crime fiction). Finally, prefixes that show no clear preferences towards any suffix are grouped near the middle of the figure, for instance *musik-* (music) and *teknik-* (technology).

5. Summary

We have used the largest corpus that, to the best of our knowledge, has ever been used for analyzing Swedish compounds. Through this, we have been able to quantify the use of different types of compounds used on Swedish blogs. Among other things, we have shown that nearly one in every thousand word instances (tokens) is a unique noun compound, helping to quantify the importance of compounding in Swedish.

---

14 We used the implementation of the Modular toolkit for Data Processing (MDP) project. Please refer to the documentation of this software for further information: http://pypi.python.org/pypi/MDP

Furthermore, we have applied our large database of Swedish compounds to create a map of the overall attitude towards different activities, based on the connotations of the words they form compounds with. This is merely a small demonstration of what kind of information can be extracted from compounding patterns. We hope that future studies studies will be able to use our data and methods to extract more of the information present in Swedish compound constructions.

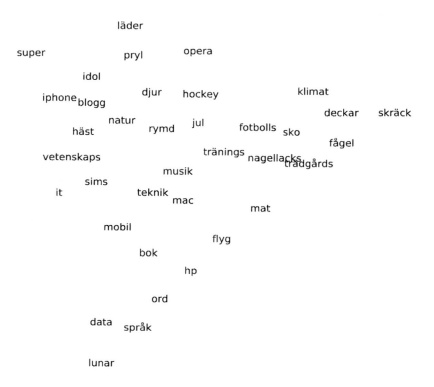

Figure 2: Attitude map based on the suffixes -bög, -fantast, -freak, -nörd, -tönt.

Acknowledgements:
We sincerely thank Professor Diana Santos for her detailed comments on our manuscript.

6. References

Baroni, M. Bernardini, S., Ferraresi, A. & Zanchett, E. (2009), The Wacky Wide Web: a collection of very large linguistically processed web-crawled corpora, *Language Resources & Evaluation* 43, pp. 209-226.

Borin, L. & Forsberg, M. (2009), All in the family: A comparison of SALDO and WordNet, in *Proceedings of the Nodalida 2009 Workshop on WordNets and other Lexical Semantic Resources – between Lexical Semantics, Lexicography, Terminology and Formal Ontologies*, Odense: NEALT, pp. 7-12.

Brodda, B. (1982), Yttre kriterier för igenkänning av sammansättningar, in Saari, M. & Tandefelt, M. (eds.), *Förhandlingar vid trettonde sammankomsten för att dryfta frågor rörande svenskans beskrivning, Hanaholmen 1981*, Helsingfors: Institutionen för nordiska språk och nordisk litteratur vid Helsingfors universitet, pp. 102-114.

De Smedt, K. (2012), Ash compound frenzy: A case study in the Norwegian Newspaper Corpus, in Andersen, G. (ed.), *Exploring Newspaper Language. Using the web to create and investigate a large corpus of modern Norwegian*, Amsterdam: John Benjamins, pp. 241-256.

Gustafson-Capková, S. & Hartmann, B. (2008), *Manual of the Stockholm Umeå Corpus version 2.0*. Stockholm University, URL spraakbanken.gu.se/parole/Docs/SUC2.0-manual.pdf

Karlsson, F. (1992) Swetwol: A comprehensive morphological analyser for Swedish. *Nordic Journal of Linguistics* 15, pp. 1–45.

Östling, R. (2013) Stagger: an Open-Source Part of Speech Tagger for Swedish. Northern European Journal of Language Technology, 2013, Vol. 3, pp. 1–18.

Santos, D. & Rocha, P. (2001) Evaluating CETEMpúblico, a free resource for Portuguese, in *Proceedings of 39th Annual Meeting of the Association for Computational Linguistics*, Association for Computational Linguistics, pp. 450-457. URL http://www.aclweb.org/anthology/P01-1058

Sjöbergh, J. & Kann, V. (2004), Finding the correct interpretation of Swedish compounds, a statistical approach, in *Proc. 4th Int. Conf. Language Resources and Evaluation (LREC)*, pp. 899-902. URL http://www.csc.kth.se/tcs/projects/xcheck/rapporter/sjoberghkann04.pdf

Sjöbergh, J. & Kann, V. (2006) Vad kan statistik avslöja om svenska sammansättningar? *Språk och stil* 1, pp. 199-214.

Stymne, S. & Holmqvist, M. (2008), Processing of Swedish compounds for phrase-based statistical machine translation, in *Proceedings of the 12th Annual Conference of the European Association for Machine Translation (EAMT)*, European Association for Machine Translation, pp. 180-189. URL http://www.mt-archive.info/EAMT-2008-Stymne.pdf

Svanlund, J. (2009), *Lexikal etablering: En korpusundersökning av hur nya sammansättningar konventionaliseras och får sin betydelse*. Stockholm: Acta Univesitatis Stockholmiensis.

Teleman, U., Hellberg, S., Andersson, E. & Christensen, L. (eds), (1999), *Svenska Akademiens Grammatik*, volume 1–4, Stockholm: Svenska Akademien/Nordstedts ordbok.

De l'influence de la langue parlée dans les forums Internet : aspects linguistiques et variation diastratique

Per Förnegård & Françoise Sullet-Nylander

Université de Stockholm

1. Introduction

Dans les domaines des sciences du langage et des sciences de la communication, la recherche sur la communication médiatisée par ordinateur (désormais CMO)[1] s'est développée en même temps que les nouvelles technologies elles-mêmes. Qu'il s'agisse de sms, de tchats ou de forums Internet, ces nouvelles pratiques d'écriture ont, depuis le commencement, intéressé grand nombre de linguistes et d'interactionnistes qui ont mené des études sur différents aspects de la CMO, des analyses portant sur l'utilisation et la fréquence des accents (Compernolle & Williams 2010; Compernolle 2011) et des émoticônes (par ex. Marcoccia & Gauducheau 2007; Marcoccia 2000), des études morphosyntaxiques plus traditionnelles (par ex. Panckhurst 1998), ainsi que des observations sur le métalangage des internautes adolescents (Marcoccia 2012) – pour n'en nommer que quelques-unes.

Si plusieurs chercheurs ont soutenu que le discours électronique est marqué par des traits appartenant à la langue parlée[2], peu de linguistes se sont basés sur des données empiriques pour montrer en quoi consiste cette oralité[3]. Pour le français, c'est avant tout dans les travaux de Compernolle et de Compernolle & Williams que l'on trouve des comparaisons formelles entre la langue parlée et le discours électronique (par exemple l'emploi du *ne* de négation dans les tchats : Compernolle 2008a ; Compernolle & Williams 2009 ; *nous* vs *on* dans les tchats : Compernolle 2008b). En outre, dans une de leurs études (Compernolle & Williams 2007), les deux chercheurs ont

---

[1] Pour des raisons de commodité, nous utiliserons l'abréviation CMO, même si le terme *Communication médiatisée par ordinateur* est inexact, étant donné que d'autres outils, notamment les téléphones et les tablettes, peuvent être utilisés pour l'échange des messages.
[2] Pour des références à ces études, voir Compernolle & Williams (2007: 56), Marcoccia (2004a), Marcoccia (2003: 18).
[3] Voir, entre autres, Compernolle & Williams (2007: 56).

montré que certains paramètres linguistiques varient considérablement d'un type de discours électronique à un autre. En analysant trois corpus qui viennent de trois types de CMO différents – l'IRC (*Internet relay chat*, le tchat relayé par Internet, synchrone), les forums Internet (asynchrone) et le clavardage modéré (synchrone)[4] –, ils constatent que la graphie utilisée dans l'IRC et celle du clavardage modéré occupent deux positions extrêmes[5]. C'est ce premier qui s'écarte le plus du français standard, tandis que le clavardage modéré en est très proche. Les forums Internet, quant à eux, se trouveraient au milieu de ces deux pôles[6]. Il est donc essentiel de bien préciser de quel type de CMO il est question lorsqu'on soutient qu'elle est caractérisée par l'oralité.

Grâce à de telles études, la réflexion linguistique sur les rapports entre la langue orale et la langue écrite a été enrichie par l'apparition de la CMO (cf. Mourlhon-Dallies 2007: 21). Les linguistes mettent en avant les frontières ténues entre l'oral et l'écrit et les phénomènes de brouillage quant à la dichotomie traditionnelle oral/écrit. Ainsi, au sujet de la communication médiatisée par ordinateur, Gadet note ceci :

> Souvent qualifié d'oral dans l'écrit (*écrit contaminé par l'oral, oralité par écrit, parler lisible, hybridation oral/écrit*[7]), la CMO permet [...] de soulever les questions de l'éventuelle émergence de genre(s) d'écrit; et du rôle qu'y jouerait la référence à l'oralité. (Gadet 2008: 513)

Certains chercheurs estiment cependant qu'il n'existe aucun continuum entre les formes orales (matériau phonique) et les formes écrites (matériau graphique) de la langue et que l'on ne peut pas parler de « discours intermédiaires » (Kerbrat-Orecchioni, à paraître) entre l'oral et l'écrit. Kerbrat-Orecchioni admet cependant que certains types de discours de l'écrit, tels les tchats, possèdent certaines propriétés de l'oral et que, inversement, – « il arrive qu'on parle comme un livre ».

En nous basant sur l'ouvrage de Blanche-Benveniste (2000) axé sur les aspects *micro-* et *macrosyntaxiques* de la langue parlée et sur certains des travaux cités ci-dessus, nous visons à identifier quelques-unes de ces structures de l'oral dans l'un des types de CMO susmentionnés, à savoir les forums Internet.

---

[4] Également appelé *tchat événementiel*. Il s'agit de dialogues entre un ou plusieurs invités et un large public, où les messages des participants sont filtrés par un modérateur.
[5] Dans leur article sont analysés l'écriture des séquences *il y a* (*y a, y'a*, etc.), *il faut* (*faut, il fo*, etc.), *tu es* (*t'es, T*, etc.), *tu as* (*t'as, ta*, etc.), *c'est* (*c, ces*, etc.) et *j'ai* (*G*) ainsi que la fréquence du *ne* de négation lorsque ces mêmes séquences (à l'exception de *il faut* et de *il y a*) sont négatives.
[6] On reviendra aux résultats de Compernolle et de Compernolle & Williams dans l'analyse.
[7] Italiques de l'auteure.

Les forums Internet sont définis par Marcoccia (2004b: 4) comme un « dispositif de communication médiatisée par ordinateur asynchrone, permettant à des internautes d'échanger des messages au sujet d'un thème particulier ». Comme d'autres discours électroniques, il s'agit d'une communication hybride : « le code utilisé est l'écrit, mais les échanges de messages entrent dans une structure dialogale » (Marcoccia 2003: 18). Les forums constituent une hybridation aussi par leur format de réception : si le message initiatif (l'ouverture d'un *fil de discussion*) s'adresse à tous les membres du forum, les réponses (les *posts*) peuvent être destinées soit à l'initiateur du fil, soit à l'auteur d'un *post* précédent du même fil[8]. En même temps, tous les *posts*, qu'ils aient un destinataire explicite ou non, sont lisibles par tous, y compris les internautes qui n'ont pas créé de profil et qui ne peuvent pas, par conséquent, participer aux discussions. Ainsi, il s'agit d'un discours qui est à la fois public et interpersonnel (cf. Marcoccia 2003: 19-28).

Blanche-Benveniste (2000: 89) met l'accent sur des modes de production caractéristiques de l'oral, tels que les *répétitions*, les *hésitations* ou les *corrections* et sur des dispositifs syntaxiques fréquents dans les productions orales, comme les *constructions clivées*, *pseudo-clivées* et *disloquées*. Pour notre propre objectif, nous ajouterons d'autres phénomènes liés aux niveaux phonético-graphique, morphosyntaxique et syntaxique (voir *infra*).[9]

Au fil de notre étude — qualitative et quantitative —, nous prendrons en compte certains paramètres variationnels liés aussi bien aux usagers qu'aux thématiques traités dans chaque forum, afin de mener une analyse comparative des trois forums sélectionnés. Les questions de recherche auxquelles nous chercherons à répondre sont les suivantes :

- quels comportements linguistiques associés à la langue orale peuvent être identifiés dans les forums ? S'agit-il d'entités graphiques, morphologiques ou syntaxiques ?
- des paramètres diastratiques, notamment le sexe et l'âge des internautes, semblent-ils jouer un rôle pour la variation linguistique ?[10]

---

[8] Ce qui peut se faire explicitement à l'aide du pseudo du destinataire ou par le biais de citations automatiques. Au sujet de la citation automatique dans les forums, voir Marcoccia (2003: 22-23).

[9] Gadet (2008) liste les traits formels suivants, considérés comme typiques par les chercheurs, cherchant à préciser la dichotomie entre l'oral et l'écrit : « types de sujets, nominalisations, types de pronoms, négations avec ou sans *ne*, formes des questions, nature et degrés d'enchâssement, longueur de séquences… ».

[10] Compernolle & Williams (2007: 58) regrettent de ne pas pouvoir explorer la variation selon l'âge et le sexe des scripteurs, étant donné l'anonymat offert par la CMO. Cependant, en ce qui concerne les participants des forums Internet, il est souvent possible – quoique laborieux – de connaître ces deux paramètres grâce aux profils ou présentations des forumeurs. En revanche, il est, bien entendu, impossible de vérifier l'exactitude de ces données (voir aussi *infra*).

Soulignons qu'il s'agit d'une étude limitée qui se fonde sur un corpus limité : nous ne nous concentrerons que sur un certain nombre de paramètres linguistiques. Après quelques observations concernant les stratégies d'ajustement et de négociation ainsi que les modes de production (3.1), nous analyserons quelques phénomènes phonético-graphiques (3.2). Ensuite suivra, au niveau morphosyntaxique, une étude quantitative de la négation (3.3). Enfin, on passera au niveau syntaxique, où seront étudiées premièrement les interrogations (3.4.1), deuxièmement les clivées, les pseudo-clivées et les dislocations (3.4.2), troisièmement les connexions causales (3.4.3). Avant de procéder à l'analyse, nous fournirons une description de la composition du corpus (2).

2. Corpus

Notre corpus se compose d'environ 22 500 mots[11]. Afin de déceler d'éventuelles variations diastratiques, nous avons choisi trois forums dont chacun présente une population relativement homogène en matière de sexe et/ou d'âge des participants (voir *infra*). Dans chaque forum ont été sélectionnés au moins 5 fils de discussion. Pour avoir davantage de variation de sujets et un plus grand nombre d'intervenants uniques, seuls les quelque 1 500 premiers mots de chaque fil sont entrés dans notre corpus. Tous les fils ont été créés entre 2008 et 2012[12].

Le premier sous-corpus provient du *Forum ados*[13] (désormais « Ado ») auquel participent, comme le nom l'indique, notamment les adolescents. Les cinq fils prélevés dans ce forum (Ado 1-5) traitent de matières diverses (l'amour, la musique classique, la vie étudiante, le sport, la mode). Les participants se répartissent comme suit :

---

[11] Est comptée comme mot chaque unité linguistique inscrite entre deux blancs graphiques. Par conséquent, deux unités séparées par une apostrophe (par exemple *l'école*) sont comptées comme un seul mot. Les émoticônes ne sont évidemment pas comptées.
[12] Nous avons choisi les derniers fils en activité dans les trois forums et leurs sous-sections. Ainsi, tous les fils étaient-ils en activité en 2012. Le fil Gross 3 a certes été créé en janvier 2008 mais continue d'être fréquenté. (Il compte aujourd'hui plusieurs milliers d'interventions.)
[13] Les *forums ados* sont hébergés sur le site *Ados.fr* qui compte plus de quatre millions de visites par mois et plus de 100 000 messages publiés par jour (Marcoccia 2012: 159).

Forum « Ados » (Ado)											
Âge	13	14	15	16	17	18	19	20	25	26	?
Hommes	–	1	1	1	1	4	1	1	–	1	5
Femmes	1	3	6	1	4	3	–	2	1	–	10
Sexe non précisé	–	–	1	–	1	1	–	–	–	–	17
Total	1	4	8	2	6	8	1	3	1	1	32
							Âge moyen 17				

Tableau 1: Les intervenants du sous-corpus Ado regroupés selon leur âge et leur sexe.

Internet étant le lieu privilégié pour la mise en scène de soi, certaines de ces données peuvent, bien entendu, être inexactes : sur Internet, il s'agit toujours de l'âge et de sexe affirmés (cf. Marcoccia 2003: 40-45; Donath 1999; Turkle 1995). Il nous semble cependant raisonnable de penser que la majorité des internautes ayant créé un profil sur un forum et ayant pris la peine d'y indiquer leur âge et/ou leur sexe ne mentent pas sur ces données. On peut par ailleurs remarquer que 20 intervenants de ce sous-corpus ne précisent pas leur sexe et 32 – c'est-à-dire presque la moitié – leur âge. Comme on le verra, ces chiffres sont très élevés par rapports à ceux des deux autres sous-corpus.

Comme on peut le constater grâce au tableau, des intervenants des deux sexes fréquentent ce forum : ce sous-corpus compte 66 % de femmes et 34 % d'hommes, parmi les intervenants qui ont précisé leur sexe dans leur profil. Soulignons que les productions des forumeurs peuvent être de nature très inégale en ce qui concerne le nombre de *posts* publiés et leur longueur. À titre d'exemple, le fil Ado 1 compte 1606 mots répartis en 152 *posts* publiés par 18 internautes différents, soit une moyenne de 11 mots par intervention. Le forumeur le plus productif a fait 38 interventions, au total 319 mots, tandis qu'un participant n'a produit qu'un seul mot.

Le thème du fil semble avoir une influence sur la longueur des *posts*. Dans Ado 1, l'intervention initiative pose une question très précise – « Quelle est la couleur de vos sous-vêtements aujourd'hui ? » – à laquelle on peut très bien répondre par un seul mot (par exemple « turquoise »). Dans Ado 2 – dont l'initiatrice souhaite des propositions de musique – les *posts* sont bien plus longs, les 21 participants ayant produit 1572 mots qui se répartissent en seulement 39 *posts*, soit une moyenne de 44 mots par intervention.

Dans le deuxième sous-corpus, dont le thème est « l'art de séduire » (« ADS »)[14], la population est très différente de celle du premier : ici participent presqu'exclusivement des hommes. En effet, le règlement du site précise qu'il s'agit d'un « forum de séduction créé pour les hommes » mais que les femmes sont « tolérées » si elles respectent certaines « règles »[15]. Les *posts* étudiés ont été rédigés par des intervenants de sexe masculin dans 94

---

[14] www.artdeseduire.com
[15] http://forum-seduction.artdeseduire.com/reglement-et-f-q/

% des cas, comme il ressort du tableau 2. Pour atteindre les 7 500 mots, nous avons dû intégrer 8 fils de discussion de ce forum (ADS 1-8).

Forum « Art de séduire » (ADS)																				
Âge	15	16	17	18	19	20	21	22	23	24	25	27	28	30	31	32	33	34	35	?
Hommes	1	3	3	11	6	2	3	1	2	2	1	3	1	2	1	2	1	1	–	3
Femmes	–	–	1	–	–	1	–	–	–	–	–	–	–	–	–	–	–	–	1	–
Total	1	3	4	11	6	3	3	1	2	2	1	3	1	2	1	2	1	1	1	3
																	Âge moyen		21	

Tableau 2: Les intervenants du sous-corpus ADS regroupés selon leur âge et leur sexe.

Dans le troisième sous-corpus, dont les discussions sont dédiées à la grossesse et aux bébés[16] (« Gross »), participent uniquement des femmes. Cinq fils de discussion de ce forum sont entrés dans notre corpus (Gross 1-5).

Forum « Grossesse/bébé » (Gross)												
Âge	19	20	22	23	24	25	26	27	29	30	34	36	?
Hommes	–	–	–	–	–	–	–	–	–	–	–	–	–
Femmes	2	2	3	7	1	2	3	7	1	2	1	1	9
Total	2	2	3	7	1	2	3	7	1	2	1	1	9
											Âge moyen	25

Tableau 3: Les intervenants du sous-corpus Gross regroupés selon leur âge et leur sexe.

3. Analyse

3.1 Genres écrits/genres oraux et modes de production

En ce qui concerne la *problématique des genres*, nous rattachons notre approche à celle de Blanche-Benveniste (2000: 62-63) qui, à partir de l'étude de Biber (1988), cherche à problématiser la question des registres et des genres à l'oral *vs* l'écrit. Elle affirme ainsi :

> L'existence de différents genres dans la langue parlée montre qu'il est bon de multiplier les angles d'observation et d'envisager plusieurs sortes de compétences linguistiques […] Au fur et à mesure que se développent les études sur les langues parlées fondées sur de grands corpus, on s'aperçoit que la part quantitative du « langage spontané » se réduit, et qu'il est bon de connaître l'ensemble des genres attestés. (Blanche-Benveniste 2000: 62-63)

---

[16] forum.doctissimo.fr/grossesse-bebe/liste_categorie.htm. Il s'agit d'une sous-section du forum santé et bien-être *Doctissimo*. Celui-ci comptait, en avril 2013, plus de 3 300 000 forumeurs inscrits.

Rappelons que l'opposition discours spontané *vs* discours préparé ne correspond pas nécessairement à l'opposition oral *vs* écrit. Ainsi postulerons-nous que les paroles diffusées dans notre corpus écrit se rapprochent de « paroles improvisées » (Biber 1988, citée par Blanche-Benveniste 2000: 56).

De leur côté, Kerbrat-Orecchioni et Traverso (2004: 41-42) considèrent que la notion de genre comporte deux composantes : une textuelle et une discursive. Elles distinguent deux genres correspondant pour le premier à des catégories de textes plus ou moins institutionnalisées et, pour le deuxième, à des types de discours regroupés autour de traits rhétorico-pragmatiques. Tentant de catégoriser les genres de l'oral, elles partent d'une distinction similaire : les uns correspondent à des « événements de communication » (les G1) définis sur la base de critères « externes » liés au contexte situationnel, tandis que les « activités discursives » (les G2) sont catégorisées à partir de critères « internes », c'est-à-dire sur le matériau linguistique et l'organisation discursive. Dans notre étude des forums, nous prendrons en considération aussi bien des facteurs « externes » que des facteurs « internes »; pour ces derniers, nous nous concentrerons sur des aspects syntaxico-discursifs.

Dans les fils étudiés, il est clair que les stratégies d'*ajustement* et de *négociation* caractéristiques des *genres conversationnels* (Maingueneau 2007: 76) font partie intégrante des échanges. À l'intérieur d'un même forum, les participants de chaque fil s'adaptent aux interventions environnantes. Souvent, les traits discursifs et interactionnels du fil dans son intégralité dépendent de l'intervention de l'initiateur. On le voit dans les exemples (1) et (2), extraits du forum Gross :

(1) *Intervenant 1 (initiateur du fil)*
Bonsoir,
Si vous êtes comme moi une future maman et que c'est prévu pour mars 2013 je vous propose de suivre nos grossesses respectives ensemble!
Je m'appelle ***[17], j'habite à côté de ***, j'ai 29 ans et j'attends bb 1.
J'en suis à trois semaines de grossesse et pour l'instant je n'ai pas de nausée mais souvent mal au bas du ventre comme si j'avais mes règles (mais pas de saignements).
Et vous alors ?
Intervenant 2
Bonjour!
Tout d'abord felicitation ☺
Je suis *** j'ai 26 ans et j'habite à côté de ***. Le bb1 est prévu pour le 16 mars 2013.

---

[17] Afin de préserver l'anonymat des participants, nous remplaçons les prénoms par trois astérisques.

>   Jai eu une 1ere echo samedi dernier car 1ere grossesse GEU et
>   seconde FC...je suis donc tres bien suivie! Etant donné mon
>   passé je psychotte pas mal...
>   Je suis à 5SA dc 3SG et ma prochaine echo est le 19/07
>   Au niveau sensations...pas de nausees, par contre ventre dur et
>   gonflé pas douloureux mais genant. Du mal à dormir et une
>   peche d'enfer jai klk coup de barre pdt la journees...
>   Voilà !
>   (Gross 4, femme, 29 ans ; femme, 26 ans)

> (2)   *Intervenant 1 (initiateur du fil)*
>   Je propose ce forum sans prise de tête sans tabou. On c'est sui-
>   vis pendant un an et faut continuer ça serai dommage d'arrêter
>   alors restons connecter entre maman ☺
>
>   *Intervenant 2*
>   coucou ma puce est née fin septembre 2011, a voir ton tickers
>   elles ne doivent pas avoir trop de différence ☺
>   sa se passe bien ?
>
>   *Intervenant 1*
>   BIENVENUE oui tous ce passe bien merci dit nous tous sur
>   ton petit lou
>
>   *Intervenant 2*
>   donc ma fille s'appelle *** et elle aura 4 mois le 28 elle à une
>   grande soeur qui à 25 mois qui s'appelle ***. elle se porte pas
>   trop mal mais apparemment ce n'est pas trop une gloutonne
>   (comparé avec d'autres bébés sur docti) !! ☺elle a fait ses nuits
>   à 1 mois...
>   et toi ?
>   (Gross 2, femme, âge non précisé ; femme, 23 ans)

Ainsi, dans (1), l'initiatrice du fil indique son prénom, son lieu de résidence et décrit le déroulement de sa grossesse, suite à quoi l'intervenant 2 construit sa réponse à l'identique.

En (2), les participantes interviennent par alternance question/réponse (« sa se passe bien ? »; « oui tous ce passe bien ») et en revenant – afin de le compléter – sur leur propre discours grâce à des marqueurs discursifs de reprise et d'ouverture, comme ici « donc » dans l'énoncé : « *donc* ma fille s'appelle *** … ».

Pour ce qui est des *modes de production* présentés comme caractéristiques de la langue parlée, quelques exemples sont pertinents pour montrer les points communs entre notre corpus et des productions orales.

Dans ADS4, par exemple, l'un des internautes produit cet énoncé :

> (3)   J'ai finalement *dormi fini par dormir* avec. (ADS 4, homme, 22 ans)

Ici, il s'agit d'un « étoffement » du syntagme verbal (Blanche-Benveniste 2000: 89), par lequel le locuteur ajoute une précision aspectuelle. On peut parler de « retouche » dans l'exemple suivant, où l'initiateur du fil commence ainsi son intervention :

(4) Bonsoir messieurs,
Aujourd'hui, enfin ce soir, a l'instant quoi, je viens de quitter une discussion d'une heure avec une demoiselle que j'ai connu dans ma jeunesse (en 6eme et 5eme) lors de nos secours longue durée dans un pays étranger. (ADS 3, homme, 32 ans)

Dans l'exemple (5), il s'agit une nouvelle fois d'une retouche, où l'intervenante se rend soudain compte que ce qu'elle est en train d'écrire n'est pas tout à fait exact :

(5) il repart toujours seul et sans KC ou NC[18]... *Ah si, une fois je l'ai vu KC,* mais fallait voir l'allure de la fille, d'ailleurs j'ai encore des doutes sur le faite que ça en été réellement une ^^ (ADS 2, femme, 20 ans)

Au lieu d'effacer ou de modifier la première phrase (« il repart toujours seul et sans KC ou NC »), l'auteure de l'intervention ajoute une exclamation (« Ah si »), après laquelle elle corrige l'affirmation précédente.

Un autre forumeur rectifie, lui aussi, l'énoncé précédent à l'aide de *Ah si,* au lieu de le modifier :

(6) Pour le moment, a part parler de nos situations respectives, de nos souvenirs a l'étranger et décider de refaire un revival de nos années collèges 🌍avec les autre que nous avons chacun retrouvé, rien de plus.

Ha si, elle m'a dit de passer lui faire un coucou le jours ou j'irais au ski, je lui ai rendu la proposition le jour ou elle passait sur Paris...
(ADS 3, homme, 32 ans[19])

Enfin, citons un autre exemple relevant, selon nous, d'un mode de production de l'oral, où le discours se construit, comme dans une conversation à bâtons rompus :

---

[18] KC est une abréviation de l'anglais « *kiss close* »; NC de l'anglais « *num close* » (« prendre le numéro de téléphone de quelqu'un »). L'emploi d'anglicismes est particulièrement prégnant dans le forum ADS, dont l'usage est d'ailleurs encouragé par les créateurs du site (http://www.artdeseduire.com/category/lexique); il s'agit, selon eux, de « termes techniques et autres raccourcis utilisés dans le monde de la séduction ». Tous les emprunts de l'anglais utilisés dans ce forum ne font cependant pas partie de ce « jargon » : il y a plusieurs anglicismes qui relèvent du vocabulaire de tous les jours, tels que *everybody, checkant, revival, cut* (« elle me cut les cheveux ») ou *old school.*

[19] L'auteur de cette intervention est le même que dans l'exemple (4).

(7) on a répondu en même temps 😊 *du coup je sais plus ce que je voulais rajouter* 😊 (Gross 3, femme, âge non précisé)

Bien qu'il s'agisse d'une communication asynchrone qui permet de rectifier le message avant de le poster, on peut donc constater qu'un certain nombre de *posts* présentent les mêmes retouches qu'une communication en face à face.

3.2 Aspects phonético-graphiques

Considérons dans un premier temps ces deux exemples :

(8) ah oui en effet, sa a été très rapide 😊.
dsl pour ta fc, *sa ne doit pas* être évident. (Gross 5, femme, 23 ans)

(9) J'ai suivi la méthode une fois. *Je peux pas dire* si c'était par amour ou par curiosité, surement un peu des deux. En tout cas ça a marché. Tu veux que je te détaille ce qui s'est passé ?
(ADS 1, homme, 18 ans)

L'exemple (8) présente plusieurs phénomènes qui s'écartent du français écrit standard : absence de majuscules en début de phrase, omission du clitique sujet et de la copule (« dsl pour... » au lieu de « Je suis désolée pour »), *sa* pour *ça*, abréviations (*dsl* (« désolé/e »), *fc* (« fausse couche »). Dans l'exemple (9), tous les phénomènes énumérés ci-dessus sont absents; ainsi cet exemple est-il, dans son ensemble, plus conforme à la norme écrite. Pourtant, dans l'exemple (8), la négation est complète, tandis qu'elle est réduite à *pas* dans (9).

De fait, un énoncé comportant des marques qui ne sont pas conformes au français écrit standard n'est pas forcément influencé par l'oral. Dans (8), ni l'absence de majuscules en début de phrase ni les abréviations ne sont mimétiques de la langue orale, car lors d'une lecture à haute voix de cet énoncé, ces déviances par rapport à la norme écrite ne s'entendent pas : par exemple, *fc* sera prononcé [foskuʃ] et non pas [efse]. En revanche, la chute du clitique sujet et de la copule dans « dsl pour ta fc » dans (8) peut être considérée comme une influence de la langue parlée, ces entités étant fréquemment omises à l'oral. Il faut donc distinguer les formes mimétiques de la langue parlée de celles qui s'écartent simplement de la norme de l'écrit. Ainsi, l'exemple (8) n'est pas, selon nous, plus marqué par l'oralité que l'exemple (9), malgré les déviances de la norme écrite.

Le pronom démonstratif *cela* et sa variante courte *ça* sont employés sous des formes différentes. Dans un grand nombre de *posts*, les participants utilisent la forme *sa* comme en (8) ci-dessus dans « *sa* a été très rapide ». Selon nous, ce phénomène confirme la primauté du mode de production de l'oral sur celui de l'écrit dans notre corpus : en utilisant le graphème *s* correspondant au phonème [s] et non le graphème *c* sans cédille – bien qu'il soit plus proche orthographiquement –, on évite une lecture fautive de « ca a été » en [kaaete]. Cependant, les stratégies d'*ajustement* mentionnées plus haut doivent également être prises en compte. Ainsi, dans certains fils, la forme « ça » est la plus fréquente. C'est le cas de ADS 7: « je trouve que ça fait classe »; « Ça dépend aussi du type de chemise » ; « Mi dehors/dedans ça ne le fait pas dans la réalité »; « Sortir sa chemise, je trouve ça vraiment beauf », etc.

L'alternance entre *cela* et *ça* (avec des graphies variables) nous paraît également intéressante quant aux paramètres registraux et variationnels. Dans une même intervention et dans la même suite, les deux formes peuvent être employées :

(10) En fac/au lycee... *Sa* depends de là ou tu es. Si c'est un endroit selec (henry 4, iep de paris, Dauphine...) tu le rentres. Sinon pour le reste *cela* depends de la chemise. Une chemise a carreau, une chemise noire scintillante...sorti. Une chemise plus "classe" type de celle que tu porterai au boulot ou alors une de marque type R.Lauren tu la rentre (ADS 7, homme, 18 ans)

Il faut toutefois noter que la forme *cela* est extrêmement rare : comme le montre le tableau 4, elle n'est utilisée que dans 4 % des cas. Partout ailleurs, on préfère la forme courte :

	Ado 1-5		ADS 1-8		Gross 1-5		Total	
	nbr	%	nbr	%	nbr	%	nbr	%
cela	2	2 %	3	4 %	6	7 %	11	4 %
ça	64	71 %	56	67 %	43	49 %	163	63 %
sa[20]	13	15 %	13	15 %	27	30 %	53	20 %
ca	11	12 %	12	14 %	12	14 %	35	13 %
Total	90	100 %	84	100 %	88	100 %	262	100 %

Tableau 4: Répartition entre les formes du pronom démonstratif neutre et ses différentes graphies.

Ces données permettent de déceler une variation entre nos trois sous-corpus. En effet, dans le sous-corpus Gross, où tous les intervenants sont de sexe féminin et où l'âge moyen est plus élevé que dans les autres forums, la variante standard avec *c* cédille n'est utilisée que dans 49 % des cas, tandis que, dans les deux autres sous-corpus, elle représente respectivement 71 % et 67 %. On peut mettre en rapport le taux réduit de *ça* dans Gross avec le

---

[20] Les attestations du *sa* possessif ont évidemment été exclues.

chiffre plus élevé de *sa* : bien qu'il s'agisse d'une variante graphique non standard, elle est « phonétiquement correcte »[21].

Ajoutons à ce sujet que, de manière récurrente, la graphie de *s'est* des formes verbales réfléchies ou pronominales est reproduite par *c'est* comme dans Gross 1 « ta grossesse *c'est* bien déroulé ? » ou dans Gross 2 : « On *c'est* suivis pendant un an »[22].

Notre corpus comporte des réductions des pronoms déictiques sujet *je* et *tu* ainsi que du pronom neutre *il* (notamment dans les séquences *il faut* et *il y a* et leurs variantes). Ces réductions sont caractéristiques de la langue parlée (Blanche-Benveniste 2000) :

(11) maintenan *ya* plus k!!!!! (Gross 5, femme, 27 ans)

(12) en me disant qu'elle n'était plus amoureuse, que y'avait plus le "petit truc" (bref vous connaissez). (ADS 1, homme, 18 ans)

Les exemples (11) et (12) peuvent être considérés comme des phénomènes « périgraphiques », c'est-à-dire des graphies s'écartant du français standard mais produites intentionnellement. (Pierozak 2003, citée par Compernolle & Williams 2007: 61). La réduction du *e* instable (13-15) et celle de *u* dans *tu* (16) constituent d'autres exemples :

(13) Mais franchement, zen, *j'me* suis inscrite après le début des cours il y a deux ans, j'ai pas eu de problème 😊 (Ado 3, sexe et âge non précisés)

(14) Coucou les filles 🐵
j'peux me joindre à vous ? 😊 (Gross 5, femme, 27 ans)

(15) Si mon copain va à l'anniversaire de son meilleur pote plutot qu'a moi, *j'serais* triste, mais *j'lui* en voudrais pas c'est quand même son meilleur pote! (Ado 5, femme, 15 ans)

(16) et essaye de reproduire les mêmes émotions que *t'avais* produite en elle quand elle était amoureuse (ADS 1, homme, 17 ans)

La réduction du *e* instable (13-15) et de *u* dans *tu* (16) dans ces exemples n'est vraisemblablement pas due à un souci de brièveté, c'est-à-dire à une volonté de réduire le nombre de caractères : *j'me* et *j'peux* comptent autant de caractères que leurs variantes standard *je me* et *je peux*, si ce n'est qu'il faut ajouter une espace dans ces dernières. Ces exemples donnent plutôt

---

[21] Dans une étude de l'emploi des signes diacritiques dans un site de rencontres, Compernolle (2011) observe que les annonces rédigées par des femmes font un emploi plus fréquent des accents aigu, grave et circonflexe que celles des hommes, tandis que les chiffres sont inversés quant à l'utilisation de la cédille.

[22] Voir aussi Compernolle & Williams (2007: 63) où la variante standard de *c'est* est utilisé dans 92 % des cas dans les forums. Dans leur corpus IRC, en revanche, elle ne représente que 44 %.

l'impression que les formes abrégées utilisées par certains forumeurs sont mimétiques des formes employées à l'oral (cf. Compernolle & Williams 2007: 57). Un inventaire complet des séquences *tu as* et *il y a* et leurs variantes suggère cependant que les phénomènes périgraphiques sont présents mais pas extrêmement répandus :

Tu as et ses variantes					
	Ado 1-5	ADS 1-8	Gross 1-5	Total	
tu as	8	14	15	37	(82 %)
t'as, ta, t'a, tas	3	4	1	8	(18 %)
Total	11	18	16	45	(100 %)

Tableau 5: La séquence *tu as* et ses variantes non standard.

Il y a et ses variantes					
	Ado 1-5	ADS 1-8	Gross 1-5	Total	
il y a	11	13	8	32	(78 %)
y a, ya, y'a	4	2	3	9	(22 %)
Total	15	15	11	41	(100 %)

Tableau 6: La séquence *il y a* et ses variantes. Sont comptées également les séquences négatives et les groupes verbaux à l'imparfait et au futur simple.

Les tableaux 5 et 6 montrent que les formes standard de *tu as* et *il y a* sont utilisées respectivement dans 82 % et 78 % des cas[23], c'est-à-dire environ 4 fois sur 5. On est donc très loin d'une systématisation de formes oralisées. À titre d'exemple, dans le corpus de français parlé familier utilisé par Compernolle & Williams (2007: 66), la suppression du clitique sujet dans *il y a*, variante prononcée [ja], se fait dans 74 % des cas. Les données de notre corpus ne permettent pas d'observer une éventuelle variation diastratique quant aux phénomènes périgraphiques.

Certaines variantes non traditionnelles donnent parfois lieu à des graphies qui sont plus encombrantes que leurs variantes standard :

(17) Simple avis, d'un mec qui *en n'a* bouffé des LTR[24]. (ADS 1, homme, âge non précisé)
(18) Et c'est vrai que les chemises de type "Slim Fit" donne un air classe, à tester pour ceux qui *en n'ont* pas encore. (ADS 7, homme, 16 ans)

---

[23] La proportion de variantes non standard de la séquence *tu as* est cependant plus élevée dans notre corpus que dans les forums qu'ont étudiés Compernolle & Williams (2007: 63), où les formes non traditionnelles représentent 8,5 % des cas. En revanche, en ce qui concerne les variantes de *il y a*, nos résultats corroborent ceux obtenus par Compernolle & Williams (2007: 61), dans le corpus desquels les formes traditionnelles représentent presque 82 % des cas.

[24] LTR, abréviation de l'expression anglaise « *long time relationship* ».

Dans (17) et (18), les forumeurs marquent la liaison obligatoire entre *en* et le mot qui suit par un *n* euphonique, comme s'ils considéraient que le matériau graphique n'était pas suffisant pour indiquer le liage entre *en* et le mot qui suit[25]. De nouveau, il nous semble que l'on pourrait interpréter ce surmarquage comme la manifestation de la primauté du mode de production de l'oral sur celui de l'écrit.

Les productions étudiées reflètent rarement un souci d'économie quant au nombre de caractères. À titre d'exemple, le syllabogramme *g* pour « j'ai » et la graphie *ke* pour « que », si fréquents dans le « langage SMS »[26], sont quasi-absents de notre corpus : seuls deux intervenants les emploient[27]. Cette très faible représentation du syllabogramme *g* dans les forums a également été constatée par Compernolle & Williams (2007: 64) : dans leur corpus, il n'est utilisé que dans 3,5 % des cas ; le reste du temps, les forumeurs choisissent la forme standard *j'ai*.

On notera par ailleurs que l'usage du « langage SMS » est proscrit dans les chartes d'utilisation des forums ici étudiés. Ainsi, dans le forum Ado, « [l]e langage dit 'SMS' est strictement interdit » (cité par Marcoccia 2012: 163); dans le règlement du forum ADS, le modérateur souligne qu'il faut écrire « dans un français correct, sans abréviations et vulgarités » et s'exprimer « de façon claire et appliquée (pas de langage SMS) »[28]; la charte du forum Doctissimo, qui héberge le sous-forum Gross, précise qu'on « participe [...] aux discussions [...] en utilisant un langage correct »[29]. Selon Marcoccia, « à peine 10 % des messages postés dans *Ados.fr* contiennent du 'langage SMS' » (2012: 163).

3.3 Aspects morphosyntaxiques : la négation

De nombreuses recherches ont pu constater que l'omission du *ne* de négation est un trait tout à fait typique du français parlé, le premier composant de la négation disparaissant dans, au moins, 80 % des cas[30] (voir études citées par Compernolle & Williams 2009). Selon les observations de Blanche-Benveniste, il y a jusqu'à 95 % d'absence de *ne* dans les conversations orales, « quels que soient les locuteurs » (2000: 39). Elle ajoute cependant que « dans certains discours publics où le langage est très surveillé, [...], le *ne* de négation est beaucoup plus fréquent ». Dans une étude plus récente,

---

[25] Panckhurst a relevé le même *n* « euphonique » dans les courriels qu'elle a analysés (1998: 51).
[26] Voir Fairon, Klein & Paumier (2006).
[27] Gross 1: 1 attestation de *g* (femme, 20 ans); Gross 5: 5 attestations de *g* et 4 de *ke* (femme, 27 ans).
[28] http://forum-seduction.artdeseduire.com/reglement-et-f-q/5-lire-reglement-ads.html
[29] http://www.doctissimo.fr/asp/forums/charte_utilisation.htm
[30] Ce chiffre s'applique au français hexagonal.

Compernolle (2009) obtient le même chiffre que Blanche-Benveniste, le *ne* étant omis dans 94 % des cas[31]. Voici le taux de maintien et de chute dans notre corpus[32] :

	Ado 1-5		ADS 1-8		Gross 1-5		Total	
	nbr	%	nbr	%	nbr	%	nbr	%
Négation complète	77	61 %	72	53 %	70	65 %	219	59 %
Négation réduite (sans *ne*)	50	39 %	64	47 %	38	35 %	152	41 %
Total	127	100 %	136	100 %	108	100 %	371	100 %

Tableau 7: Négations complètes et négations réduites dans les trois forums[33].

Comme il ressort de ce tableau, le *ne* tombe dans 41 % des négations de notre corpus, chiffre suffisamment élevé pour pouvoir parler d'une vraie influence de la langue parlée, même si l'on est loin d'un mimétisme systématique de l'oral. On peut également observer une variation diastratique : c'est dans ADS – fréquenté presque exclusivement par des hommes – que l'absence de *ne* est la plus fréquente. Parmi les 8 fils étudiés de ce forum, seul un fil (ADS 8) compte plus de négations complètes que de négations réduites.

Nombreux sont les forumeurs qui se servent tantôt de la forme complète, tantôt de la forme réduite de la négation. L'exemple (10) provient du message initiatif du fil ADS 3 :

(19) Je l'ai retrouvé via FB il y a environ 6 mois et nous *ne nous étions jamais* vraiment reparlé. [...] *Je sais pas* trop comment gamer, et *j'ai pas* envie d'être relou a lui parler tout les jours. (ADS 3, homme, 32 ans)

Cette variation peut même être observée dans un seul et même énoncé :

(20) en effet je sais que la possibilité *n'est pas* nulle, mais *j'arrive pas* à réaliser. :/ J'espère *ne pas tomber* de trop haut en cas d'échec. (ADS 1, homme, 18 ans)

---

[31] En outre, Compernolle observe que les *ne* maintenus en français parlé s'emploient dans des contextes marqués prosodiquement, comme le débit ralenti (2009). Son corpus – assez limité comme il l'admet lui-même – se compose de productions orales de locuteurs jeunes. La majorité d'entre eux sont de sexe féminin.

[32] On peut noter que, dans son analyse de courriels de 1998, Panckhurst constate que les négations demeurent quasiment intactes (1998: 57).

[33] Si Compernolle et Williams (2007: 67-68) étudient le maintien du *ne* dans leur corpus forum, ils n'étudient pas l'ensemble des occurrences mais seulement l'emploi de la négation dans certains environnements immédiats, ce qui réduit fortement le nombre d'occurrences.

D'autres forumeurs n'utilisent jamais le *ne* de négation dans leurs interventions :

>   (21)   au début j'avais peur de *pas savoir* gérer le boulot et 1 enfant, mais *j'ai pas* eu le choix, il a fallu retravailler... Et finalement ça se passe très bien, et pourtant mon fils *nous fait pas* toujours des nuits de rêve !!! bonne nuit !!! (Gross 5, femme, 25 ans)

Pour résumer, l'emploi de la négation dans notre corpus révèle une nette influence de la langue parlée mais, en même temps, on est loin de la chute systématique du *ne* observée à l'oral.

3.4 Aspects syntaxiques

3.4.1 Interrogations

Le français possédant trois manières différentes de poser des questions, une étude syntaxique des interrogations peut permettre d'observer une éventuelle influence de la langue parlée quant à la forme des énoncés interrogatifs. La première construction, celle avec inversion, est, selon Riegel, Pellat & Rioul (2009: 671), « réservée à l'écrit, en particulier littéraire », tandis que la deuxième avec *est-ce que* est aujourd'hui utilisée aussi bien à l'oral qu'à l'écrit. Dans la troisième variante, qui correspond à l'interrogation intonative (sujet-verbe), seul le point d'interrogation indique, à l'écrit, que l'on a affaire à une question en cas d'interrogation totale. À ce sujet, Panckhurst constate, dans son corpus courriel (1998: 58-59), une quasi absence de formes qui correspondent à l'interrogation intonative (sujet-verbe) et conclut à une opposition « très nette » entre la CMO et l'oral.

Quant à notre corpus, les trois variantes canoniques sont présentes, aussi bien les questions avec inversion (22, 23), qu'en *est-ce que* (24, 25), que la question sans inversion (26, 27). Toutes les trois sont en outre utilisées aussi bien pour l'interrogation totale (22, 24, 26) que pour l'interrogation partielle (23, 25, 27). Il existe également un certain nombre d'interrogations incomplètes, c'est-à-dire sans verbe conjugué (28) :

>   (22)   *est-ce* vraiment une règle absolue d'éviter le noir en relooking ? (ADS 6, homme, 19 ans)

>   (23)   C'est un peu compliqué : relation à distance, vous avez tout deux une vie de famille contraignante... *Qu'envisages tu* vraiment, *qu'est elle* à tes yeux ? (ADS 3, femme, 17 ans)

>   (24)   Cependant, et ça n'a rien à voir, mais ton sujet n'a rien à faire ici, alors dis moi : *est ce que c'est un S.O.S ?* Ou *est ce que* c'est une sorte de journal ? (ADS 1, homme, 27 ans)

(25) Et *qu'est-ce que* tu vas dire si elle reviens vers toi et qu'elle te demande *qu'est ce qui* t'arrive de si bien dans ta vie ?? (ADS 1, homme, 18 ans)

(26) félicitation ***! *tout se passe bien* avec ton bout de chou *? ta grossesse c'est bien déroulé ?* (Gross 1, femme, 19 ans)

(27) et toi alors *comment sa se passe* pour le moment ? (Gross 1, femme, 20 ans)

(28) Des jeans en microfibre ? (Ado 1, homme, 18 ans)

Selon Mosegaard Hansen (2001:464), l'alternance des trois variantes de la question totale à l'oral – inversion / *est-ce que* / intonation ascendante – ne dépend pas uniquement du registre. Selon elle, le degré de « formalité » ne constituerait qu'un épiphénomène derrière lequel se cacheraient d'autres paramètres sémantiques et pragmatiques plus solides. Deux grandes propriétés sont attribuées aux questions totales :

a) le locuteur signale à l'interlocuteur qu'il est pertinent de se poser une question sur la validité du contenu propositionnel exprimé;
b) le locuteur demande une réaction de l'interlocuteur au sujet de cette proposition.

Les questions avec inversion et avec *est-ce que* ont grammaticalisé la première de ces propriétés, avec en plus pour *est-ce que* une construction plus « emphatique ». Pour la question intonative, la structure syntaxique est celle de l'assertion. Pourtant, l'intonation montante signale l'incertitude et fonctionne comme une ouverture, un appel vers l'interlocuteur. La question avec intonation ascendante renferme donc plus systématiquement la deuxième des propriétés. En outre, le statut des participants ainsi que leur relation d'égalité ou d'inégalité dans l'interaction sont également susceptibles d'influer sur la forme des questions (Mosegaard Hansen 2001: 477). Les interrogations avec inversion et avec *est-ce que* se prêteraient mieux à la relation de « déférence » entre les partenaires, étant donné qu'elles codifient explicitement l'incertitude sur le contenu de la proposition. En revanche, l'interrogation intonative serait plus prévisible dans un contexte informel où les participants sont à égalité dans l'interaction.

Ces observations de Mosegaard Hansen (2001) faites sur des productions orales nous permettent-elles de discerner des tendances dans notre corpus d'interactions écrites ? Dans le contexte interactif des forums, où les participants sont dans une relation de relative égalité[34], on pourrait formuler l'hypothèse que les questions sans inversion, se démarquant de l'assertion à

---

[34] On peut noter que dans les trois sous-corpus étudiés ne figure aucune attestation de *vous* au singulier, bien que les forumeurs ne se soient vraisemblablement jamais rencontrés.

l'écrit uniquement par un point d'interrogation, seront plus fréquentes que les autres formes.

Voici la répartition des différents types d'interrogations dans nos trois sous-corpus :

		Ado 1-5		ADS 1-8		Gross 1-5		Total	
Interrog. totale	Inversion	7	(30 %)	8	(36 %)	3	(7 %)	18	(20 %)
	Ordre SV	16	(70 %)	11	(50 %)	31	(70 %)	58	(65 %)
	est-ce que	0	(0 %)	3	(14 %)	10	(23 %)	13	(15 %)
	Total	23	(100%)	22	(100 %)	44	(100 %)	89	(100 %)
Interrog. partielle	Inversion	7	(39 %)	6	(55 %)	5	(36 %)	18	(42 %)
	Ordre SV	9	(50 %)	2	(18 %)	8	(57 %)	19	(44 %)
	est-ce que	2	(11 %)	3	(27 %)	1	(7 %)	6	(14 %)
	Total	18	(100 %)	11	(100 %)	14	(100 %)	43	(100 %)
Interrog. incomplètes		12		1		4		17	
Total : Interrogations		53	(36 %)	34	(23 %)	62	(41 %)	149	(100 %)

Tableau 8: Les différents types d'interrogations dans les trois forums.

Les chiffres du tableau 8 confirment l'hypothèse selon laquelle les questions sans inversion seraient les plus nombreuses. En effet, 58 % des interrogations complètes (totales et partielles), prennent l'ordre des mots sujet-verbe. Ce sont cependant les questions totales – où seul le point d'interrogation (ou, à l'oral, l'intonation ascendante) montre qu'il s'agit d'une question – où cette tendance se dégage le plus : 65 % des interrogations totales mais seulement 44 % des interrogations partielles. Ainsi, dans chaque sous-corpus, l'inversion est plus fréquemment utilisée dans les interrogations partielles que totales.

On peut noter des variations entre les trois sous-corpus. Dans Ado, 34 % des questions complètes se construisent avec inversion, 61 % avec l'ordre SV. Dans ADS, où l'usage de *est-ce que* est plus fréquent qu'il ne l'est dans Ado, l'inversion, utilisée dans 42 % des cas, compte plus d'attestations que l'ordre SV (39 %). Dans Gross, enfin, c'est, de loin, l'interrogation sans inversion qui est préférée : 67 % des questions complètes se construisent de cette manière, l'inversion étant utilisée dans seulement 14 % des cas. Cette différence significative entre Gross et les deux autres sous-corpus, faut-il l'expliquer en termes d'*égalité* et d'*inégalité* (voir *supra*), c'est-à-dire que les intervenantes de Gross, qui sont toutes mères ou futures mères, s'adresseraient à un public plus homogène dont la relation d'égalité serait plus prégnante que celle des deux autres ? Cependant, on pourrait considérer que les participants d'ADS constituent également une communauté homogène : les termes d'adresse montrent bien que les forumeurs-hommes s'adressent à des personnes appartenant au même groupe qu'eux : « Salut les mecs » (ADS 2), « Bonsoir messieurs » (ADS 3). Cette différence serait-elle plutôt due à des facteurs diastratiques ? Les forumeurs de sexe féminin emploieraient-elles un ton plus informel quand elles communiquent entre elles ?

Ce n'est pas seulement entre les sous-corpus que l'on peut constater une variation syntaxique ; on peut également observer une différence entre message initiatif et réponse. Ainsi les constructions avec inversion et *est-ce que* sont-elles légèrement plus fréquentes dans le premier *post* du fil. À titre d'exemple, le message initiatif de Gross 3 présente 3 interrogations avec *est-ce que* et 1 avec inversion. À notre avis, cette façon de poser des questions au début d'un fil peut être mise en rapport avec l'hypothèse de Mosegaard Hansen (voir *supra*), selon laquelle ces constructions codifient l'incertitude de la proposition. Dans le genre discursif que constituent les forums, on peut s'attendre en effet à ce que les scripteurs utilisent plus fréquemment cette forme d'interrogation dans un message initiatif, dans la mesure où celui-ci correspond, la plupart du temps, à une vraie demande de conseil ou d'information[35].

Une dernière différence qui peut être constatée entre les trois sous-corpus est le nombre d'interrogations. Dans ADS, où 94 % des intervenants sont de sexe masculin, 34 questions sont posées (y compris les questions incomplètes), tandis que Gross en compte 62. Ainsi, ce dernier présente 88 % plus de questions que ADS. Ces chiffres semblent confirmer l'hypothèse fréquemment émise – surtout dans les années 1980 et 1990 et avant tout par des chercheurs anglo-saxons – selon laquelle il y aurait une asymétrie entre hommes et femmes en ce qui concerne les interrogations : selon ces travaux, les femmes, qui, à la différence des hommes, seraient sur un mode d'échange « coopératif », poseraient plus fréquemment des questions que les hommes (voir par exemple Moïse 2002). D'autres études, par exemple celle de Freed & Greenwood (1996), récusent cependant cette hypothèse, soutenant que la fréquence de questions posées dans une conversation n'est pas due à des facteurs sexuels mais à d'autres facteurs externes, comme le contexte et le thème traité. Quoi qu'il en soit, il y a une différence nette entre ADS et Gross en ce qui concerne aussi bien le nombre de questions posées que leur construction syntaxique. Dans un travail ultérieur basé sur un corpus élargi, nous espérons pouvoir revenir à ces questions afin de déterminer si la variation observée est due à des facteurs sexuels ou bien contextuels.

---

[35] Il arrive ainsi que, lorsque le créateur d'un fil ne s'adapte pas aux règles du genre, c'est-à-dire qu'il ne pose pas de question, l'intervenant suivant le rappelle à l'ordre : « [...] ton sujet n'a rien à faire ici, alors dis moi : est ce que c'est un S.O.S ? Ou est ce que c'est une sorte de journal ? » (ADS 1, homme, 27 ans; cf. ex (24)).

3.4.2 Clivées, pseudo-clivées et dislocations

Blanche-Benveniste (2000: 96-101) se penche sur divers dispositifs syntaxiques fondamentaux spécifiques de l'oral « qui livrent autant de façons différentes de traiter l'information ». Nous ferons tout d'abord quelques observations sur les *constructions clivées* et *pseudo-clivées* de notre corpus. En particulier la tournure pseudo-clivée constitue, selon Blanche-Benveniste (2000: 99), une « forme naturelle de réponse à une question, avec reprise du verbe de la question ». Elle fournit l'exemple suivant comme illustration : « *Qu'est-ce que* tu aimes sur la scène ? – *Ce que* j'aime, euh à la fin, *c'est* les applaudissements ». Cette tournure serait souvent suivie par une clivée qui semble confirmer l'information donnée par le verbe : « *Ce que* j'aime pas euh *c'est* la violence en même temps quoi [...] *c'est* ça *que* j'aime pas ». Dans notre corpus, les deux constructions fonctionnent rarement comme réponse à une question, comme c'est le cas dans l'exemple de Blanche-Benveniste indiqué ci-dessus. Ces constructions apparaissent plutôt dans des séquences argumentatives. En voici quelques réalisations dans nos trois forums :

(29) C'est un choix à faire ☺
Ce qui peut aussi peser dans la balance, c'est le papa. Si tu sais qu'il s'occupera aussi du bébé, qu'il te soutiendra, et que c'est le genre de gars qui est capable de passer l'aspirateur pour te permettre de bûcher tranquille, c'est un élément à prendre en considération. (Gross 3, femme, âge non précisé)

(30) Oui, c'est sur que je pense aussi que la voiture est plus avantageuse mais *ce que je voulais dire par là, c'est que ce n'est pas injouable* et *** a précise qu'il était en banlieue proche donc il s'évite l'heure de RER pour arriver a 20 km de Paris (ADS 8, homme, 16 ans)

(31) Tu sais, j'ai le droit d'aimer ces artistes-là, et *ce n'est pas parce que ça n'est pas de ton goût que tu dois te sentir obligé d'envoyer chier les gens* ☻ (Ado 2, femme, 15 ans)

Dans (29), la pseudo-clivée permet au forumeur d'introduire un nouvel argument concernant la discussion sur la décision de mettre un enfant en route alors qu'on est en thèse de doctorat. Dans l'exemple (30), le forumeur revient sur sa propre argumentation quant à l'utilité de posséder une voiture comme « élément de séduction fort ». Enfin, dans le dernier exemple (31), avec la construction *ce n'est pas parce que... que*, le forumeur reprend et rejette en même temps les propos d'un autre participant. Bien que très peu nombreuses dans notre corpus (voir tableau 9 ci-dessous), les tournures clivée et pseudo-clivée semblent tout à fait efficaces dans ce contexte dialogique et argumentatif :

	Ado	ADS	Gross
clivées et pseudo-clivées	9	7	3
dislocations	14	8	22

Tableau 9: Distribution des constructions clivées, pseudo-clivées et disloquées dans nos sous-corpus.

Il ressort du tableau 9 que les participants de Ado et ADS se servent de loin en loin de clivées et de pseudo-clivées. Dans Gross, par contre, elles sont rarissimes. En ce qui concerne les *dislocations*, c'est le cas inverse : c'est dans Gross qu'elles sont les plus fréquentes.

La dislocation est définie comme une forme de construction dans laquelle on a d'une part un pronom qui assure la fonction de régi et, d'autre part, une réalisation lexicale détachée, soit avant le verbe, soit après le verbe (Blanche-Benveniste 2000: 158). Il s'agit d'une construction « très fréquente en français oral et [qui] joue un rôle central dans la construction des énoncés » (Engel 2010: 20)[36]. Les dislocations trouvées dans notre corpus sont de formes peu variées. En effet, il s'agit en majeure partie de formes du type canonique *Moi, je* (32, 33) ou SN + *ça* (34). En voici trois exemples :

(32) Tout depend aussi de ta morphologie et de la largueur de ton bassin et 4mois c'est encore tot mais on est tjrs si pressé d'avoir un gros bidon !! ☺ *Moi j'ai* une petit boué en dessous du nombril mais a part moi je ne pense pas que de l'exterieur on puisse le remarquer. (Gross 1, femme, 19 ans)

(33) *Toi tu* trouves peut être ça laid mais pas moi, il suffit de regarder toutes les célébrités sur les magazines et tu t'apercevas que j'ai raison... Quelqu'un saurait-il comment s'y prendre ? (ADS 7, homme, 24 ans)

(34) Sinon *le noir ça amincie*, donc bof quoi... ☺ (Ado, homme, 18 ans)

Comme pour les constructions clivées et/ou pseudo-clivées, on voit combien cette « redondance syntaxique » (Blanche-Benveniste 2000: 37) est efficace dans la situation d'énonciation des forums où il s'agit à la fois de se placer dans la chaîne dialogique des fils tout en se démarquant des autres forumeurs afin de mettre en avant sa propre argumentation.

3.4.3 Conjonctions causales

Dans un article récent, Engel, Forsgren & Sullet-Nylander (2012: 192) ont montré que les connexions causales sont jusqu'à cinq fois plus fréquentes à

---

[36] Voir aussi Blanche-Benveniste (2000: 67-68) et Gadet (2007: 17).

l'oral qu'à l'écrit[37]. Selon eux, un nombre plus élevé de conjonctions causales est ainsi un trait typique du discours oral dialogué[38]. Si l'on regroupe en deux blocs, oral et écrit, les différents corpus étudiés par les trois chercheurs, on constate en effet que la fréquence de connexions causales marquées par *parce que*, *puisque* et *car* est nettement plus élevée à l'oral :

	Corpus oraux		Corpus écrits			
			journalistique		littéraire/scientifique[39]	
	occ.	occ./1000 mots	occ.	occ./1 000 mots	occ.	occ./1 000 mots
parce que	954	4,04	41	0,30	360	env. 0,55
puisque	85	0,36	18	0,13	129	env. 0,20
car	10	0,04	53	0,39	306	env. 0,47
Total	1 049	4,44	112	0,82	795	env. 1,22

Tableau 10: Distribution des conjonctions causales marquées par *parce que*, *puisque* et *car* dans les corpus étudiés par Engel, Forsgren & Sullet-Nylander (2012:190).

Il ressort de ce tableau que les cadences moyennes (nombre d'occurrences / 1 000 mots) sont bien plus élevées à l'oral qu'à l'écrit : à l'oral, les conjonctions *parce que*, *puisque* et *car* ont une cadence moyenne de 4,44. À l'écrit, la cadence n'est que de 0,82 (prose journalistique) et d'env. 1,22 (littérature, science)[40].

Les résultats obtenus par Engel, Forsgren & Nylander sont confirmés par un autre corpus de français parlé, Corpaix (Véronis 2000), qui se compose de 1 000 000 mots :

---

[37] Pour l'oral, il s'agit de quatre corpus différents, dont un composé de journaux télévisés, un deuxième de conversations à bâtons rompus, un troisième d'interviews, un quatrième de débats télévisés. Pour l'écrit, Engel, Forsgren & Sullet-Nylander utilisent un corpus journalistique et un corpus littéraire et scientifique (voir ci-dessous). Pour davantage de précisions sur ces corpus, voir Engel, Forsgren & Sullet-Nylander (2012: 189).

[38] Cela ressort clairement du corpus composé de journaux télévisés employé par les trois chercheurs, où « presque toutes les séquences causales se retrouvent dans des parties dialogales (interviews) » (Engel, Forsgren & Sullet-Nylander 2012: 192 et n.).

[39] Ce corpus se compose d'une part d'ouvrages littéraires (80 %), d'autre part d'essais ou de travaux scientifiques (20 %), publiés après 2009 et entrés dans la base textuelle *Frantext* (http://www.frantext.fr). Le nombre total de mots est estimé par Engel, Forsgren & Sullet-Nylander à environ 650 000 mots (2012: 190).

[40] Peut-être la cadence moyenne plus élevée dans le corpus littéraire et scientifique pourrait-elle être expliquée par le fait que les ouvrages littéraires analysés contiennent des parties dialoguées.

Corpus oral : Corpaix	
	occ.	occ./1 000 mots
parce que	4577	4,58
puisque	478	0,48
car[41]	164	0,16

Tableau 11: Distribution des conjonctions causales *parce que*, *puisque* et *car* dans Corpaix.

Les tableaux 10 et 11 permettent de constater que ce n'est pas uniquement la fréquence de connexions causales en tant que telles qui se distingue entre les données écrites et orales : Engel, Forsgren & Sullet-Nylander notent également que « *parce que* domine à l'oral, tous genres confondus » (2012: 191). Cette observation est, elle aussi, confirmée par Corpaix; en effet, l'emploi de *puisque* et de *car* peut être qualifié d'extrêmement rare. Quant aux corpus écrits, en revanche, *parce que* et *car* ont quasiment la même fréquence, tandis que le recours à *puisque* est bien plus rare. À l'oral, en revanche, les tableaux 10 et 11 montrent que *puisque* est plus fréquent que *car*. Cette faible représentation de *car* à l'oral pourrait s'expliquer par le fait que *car* est « intuitivement perçu comme plutôt formel, *i.e.* comme appliquant la norme du français dit standard » (Engel, Forsgren & Sullet-Nylander 2012: 192; voir aussi Bracops 1996: 15).

Traditionnellement, la différence sémantico-pragmatique entre les conjonctions causales est expliquée en termes de *justification* et d'*explication*. Or les contre-exemples authentiques fournis par Bracops (1996: 402-404) et Engel, Forsgren & Sullet-Nylander (2012: 201, 207) montrent que cette distinction n'est pas toujours facile à détecter, surtout dans les données orales : on trouve *puisque* là où l'on pourrait s'attendre à *parce que* et vice-versa. À propos de *car*, Bilger & Blanche-Benveniste (1999) ont par ailleurs émis l'hypothèse que son emploi est caractérisé par une certaine variation diaphasique.

Qu'en-est-il de notre corpus de forums Internet ? Se rapproche-t-il plutôt de l'emploi écrit ou oral ? Le tableau 12 montre la distribution des conjonctions causales dans nos trois sous-corpus. Pour avoir une image plus complète de la connexion causale dans notre corpus, nous intégrons dans ce tableau les attestations de la conjonction *comme* ainsi que les locutions *vu que* et *étant donné que*.

---

[41] Ce corpus n'étant pas lemmatisé, il n'est pas exclu que quelques attestations du substantif *car* se cachent derrière ce chiffre, ce qui diminuerait encore la fréquence d'emploi de cette conjonction à l'oral. On ne peut pas inclure *vu que*, *étant donné que* et *comme* causal dans le tableau 11, car les deux composants de *vu que* et les trois composants de *étant donné que* ont été séparés et figurent respectivement sous *vu*, *que*, *étant* et *donné*, tandis que les attestations de *comme* conjonction et *comme* adverbe ont été confondues.

	Ado		ADS		Gross		Total	
	occ.	occ./1 000 mots	occ.	occ./1 000 mots	occ.	occ./1 000 mots	occ.	occ./1 000 mots
parce que	12	1,53	8	1,04	11	1,43	31	1,33
puisque	0	0	0	0	0	0	0	0
car	14	1,78	12	1,55	21	2,73	47	2,02
Total partiel	26	3,31	20	2,59	32	4,16	78	3,35
comme[42]	2	0,25	1	0,13	2	0,26	5	0,21
vu que	8	1,02	6	0,78	3	0,39	17	0,73
étant donné que	0	0	1	0,13	1	0,13	2	0,09
Total	36	4,58	28	3,63	38	4,94	102	4,38

Tableau 12: Distribution des conjonctions causales dans nos trois sous-corpus.

En ce qui concerne la fréquence de connexions causales, on peut noter qu'elle se rapproche bien plus de l'emploi constaté à l'oral qu'à l'écrit; les deux conjonctions *parce que* et *car* (*puisque* n'est pas attesté; voir *infra*) comptent en effet 3,55 occurrences par 1 000 mots. Quant à la distribution des trois conjonctions, l'emploi s'avère cependant complètement différent des corpus oraux présentés ci-dessus : *car* est la conjonction causale la plus fréquente dans chaque groupe et a une cadence moyenne de 2,02 tous sous-corpus confondus. Son nombre d'occurrences pour 1 000 mots n'est donc pas seulement bien supérieur à celui constaté dans les corpus oraux mais aussi à celui observe dans les corpus écrits. La conjonction *parce que*, quant à elle, est, avec sa cadence moyenne de 1,33, d'une fréquence supérieure à celle des corpus écrits mais, en même temps, bien inférieure à celle des corpus oraux.

Puisque étant absent de tous les sous-corpus, c'est la locution *vu que* qui occupe la troisième place. Dans leur étude, Engel, Forsgren & Sullet-Nylander (2012), notent que *puisque* est le moins employé au total (productions écrites et orales confondues). De plus, ils précisent que *puisque* et *car* « se 'complètent' quantitativement au sein des corpus écrits et oraux » (Engel, Forsgren & Sullet-Nylander 2012: 199), *puisque* pour l'oral, *car* pour l'écrit.

Cette fréquence remarquable de *car* pourrait-elle s'expliquer par un souci d'économie ? Il est, en effet, possible que la brièveté joue un rôle, la conjonction étant présente dans des énoncés qui se caractérisent par la concision :

>   (35)   Jai eu une 1ere echo samedi dernier *car* 1ere grossesse GEU[43] et seconde FC...je suis donc tres bien suivie! (Gross 4, femme, 26 ans)

---

[42] Les attestations où la conjonction *comme* sert à établir une comparaison ne sont évidemment pas prises en compte.

Le style rapide de l'exemple (35) est patent avec la proposition incomplète (« car 1ere grossesse... »), l'absence d'apostrophes (*Jai*) et l'emploi d'abréviations et de sigles (*1ere, echo, GEU, FC*). Ici, il se peut donc que la conjonction *car* ait été choisie à cause de sa brièveté.

Or comme il a été dit plus haut, le souci d'économiser le nombre de caractères ne semble pas être très répandu dans notre corpus. Aussi *car* est-il très fréquent également chez les forumeurs qui n'utilisent pas un style rapide; c'est le cas des exemples (36) et (37) :

(36) J'hésite pas une seconde j'irai a celle [=la fête] de mon meilleurs amis
et comme les fêtes de se styles sont le plus souvent le soir
je passerai la journée avec ma copine en lui offrante mon cadeau
des p'tits calins et tout ..

Car si mon meilleurs amis ne vient pas a mon anniversaire de 18 ans
Pour aller a la fête d'anniversaire de sa copine
Sa me ferait très très mal et sa ferai un grand vide dans mon anniversaire (Ado 5, homme, âge non précisé)

(37) J'ai eu l'idée d'un projet à organiser au sein de mon lycée à propos des diverses théories sur l'homosexualité, suite au débat sur cette question dans la section débat.
Je le sais très ouvert, et je pense qu'il sera intéressé, et également pour obtenir l'adresse mail de ma prof de bio, concerné par le sujet. D'ailleurs, j'en ai un peu discuté avec elle, et elle est intéressé (c'est celle à qui je t'avais cité en exemple, si tu te souviens bien).
Car le programme de bio est censé nous parler de l'homosexualité, mais dans le manuel, il est rappelé que ça fait partie de "la vie privée et que l'homophobie est punie par la loi" 😊. (Ado 1, homme, 16 ans)

Compte tenu de la très haute fréquence de *car* dans notre corpus, il y a lieu de se demander si les restrictions d'emploi de cette conjonction par rapport à *parce que* décrites par les grammairiens ne devraient pas être rediscutées. Selon Bracops (1996: 15), « les locuteurs – du moins les jeunes gens [...] rattachent [*car*] à un registre élevé, souvent qualifié par eux de 'littéraire' ». Cela ne semble pas être le cas de nos trois sous-corpus, où *car* est donc la conjonction causale la plus fréquente. Il s'utilise souvent en co-texte informel, comme dans les exemples suivants :

---

[43] GEU, abréviation de « grossesse extra utérine ». Comme c'est également le cas de ceux de ADS, les participantes de Gross utilisent du jargon abrégé comme 5SA (cinq semaines d'aménorrhée) et PDS (prise de sang). La signification de ces abréviations n'est pas toujours claire aux non initiées. Ainsi, une participante du fil Gross 4 demande-t-elle des clarifications : « Par contre, je ne suis pas très familière de tous ces termes : GEU, FC, 5SA, 3SG,... Peux-tu m'aiguiller ? »

(38) en effet, se retrouver dans une fac seul/e la rentrée est à la fois 'excitant', nouveau mais un peu stressant *car* on connait personne (Ado 3, femme, 18 ans)
(39) Sinon, chapeau pour l'allaitement *car* ça doit pas être facile, moi j'ai essayé un jour et j'avais les seins en feu lol. (Gross 2, femme, 27 ans)
(40) mais j'ai moins de lait donc ça me soule *car* j'adore allaiter ma fille etje trouve ça moins contraignant que le biberon c'est plus rapide et pas besoin de préparation lol (Gross 2, femme, âge non précisé)

Dans ces trois exemples, les co-textes de *car* peuvent être considérés comme informels : dans (38) et (39) la négation est réduite (*personne* et *pas*), tandis que dans (40), la conjonction vient juste après l'expression familière « ça me soule ». On peut difficilement parler ici de « registre élevé » ou de style « littéraire ». Notre corpus contient de nombreux exemples de *car* en co-texte informel.

Comme il ressort du tableau 12, la fréquence de connexions causales varie d'un sous-corpus à l'autre. Dans ADS, celles construites avec *parce que* et *car* représentent 2,59 occ. / 1 000 mots. Si on compare ce chiffre à ceux obtenus par Engel, Forsgren & Sullet-Nylander (tableau 10), il se trouve ainsi à mi-chemin entre discours oral (4,44) et discours écrit (0,82 / 1,22). Dans Ado, la cadence moyenne est plus élevée, les connexions causales avec *parce que* et *car* représentant 3,31 occ. / 1 000 mots. Dans Gross, enfin, l'emploi de connexions causales avec ces deux conjonctions, s'élève à 4,16 occ. / 1 000 mots, un chiffre proche des discours oraux étudiés par les trois chercheurs. Ces résultats peuvent être mis en rapport avec les observations faites au sujet des interrogations, c'est-à-dire que le sous-corpus Gross possèdent des traits que l'on retrouve dans un discours dialogué oral qui procède par questions/réponses. Dans ADS, en revanche, le caractère dialogal est bien plus faible : ce sous-corpus présente moins de questions (voir 3.4.1 *supra*) et également moins de connexions causales. Or, si l'on regarde la distribution des différentes conjonctions causales, l'influence du français écrit serait *plus grande* dans Gross que dans les deux autres sous-corpus, puisque, dans 55 % des cas, les conjonctions causales se font à l'aide de *car* – conjonction réservée à l'écrit selon Engel, Forsgren & Sullet-Nylander. Les connexions causales de notre corpus révèlent ainsi une vraie hybridation entre l'oral et l'écrit.

4. Conclusion

Au terme de cette analyse de la langue des forums Internet, certaines tendances concernant le rapport oral/écrit peuvent clairement être mises en évidence. Tout d'abord, on a pu déceler des traits pointant sur un mode de production parfois plus proche du parlé que de l'écrit. Ainsi les productions des forumeurs semblent-elles en grande partie spontanées, bien qu'il s'agisse d'une communication asynchrone : les énoncés s'improvisent au fur et à mesure que les internautes avancent dans leurs discours, ce qui peut aboutir à des étoffements, retouches et reformulations, caractéristiques de l'oral.

Au niveau phonético-graphique, cependant, les phénomènes périgraphiques, comme la réduction du *e* instable et la chute du clitique sujet, ne sont pas très fréquentes par rapport à l'oral : l'influence de la langue parlée paraît ici assez faible.

Ensuite, au niveau morphosyntaxique, si l'influence de la langue orale s'avère plus grande, le *ne* de négation étant supprimé 4 fois sur 10, on est pourtant loin des 9 fois sur 10 constatées dans les productions orales spontanées. On peut toutefois observer une variation entre nos trois sous-corpus quant à l'emploi de la négation : dans ADS, fréquenté presque exclusivement par des hommes, la négation tombe quasiment 1 fois sur 2. En effet, dans 7 des 8 fils étudiés de ce forum, la négation sans *ne* est plus fréquente que la négation complète. Dans le sous-corpus Gross, dont la population est entièrement composée de femmes, en revanche, le *ne* de négation est maintenu dans 65 % des cas.

Au niveau syntaxique, enfin, la forme privilégiée de l'interrogation totale, correspondant à l'interrogation intonative à l'oral, est l'ordre SV. Cette construction est également la plus fréquente à l'oral et indique un degré d'interaction plus élevé que les deux autres formes d'interrogation : presque 6 questions sur 10 utilisent l'ordre SV. Sur cet aspect, il ressort de l'étude une différence nette concernant la variation hommes/femmes. En effet, le forum Gross, fréquenté par des femmes, comporte, au total, presque deux fois plus de questions que celui où la quasi-totalité des intervenants sont de sexe masculin (ADS). C'est également dans le sous-corpus féminin que les questions sans inversion sont les plus fréquentes.

L'analyse se clôt sur une étude quantitative des connexions causales qui révèle une vraie hybridation entre l'oral et l'écrit. D'un côté, la fréquence élevée de connexions causales se rapproche de l'emploi observé à l'oral. D'un autre côté, la conjonction causale la plus fréquente est *car* – et cela dans tous les sous-corpus –, conjonction réservée à l'écrit. La brièveté de cette conjonction ne peut que partiellement expliquer sa forte présence dans notre corpus. Il y a, en outre, une grande variation entre nos trois sous-corpus : les connexions causales sont nettement plus fréquentes dans le forum Gross (100 % femmes) que dans ADS (94 % hommes), tandis que le sous-corpus fréquenté par les deux sexes (Ado) se trouve entre ces deux pôles. Dans une étude ultérieure fondée sur un corpus élargi, nous aurons l'occasion de revenir à cette variation afin de déterminer s'il s'agit d'une variation diastratique ou plutôt contextuelle.

Pour terminer, insistons sur le fait que cette étude ne couvre que quelques aspects langagiers du corpus et qu'il reste bien des phénomènes, au croisement de l'oral et de l'écrit (le code) d'un côté et du formel et de l'informel (le registre) de l'autre, à explorer dans les forums Internet.

5. Références bibliographiques

Biber, D. (1988), *Variation across speech and writing*, Cambridge: Cambridge University Press.
Bilger, M. & Blanche-Benveniste, C. (1999), Français parlé-oral spontané. Quelques réflexions, *RFLA: Dossier «l'oral spontané»*, IV/2, pp. 21-30.
Blanche-Benveniste, C. (2000), *Approches de la langue parlée en français*, Gap/Paris: Ophrys.
Bracops, M. (1996), *Le système de car. Étude grammaticale, sémantique et pragmatique*, vol. 1. Bruxelles: Université Libre de Bruxelles (thèse).
Compernolle, R. A. van (2008a), Morphosyntactic and phonological constraints on negative particle variation in French-language chat discourse, *Language Variation and Change* 20 (2), pp. 317-339.
Compernolle, R. A. van (2008b), *Nous* versus *on*: Pronouns with first-person plural reference in synchronous French chat, *Canadian Journal of Applied Linguistics* 11 (2), pp. 85-110.
Compernolle, R. A. van (2009), Emphatic *ne* in informal spoken French and implications for foreign language pedagogy, *International Journal of Applied Linguistics* 19 (1), pp. 47-65.
Compernolle, R. A. van (2011), Use and variation of French diacritics on an Internet dating site, *Journal of French Language Studies* 21 (2), pp. 131-148.
Compernolle, R. A. van, & Williams, L. (2007), De l'oral à l'électronique: La variation orthographique comme ressource sociostylistique et pragmatique dans le français électronique, *Glottopol* 10, pp. 56-69, disponible sur: http://www.univ-rouen.fr/dyalang/glottopol/telecharger/numero_10/gpl10_04compernolle.pdf
Compernolle, R. A. van, & Williams, L. (2009), Variable omission of *ne* in real-time French chat: A corpus-driven comparison of educational and non-educational contexts, *Canadian Modern Language Review* 65 (3), pp. 413-440.
Compernolle, R. A. van, & Williams, L. (2010), Orthographic variation in electronic French: The case of *l'accent aigu*, *French Review* 83 (4), pp. 820-833.
Corpaix = Véronis, J. (2000), *Fréquence des mots en français parlé («Corpaix»)*, disponible sur: http://sites.univ-provence.fr/~veronis/data/freqmots-oral.html
Donath, J. (1999), Identity and Deception in the Virtual Community, in Smith, M. A. & Kollock, P. (éds), *Communities in Cyberspace*, London/New York: Routledge, pp. 29-59.
Engel, H. (2010), *Dislocation et référence aux entités en français L2. Développement, interaction, variation*, Stockholm: Stockholms universitet (Forskningsrapporter/ Cahiers de la Recherche 43).
Engel, H., Forsgren, M. & Sullet-Nylander, F. (2012), Un classique revisité: *car, parce que, puisque*. Entre théorisation et observation sur données authentiques, in Ahlstedt, E., Benson, K., Bladh, E., Söhrman, I. & Åkerström, U. (éds), *Actes du XVIIIe congrès des romanistes scandinaves* (Romanica Gothoburgensia 69), Göteborg: Acta universitatis Gothoburgensis, pp. 187-209.

Fairon, C, Klein, J.-R. & Paumier, S. (2006), *Le langage sms. Étude d'un corpus informatisé à partir de l'enquête «Faites don de vos sms à la science»*, Louvain: UCL Presses Universitaires de Louvain.

Freed, A.F. & Greenwood, A. (1996), Women, men and type of talk: What makes the difference?, *Language in Society* 25 (1), pp. 1-26.

Gadet, F. (2007), *La Variation sociale en français*, Paris: Ophrys.

Gadet, F. (2008), Ubi scripta et volant et manent, in Stark, E., Schmidt-Riese, R & Stoll, E. (éds), *Romanische Syntax im Wandel*, Tübingen: Gunter Narr Verlag, pp. 513-529.

Kerbrat-Orecchioni, C. & Traverso, V. (2004), Types d'interactions et genres de l'oral, *Langages* 153, pp. 41-51.

Kerbrat-Orecchioni, C. (à paraître), De l'analyse du discours à l'analyse des discours, in Soulages, J.-C. (éd.), *Hommages à Patrick Charaudeau*, Paris: L'Harmattan.

Maingueneau, D. (2007), *Analyser les textes de communication*, Paris: Armand Colin.

Marcoccia, M. (2000), Les smileys: une représentation iconique des émotions dans la communication médiatisée par ordinateur, in Plantin, P, Doury, M. & Traverso, V. (éds), *Les émotions dans les interactions*, Lyon : Presses Universitaires de Lyon, pp. 249-263.

Marcoccia, M. (2003), Parler politique dans un forum de discussion, *Langage et société* 104, pp. 9-55.

Marcoccia, M. (2004a), La communication écrite médiatisée par ordinateur : faire du face à face avec de l'écrit, in *Journée d'étude de l'ATALA «Le traitement automatique des nouvelles formes de communication Écrite (e-mails, forums, chats, SMS, etc.)»*, 5 juin 2004, ENST Paris, disponible sur: http://sites.univ-provence.fr/veronis/je-nfce/Marcoccia.pdf

Marcoccia, M. (2004b), L'analyse conversationnelle des forums de discussion: questionnements méthodologiques», *Les Carnets du Cediscor* 8, disponible sur: http://cediscor.revues.org/220

Marcoccia, M. (2012), Définitions et négociations de la norme scripturale dans un forum de discussion d'adolescents, *Ela. Études de linguistique appliquée* 166, pp. 157-169.

Marcoccia, M. & Gauducheau, N. (2007), L'analyse du rôle des smileys en production et en réception: un retour sur la question de l'oralité des écrits numériques, *Glottopol* 10, pp. 39-55, disponible sur: http://www.univ-rouen.fr/dyalang/glottopol

Moïse, C. (2002), Pratiques langagières des banlieues: où sont les femmes?, in *Rapports de sexe, rapports de genre, entre domination et émancipation* (*VEI Enjeux* 128), Paris: Centre National de Documentation Pédagogique, pp. 46-61.

Mosegaard Hansen, M.-B. (2001), Syntax in interaction. Form and function of yes/no interrogatives in spoken standard French, *Studies in language* 25(3), pp. 463-519.

Mourlhon-Dallies, F. (2007), Communication électronique et genres du discours, *Glottopol* 10, pp. 11-23, disponible sur: http://www.univ-rouen.fr/dyalang/glottopol

Panckhurst, R. (1998), Analyse linguistique du courrier électronique, in Guéguen, N. & Tobin, L. (éds), *Communication, société et internet*, Paris: L'Harmattan, pp. 47-60.

Pierozak, I. (2003) *Le français tchaté. Une étude en trois dimensions – sociolinguistique, syntaxique et graphique – d'usages IRC*, Université d'Aix-Marseille (thèse).

Riegel, M, Pellat, J.-C. & Rioul, R. (2009) [1994], *Grammaire méthodique du français*, Paris: Presses universitaires de France.
Turkle, S. (1995), *Life on the Screen. Identity in the Age of Internet*, New York: Simon & Schuster.
Véronis, J. (2000), v. *Corpaix*

6. Appendice: corpus

forum.ados.fr (« Ado ») :

    Ado 1 : fil créé le 21 avril 2012, interventions du 21 au 25 avril 2012 (1607 mots)

    Ado 2 : fil créé le 2 mars 2011, interventions du 2 mars 2011 au 29 javier 2012 (1572 mots)

    Ado 3 : fil créé le 20 juillet 2012, interventions du 20 au 23 juillet 2012 (1440 mots)

    Ado 4 : fil créé le 3 juin 2012, interventions du 3 au 13 juin 2012 (1715 mots)

    Ado 5 : fil créé le 2 octobre 2012, interventions du 2 au 8 octobre 2012 (1530 mots)

www.artdeseduire.com (« ADS ») :

    ADS 1 : fil créé le 29 août 2012, interventions du 29 au 31 août 2012 (1593 mots)

    ADS 2 : fil créé le 28 septembre 2012, interventions du 28 septembre au 4 octobre 2012 (618 mots)

    ADS 3 : fil créé le 5 septembre 2012, interventions du 5 au 6 septembre 2012 (301 mots)

    ADS 4 : fil créé le 29 septembre 2012, interventions du 29 au 30 septembre 2012 (2028 mots)

    ADS 5 : fil créé le 24 août 2012, interventions du 24 août 2012 (356 mots)

    ADS 6 : fil créé le 6 juin 2012, interventions du 6 au 7 juin 2012 (941 mots)

    ADS 7 : fil créé le 5 septembre 2012, interventions du 5 au 6 septembre 2012 (1012 mots)

    ADS 8 : fil créé le 23 août 2012, interventions du 23 au 26 août 2012 (876 mots)

http://www.doctissimo.fr/html/grossesse/grossesse.htm (« Gross »)
- Gross 1 : fil créé le 17 février 2012, interventions du 17 au 18 février 2012 (1518 mots)
- Gross 2 : fil créé le 21 janvier 2012, interventions du 21 au 22 janvier 2012 (1567 mots)
- Gross 3 : fil créé le 15 janvier 2008, interventions du 15 au 17 janvier 2008 (1556 mots)
- Gross 4 : fil créé le 8 juillet 2012, interventions du 8 au 17 juillet 2012 (1543 mots)
- Gross 5 : fil créé le 31 janvier 2012, interventions du 31 janvier au 3 mars 2012 (1504 mots)

Spelling and identity in Scottish internet discourse

Philip Shaw

1. Introduction

The rise of computer-mediated communication has resulted in a quite large area of publicly visible written language which is not edited and is not consistently constrained by prescriptive spelling rules or other standardization. In synchronous media like instant messaging, chatrooms and asynchronous ones like SMS text messages, blogs, email, and Facebook homepages, writers are free to use the spelling and letter-pronunciation conventions of their language creatively. French writers can write <g> for *j'ai,* and English ones can write <2nite> for *tonight.*

The best known affordance of this freedom is the one just illustrated, that one can use creative spellings for normal words or phrases in the standard language. A second is that one can represent spoken language more closely, with structures in French like *lu ... heu bon koi dire a par mapel tanguy* ("hi ... uh so wht 2 say bsides my name is tanguy") (Volckaert- Legrier et al 2009:174) or in English like *giv us bell or somink init m8 l8ron* (Shaw 2009:268).

A rather less widely-discussed affordance is the potential to represent non-standard sociolects and regional dialects where the genre and context allow or encourage it. This is documented from several diglossic situations. Siebenhaar (2006) shows how the users of a Swiss internet chatroom code-switch between standard German and Swiss German (which was not traditionally written and has no standard orthography). They used mainly dialect in a regional chatroom and a more even mixture of standard and dialect in a superregional one. Similarly, Themistocleous (2010) carried out a survey on Cypriot internet users showing positive attitudes to and frequent use of Cypriot Greek (again a normally unwritten variety) in informal internet writing. A comparable, if more complicated, situation is reported by Warschauer et al (2002) from Egypt. The group they studied wrote formal emails predominantly in English, but in informal email and especially in chat there was more Arabic. Some of the Arabic was the standard written form, but in these less formal genres it was predominantly non-standard Egyptian Arabic.

Internet language in diglossic situations is thus characterized by frequent, and obviously deliberate, switching between the H and L codes and, apparently, a predominance of written L. By choosing L the writer asserts an identity which is informal and also, at least in the Cypriot and Swiss cases, self-consciously marked as local.

Local characteristics may also be revealed unselfconsciously in respellings of the first type (that is innovative spellings of standard-language words) and the second (that is representations of spoken forms). Shaw (2008, 2009) found that US writers spelled *what* and *because* as <wut> and <cuz> while British writers used <wot> and <coz>, reflecting probably differences in rounding; <o> is associated with a rounded vowel. English words with the irrational <gh> standard spellings are obvious targets for respellings and these are likely to reflect the writer's own phonology. The noun or past-tense verb *thought* is interesting in this respect because in many varieties outside England and the Southern Hemisphere the vowel is the same as that in CLOTH and quite unlike that in NORTH (because in these varieties there is a /r/ phoneme in the pronunciation), while in large parts of England, both south and north, the vowel of THOUGHT is different from CLOTH (and LOT) and the same as NORTH (Wells 1983). Hence spellings like < thot> are quite common in the US but not found in England, and correspondingly spellings like <thort> or <fort> occur in England but not in the US (Shaw 2008:47). The relation between the vowel of THOUGHT and that of CLOTH is complicated and not a sociolinguistic variable (unlike the differences in rhoticity between the varieties), so the appearance of these distinctive spellings is likely to be revelation of the variety associated with display of a rebellious or even ironically childish identity. Higher-level features may sometimes also be taken to be revelation; in the example quoted above *giv us bell or somink init m8 l8ron* "give us a bell [=phone me] or something, *innit* [=won't you], mate, later on" is clearly Southern English in phonology and phraseology and *So ne other crc wit ya?* "So is there any other craic [news/gossip] with you [=Brit/US have you got any...]" is clearly Irish..

The two types of examples (deliberate use of one's own colloquial speech by using marked variants and revelation of this colloquial speech by choice of spellings, etc.) above may be genuine reproductions of the writer's own speech. But there are also cases discussed in Shaw (2008, 2009) where spelling indicates a persona which is unlikely to be that of the writer. A spelling <da> for *the* suggests a stop followed by a low realization of schwa, which is associated with African-American Vernacular English (AAVE) or Jamaican speech. Spellings of this kind, with <d> for <th> are very common, much more so than actual pronunciations of this form. Many people who pronounce *the* as / ðə/ seem to write it as <da>. Even if such spellings are shorter than those with <th> they are presumably also an attempt to borrow the counter-cultural prestige of AAVE or Jamaican. Similarly when an English writer produces <fink> for *think* the spelling of <th> is likely to result from a decision, perhaps ironic, to represent the writer as a speaker of the modern South-eastern variety called Estuary English, even if in fact they are not.

Locally tinged writing can thus occur in CMC in at least three forms: code-switching into the writer's own non-standard variety for long stretches of text as in the Swiss German, Cypriot Greek, and Egyptian Arabic examples; revelatory respelling and word/phrase choice which the writer would not recognize as local; and invocation of a pronunciation which may or may not be the writer's own, but whose characteristics are recognizable to her or him. (cf. Ifukor 2011 for Nigerian examples).

Shaw (2008, 2009) shows that the last two types of localism (or glocalism, since they involve appropriation of forms from far away as well as use of local ones) are frequent in English, Irish, and US computer-mediated communication. But in these non-standard varieties of English there is no background of diglossia as in the examples from German, Greek and Arabic, merely the movement from a more formal to a more vernacular style (in Labov's (1972) terms) found in most communities.

There are, however, several cases in the English-speaking world where the local non-standard variety has a more established form and has been used in various ways in writing. Three examples are Creole and Jamaican Standard in Jamaica, Singlish and Singapore Standard, and Scots and Scottish Standard (cf. Görlach 1991). Scottish Standard English (SSE) is a variety analogous to English, Irish or US Standard English, that is, it is distinguished from other standard varieties by a particular pronunciation, a few lexical items, and a very few grammatical features. In particular, SSE is normally rhotic, that is written <r> is pronounced in all positions, as in most types of American English. But alongside SSE there is Scots, a dialect (or a collection of local varieties) sharply different from any variety of Standard English in phonology, lexicon, and syntax. This was the autonomous language of Scotland before the union of the crowns in 1603 and many would grant it the status of an independent language today. Scots (and the closely related Ulster-Scots in Northern Ireland) are covered by the EU's Regional and Minority Languages policy. There are many modern literary works in varieties of Scots or with representations of Scottish vernacular. The text of Irvine Welsh's novels has Scottish features in the narrator's voice. In Example 1 Scottishness is indexed by the negative *didnae huv* 'hadn't', the reduced form *ay* 'of', and the spellings *huv* 'have' and *wis* 'was'.

1. This cunt has cold black eyes set in a white face. If he didnae huv a dark pudding-basin haircut and his neb wis bigger, he'd be like one ay Moira and Jimmy's budgies. (Welsh 2012)
    (….If he didn't have a dark pudding-basin haircut and his nose was bigger, he'd be like one of ….)

But Scots is also used for non-fiction texts, usually as a conscious effort to regain the domain in question. Examples 2, 3 and 4 are taken from Scots-language Wikipedia on modal verbs:

2. The praisent tense o verbs ends in –s in aw persons an nummers cept whan a singil personal pronoun is neist the verb, *Thay say he's ower wee, Thaim that says he's ower wee, Thir lassies says he's ower wee* etc. *Thay'r cummin an aw* but *Five o thaim's cummin, The lassies? Thay'v went* but *Ma brakes haes went. Thaim that cums first is ser'd first. The trees growes green in the simmer.* (http://sco.wikipedia.org/wiki/Scots_leid)

   (the present tense of verbs ends in –s in all persons and numbers except when a single personal pronoun is next to the verb…)

3. The modal verbs *mey, ocht tae,* and *sall* isna aften bruikit in Scots an thir's historic but is whyls still fund in anglifee'd leiterar Scots. *Can, shud,* an *will/wul* is the prefer'd Scots maks. Scots employs doobil modal maks *He'll no can cum the day, A micht cud cum the morn, A uised ti cud dae it, but no nou.* (http://sco.wikipedia.org/wiki/Scots_leid)

   (The modal verbs *mey, ocht tae* and *sall* [compare English *may, ought to, shall*] are not often used in Scots unless in historical contexts, but are sometimes still found in anglified literary Scots. *Can, shud* and *will/wull* are the preferred Scots forms. Scots makes use of double modal forms… [*He'll no can cum the day,* = He won't be able to come today, *A micht cud cum the morn,* = I might be able to come tomorrow, *A uised ti cud dae it, but no nou* = I used to be able to do it, but not now])

4. The main differs in soond atween Doric an ither Scots dialects is as follaes: …*wh* is said /f/ stead o /ʍ/ — "whit" /fɪt/ stead of /ʍɪt/, "wha" /faː/ stead o /ʍaː/ or /ʍɒː/. (http://sco.wikipedia.org/wiki/Scots_leid)

   (The main differences in sound between [the dialect called] Doric and other Scots dialects are as follows: ….wh is pronounced /f/ instead of /ʍ/ — WHAT /fɪt/ instead of /ʍɪt/, WHO /faː/ instead of /ʍaː/ or /ʍɒː/)

In the present context it is worth noting the participle in *–in* rather than *–ing*, the negations *isna* and *'ll no*, the pronouns *a* 'I' and *whit* 'what', and the use of the voiceless labiovelar /ʍ/ where the spelling has <wh>. We will also meet representations of the pronunciation of <wh> as /f/, as in Doric, a dialect of the Northeast Lowlands. It is also significant that Scots and English representations of *the* are identical (there is no tendency for the <th> sounds to be pronounced as stops in the variety of Scots represented here).

The status of Scots is not secure. Models are available for writing the language, but they are not standardized. The many attempts to devise an agreed standard written form for the language have not yet been successful. Furthermore there is little political interest in supporting Scots in Scotland – political nationalism does not focus on language, possibly because a Lowland Scots identity might clash with a Highland/Hebrides Gaelic one.

In this paper I take the example of Scotland and ask whether the pattern of use of local forms is the same as in England, Ireland and the US or whether the special status of Scots is still visible in the twenty-first century. Where does Scottish CMC sit between the poles of consistent L variety use and occasional occurrence of identifiable local or ethnic markers drawn from both the local and the global environment?

2. Method

The procedure adopted here was as close as possible to that in Shaw (2008, 2009), so that results for Scotland could reasonably be compared with those for England. What follows describes, mutatis mutandis, the procedure in the earlier publications as well.

The text type examined is the homepage (Karlsson 2002) as nowadays provided by Facebook. The data discussed here, however, were collected in 2008-2009 from a precursor of Facebook, the Bebo homepage, which was used by many people in the 15-30 age-group, particularly in Britain. Three sections of the homepage were included in the analysis. The first is personal details: age, gender, hometown, some comments on 'what I like' 'what I hate', etc. (often in non-standard spelling), and often quite extensive quotations in the form of quizzes, song lyrics, poetry or wise words (often in standard spelling). This is written or selected by the homepage owner and it was assumed to represent an individual or at least a persona/avatar representative of the location claimed under 'hometown'. The second genre is comments: short observations, greeting, invitations, and post-card like narratives from a variety of writers, some in standard orthography, some in varying degrees of non-standard. The third genre considered was the page owner's blog, if any. The Bebo format makes it possible to publish a blog on one's page, but most are fairly short.

In the earlier papers searching on the domains *us, uk,* and *ir* produced appropriate numbers of pages from each of the target countries, but this method does not work for Scotland. Hence thirty homepages each were selected from Scotland by the following method. Google searches were run on the domain *bebo.com* and the word *wee*. This produced lists of homepages which included the word *wee* and thus were likely to come from Scotland

and to use some local forms. (In fact many came from Northern Ireland, where a variety close to Scots is spoken. The modern Northern Ireland youth identity can perhaps be defined by saying that searching for pages containing both Scots *wee* and Irish *craic* produces many texts from Northern Ireland!). Each page was opened in turn and those which recognisably named a hometown in Scotland were selected. Those which did not contain more than 100 words of connected text, or which advertised a band rather than an individual were discarded. Selection continued until thirty home pages had been found. These were then saved as text files to enable search with a concordancer. It is worth admitting that this process destroys the rich multimodality of the pages, hiding pictures, background, embedded songs, links, and layout.

The thirty texts were non-homogenous in a variety of ways. They were of different lengths. The writers (or their personae) varied in age, gender, maturity, and ethnicity, and so did the numerous writers of comments on each page. Furthermore the roles adopted by the writers/personae varied from expert to friend to mocker and their choice of register varied following this.

I read through the home pages to get a feel for what was likely to be worth investigating and came up with two sets of features. The first were the variables studied in Shaw (2008, 2009) including both features relatable to sociolinguistic variables (Labov 1972) like representations of *-ing,* and words beginning with <th>, and the sociolinguistically non-significant patterns of regularisation in *what,* and *thought.* In Scotland there are also spellings of *what* that represent pronunciations that are sociolinguistic variables in the sense that they are known markers of some dialects, namely those with <i> and those in which initial <wh> is replaced by <f> as in Doric, and a search was therefore made not only on w*t but also on f*t. A search was also made on *?a, producing words of at least two letters ending in <a>. In England such a search produces spellings like <afta, 2getha, neva> which show non-rhoticity (<er> represented as <a>), and might therefore not be expected in Scotland.

The second set of features was non-standard-English auxiliary forms, particularly negatives like *wudna, cudna, didna/dinna.* In the Irish, English and US corpora spoken forms like *don't* were common, of course, and also non-standard *ain't,* which like *–in'* for *–ing* is a sociolinguistic variable marking vernacular speech anywhere in the world. But otherwise the verb-phrase syntax and morphology is that of standard English. By contrast it was clear that the Scottish CMC sample included elements which look more like Scots as exemplified above. Consequently a search was also made for the first-person pronoun forms *I*/ *my* and *a*/*ma* which were expected to be frequent and to show unmarked 'English' or marked 'Scots-like' usage respectively.

Using the AntConc program (Anthony 2007) I searched broadly to get an idea of the realisations of the target words that occurred in the texts. For example, a search on *??a* produced all words of three or more letters ending in *a*, which including both target forms like *neva* "never" *dinna* "did not" and non-target words like *Africa* and *gonna/wuda*. The next search was for all representations of the target words in the corpus. The number of homepages using any representation (e.g. of WHAT) was noted, and also the number using each individual representation (e.g. *what wat, wot, wut, whit, wit*). It is necessary to check that the example actually represents WHAT, since there can be homographs: *wit* can represent *with* as well as *what*. This produced statistics like '20 homepages using some representations of WHAT; 18 with *what* 9 with *wat*, 6 with *wot*'. The number of texts with a given spelling or form could then be expressed as a percentage of the total number of texts with any instance of the word. The number of texts using a particular spelling was counted, rather than the numbers of cases of a spelling, because individual homepages are often highly repetitive, with contributors quoting one another, and including repeated logos or song lyrics, etc.

3. Results

As noted above, Bebo sites include many voices. Quoted material is often in standard spelling, and many posters consistently spell in a standard manner, so that all sites can be expected to include instances of the standard spellings of common words. The sites chosen are all apparently based in Scotland, and it is reasonable to suppose that (a) many of their owners are Scottish, and (b) that many of the members of their networks who post on their sites are also Scottish. It is therefore reasonable to suppose that the Scottish sample of sites includes many more Scottish writers than the English sample. But obviously both samples include writers from a variety of backgrounds. A number of the writers refer to university studies and even to a year abroad in Paris, and it is clear that these individuals are likely to have networks including quite a lot of non-Scottish people. Consequently we are looking at the spellings in Scotland-related networks, not the spellings of speakers of Scottish varieties. The advantage of this type of data is that it samples the genuine linguistic environment of young(ish) people based in Scotland in a globalized world.

As noted above, the morpheme ING is very common in English and the spelling <in> for the ING form of verbs is very common in English-language CMC. Alveolar realizations of ING are apparently universal indices of vernacular register, and are genuine components of nearly all vernaculars as well (for example Labov 1972, Trudgill 1974, Cheshire 1982). Cheshire (1982) found, for example, that alveolar representation of ING are chosen by those who aspire to 'covert prestige'. The spelling <in> often indexes informality everywhere in the English-speaking world and one can say that writers who use <in> are enacting informality and possibly but not necessarily representing features of their own speech. All 30 Scottish sites examined have participle/gerund representations in both <ing> and <in>, but this is true of virtually all the Irish, English and American sites examined in Shaw (2008, 2009) too. Consequently, although Scots consistently uses <in> spellings for this morpheme, the sites cannot be said to be particularly Scottish in this respect.

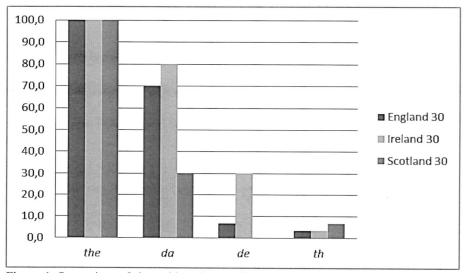

Figure 1: Proportions of sites with various realizations of *the* (English and Irish data from Shaw 2008, 2009).

It is very common in CMC to represent words with a standard spelling in <th>, and standard pronunciation with a voiced dental fricative, by a spelling in <d>. As noted above, this spelling could, like participles in <in>,be an an appeal for some sort of covert-prestige status – in this case Irish or stereotype 'creole' or African-American. However, <d> spellings are not as universal or consistent as <in> spellings of –ING. Figure 1 shows that the spelling *da* of *the* was less common in Scottish sites than in English or Irish, and that *de* did not occur, and Figure 2 shows that the pattern is the same for *this* and *that*. This difference seems to be related to differences in actual pronunciation or the stereotype of local covert-prestige pronunciation. We noted above that representations of (mainland) Scots consistently spell TH with <th>. TH-stopping is of course actually more common in Irish English (Wells 1983) than in English or Scottish, and one can infer that using features of London Jamaican is also less common or less attractive in Scotland than in England. While Scottish CMC writers do use spellings representing stopped TH, in this sample they do so less than other writers from the British

Isles and this might be because they have other resources for showing a vernacular identity.

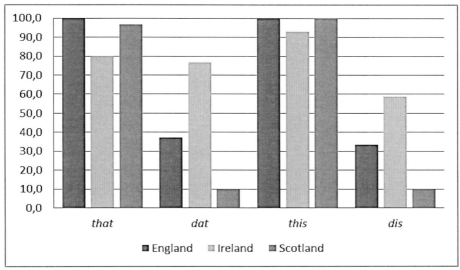

Figure 2: Proportions of sites with various representations of *this* and *that*.

Two words were chosen as candidates for showing genuine phonological differences. One is the word WHAT. Non-standard spellings of the word WHAT in English and US always omit the <h>, which for nearly all speakers of the relevant varieties is a mere spelling convention. While they often retain the <a>, giving a spelling *wat*, they also often respell it, giving *wot* in England and Ireland but *wut* in the US. In Scotland one might expect non-standard spellings which would retain the <h>, since many speakers of Scottish varieties, including Scottish Standard English, maintain a distinction between a voiceless and a voiced labiovelar approximant, corresponding to the spellings <wh> and <w> respectively. One might also expect spellings with /f/ for <wh> and with the vowel <i>, as noted above.

Figure 3 shows that among the forms found by searching on *w*t* it is *what*, *wat*, and *wot* that predominate. The numbers are very similar to those on English and Irish sites. The form *wut* which is common in the US is infrequent, but so are forms with the vowel <i> which can be referred to Scots. In particular there are unexpectedly few <wh> spellings, given what is generally taken to be the predominance of voiceless pronunciations of WH in Scotland; this may reflect an actual change towards voiced realizations. A single instance of *wht* occurs in a Scots-sounding context: *so wht e dain eh nyt* 'So what [are] you doing tonight'. A search on f*t only produced two sites with instances of *fit*. (Examples 5 and 6).

5. Thats fit am for! Ti bully yi! haha. Am sure ucould give as good as you get! ('That's what I'm for ! To bully you!....')
6. fit time on saturday is the inflation? (What time....)

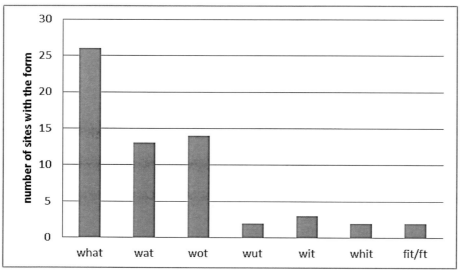

Figure 3: Number of 30 Scottish sites which use various forms of WHAT.

Thus in this area the Scottish sites seem mainly to follow the conventions of sites in other areas and not to mark voiceless WH or show Scots vowels.

The word *thought* is quite frequent in these texts, and the potential non-standard spelling is interesting. The reason is that, as noted above, in Scottish and Irish varieties the vowel is the same as that in CLOTH and quite unlike that in NORTH (because in these varieties there is a /r/ phoneme in the pronunciation, while in large parts of England, both south and north, the vowel of THOUGHT is different from CLOTH (and LOT) and the same as NORTH. Figure 4 shows that a substantial minority of websites used non-standard spellings for the vowel in THOUGHT, and that the vowels are distributed as one would expect: <o> spellings making *thot* rhyme with *hot* occur in Scotland and Ireland, <or> spellings making *thort/fort* rhyme with *sort* occur only in England. However the fact that THOUGHT rhymes with HOT in Scottish English is not common knowledge, so that spellings that show this rhyme are likely to reflect the speaker's own phonology rather than an imitation of some other variety. A similar case is SPEAK. In Scottish varieties of English it is common for the tense and lax vowels of English English/US English to merge, so *fool* and *full, pit* and *peat* have the same vowel. This is a fairly esoteric piece of knowledge, so that the spelling of *speak* as *spik* on two sites *(spik ti ye l8r on)* may also be revelation of Scottish phonology.

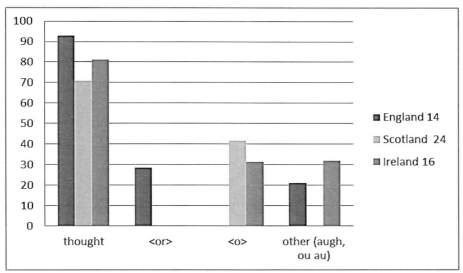

Figure 4: Proportions of sites with various representations of the vowel in thought.

The issue is complicated however. Neither *thot* nor *spik* are necessarily invented by their users. The former could be taken from other CMC writing (which the writers have probably seen) and the letter from literary Scots (which they may have done). *Thot* spellings are not in literary Scots (where *thocht* would be expected) but they are shared with Irish and US CMC, and could represent influence from them. The spelling *spik* is uniquely Scottish in CMC but shared with literary Scots, so it could conceivably represent influence from Scots spelling. Nevertheless it is quite possible that both simply represent their writers' phonology.

The consonants in THOUGHT also conform to expectations: <th> is the most frequent (as the standard always is) but in England <f> is quite common, in Ireland <t> is common and <f> also occurs, and in Scotland <th> predominates, with no cases of <t>, and only one of <f>. In the case of the consonants however, the spelling may be a representation of variety identity – fronting to /f/ and stopping to /t/ of /θ/ are familiar sociolinguistic varaibles marking Southern English and Irish vernacular respectively.

We noted above that as Scottish pronunciation is typically rhotic>; one would expect rather few <-a> spellings of words in <-er>. Shaw (2009) shows that even in England there are about four times as many sites with <er> spellings of BETTER, AFTER, NEVER, and LATER as with <-a> spellings. Searches for this investigation on aft*, n*v*, bet*, and l8* and lat* showed that forms with <-er> or <r> were even more predominant over <-a> spellings in Scotland than in England. Nevertheless two sites (out of 15 with AFTER) had *afta*, two others (out of 11) had *neva*, three more (out of 22) had *beta* and one had *18a*, making at least ten sites with instances of non-rhotic representations of <-er>. These may well come from messages written by English or other non-rhotic speakers, of course.

Thus it is clear that some of the spellings on Scottish sites bear the same sort of relationship to national and international sociolingustic variables and to local pronunciation as we have shown for English, Irish, and US sites. Sites use international standard and non-standard conventions, they reflect the local phonology of standard English, and they imitate or perform features from other varieties. However in the Scottish sites there are local features which might have a different character from these. They reflect the existence of everyday features of modern Scottish English which diverge much further from standard English than most vernaculars in England and Ireland. One could call these using Scots as if it was an alternative code like the L codes in the classic Swiss and Cyprus diglossia discussed above.

This feature of the Scots sites is most easily exemplified from patterns of negation. In the English, Irish and US texts negation involves affixation of <nt> to a modal or copula in the Standard for *isn't* or *hasn't/haven't*. Although part of standard spelling, it has similar connotations to <in> for –*ing*. The only non-standard feature is *aint* which is a widely-used non-standard form. But in the Scottish texts there are many instances of negatives with Scots forms. Searches for words that end in *na, nae, no* or *ny* produce many examples like these five:

7. Av nae been doin much cos ive been ill 4 about a week; (I haven't been..)
8. Canna believe yi didnae pull up yon night" a was affa hurt; (Can't believe you didn't...)
9. am gonna be wreacked canny wait to go out now; (.....can't wait to..)
10. i hav prob sn it b4 bt cna mind wat it looks lyk!!; (...but can't *mind* (=remember) what it looks like.)
11. U seen ma otha half comment yetz?! heehee!! i jst cudnae resist!! lol! (....I just couldn't resist)

In these cases the negated auxiliaries are: 7. *av nae* ('I've not'); 8. *canna* ('can't'), *didnae* ('didn't'); 9. *canny* ('can't'); 10. *cna* (can't); 11. *cudnae* ('couldn't'). These examples are typical of the environments Scots-like negation occurs in, and the variation in its spelling. Most (7, 9, 10, and 11) seem to be in Standard (Scottish) English (CMC) spelling with the Scots negation the only local feature in the sentence, though in 10 the whole phrase *cna mind* ('can't remember') is Scots. Only one –number 8 – could be said to be written systematically in Scots with *yi* 'you/u', *yon* 'that' (third member in the *this, that, yon* set), *a* 'I' and *affa* ('awful').

A search on *na/*nae/*ni/*nie/*ny and no produced around 35 instances of verbal negation. The spellings of CAN'T included *canna, cana, cani,* *canni, cannie,* and *canny* (as in example 3 above). Other common forms were *wasna, wasnae,* and *didnae.* Although *havna* occurred, the most common 'Scots' negation of HAVE was with contraction of the auxiliary and full *nae/ no* as in example 1 above or *av no seen you in ages eh.* But although it is easy to find forms like this, they are not by any means the most frequent in these sites. All thirty sites included negations with English *not* or (mostly) *n't,* usually numerous, while less than half included any instance of Scots-like negation, and in very few of these were there more than one or two examples.

Pronouns are also possible sites for use of Scots-like spellings. Checking YOU showed that 29 out of 30 sites used *u,* 25 *ya* and 14 *you,* a pattern almost identical to the English, Irish and US sites (Shaw 2008). However 14 Scottish sites used *ye* which otherwise only occurred in Irish sites (12 out of 30) and three used *yi.* The spelling *ye* for modern YOU (not archaic and biblical nominative plural *ye* in that there is no contrast with an accusative) is therefore Scottish (and Irish); it is widespread in written Scots. As Example 12 shows, the first-person pronoun *a* 'I' may appear as an independent word homonymous with the indefinite article or contracted with an auxiliary, as in *ad* 'I'd', *al* 'I'll', *am* 'I'm':

> 12. Jst thot ad leave ya a wee comment since a aint left ya 1 da dy
> (Just thought I'd leave you a little comment since I haven't left you one today)

I searched on *a* and on *a?* and identified pronouns manually. Some form of nominative *a* occurs in at least 24 of the 30 sites. 16 have *a* or *ah* as an independent word. A further five have *av* 'I've' or *al* 'I'll' but no independent first-person pronoun of this type. A remaining three or so only have *am* 'I'm', in Scots contexts like:

> 13. *am gid yah hw aboot dee?*('I'm good [well], yeah, how about *dee* [Dee? thee? today?])

The form *am* in other contexts is hard to distinguish from a subjectless verb in diary style as in *Berlin was amazing! Am now back in France where i am working as an au pair.* The possessive *ma* 'my' occurs in 20 Scottish sites, mostly in Scots-looking contexts, but it also occurs in 10 English and eight Irish sites. It is a feature of international CMC style that happens to coincide with a Scots spelling and thus appears especially often on Scottish sites.

Other frequent Scots items, not analysed in detail include: *Aye* 'yes' in nine sites; *fae* 'from' in eight sites; *the/da nite/night* 'tonight' in six sites; *the day,* etc 'today' in five; *the mor(r)a* 'tomorrow' in four.

4. Discussion

The forms discussed fall into different categories as noted above, but the sites they occur in are also characterized by different categories of occurrence, and both types of category are of interest in understanding the Scottishness of these texts.

The majority of the forms found are in standard spelling. This is partly due to quoted material like jokes or song titles, but standard spelling is also a feature of many contributions. Where spelling is nonstandard, a majority represent an international CMC English register: *goin, ya, tonite, l8r, da, 2, gonna,* etc. Here we may also include pan-British Isles spellings like *wot* and *coz* (vs US *wut, cuz*)

The minority of non-standard forms that can be associated with Scottish Standard English or Scots fall into two categories, those that can scarcely be deliberate, and those that may be. First, the spelling *thot* 'thought' is different from all the others discussed here, in that it represents the actual phonology of Scottish Standard English and is not Scots (where the corresponding form would be *thocht*). Furthermore, as we noted above, it is part of complex lexical distribution pattern and it is unlikely that anyone would choose the spelling deliberately to display Scottishness. We are arguing, therefore that it reveals the writer's Standard Scottish English phonology. There is a counter-argument, and that is that *thot* is frequent US respelling in line with US English phonology, so the writers may be simply adopting what they take to be an international CMC form. The one occurrence of *fot* (Example 13 below), however, shows the writer deliberately adopting a Southern English initial consonant but nonetheless writing an extremely unSouthern English vowel, revealing his own phonology.

The second category includes forms that more or less resemble those of Scots: vocabulary items, negation forms, pronouns, etc. These often occur as part of a general CMC vernacular, like the locally-marked features in sites from other regions.

> 14. *awrite m8 you enjoy yar sel on sat, a fot it was kwlaity likes*
> (All right, mate, [did] you enjoy yourself on Saturday, I thought it was quality, like)

In Example 14 the Scottish forms *awrite, yar sel, a* and *–ot* co-occur with the British *m8* and the specifically English *f-* for TH. All of these may be merely markers of a vernacular register.

Sometimes it seems possible that there is metaphorical code-switching (i.e code-switching to assert one's linguistic identity, Blom & Gumperz 1972), although one cannot determine motivation from this type of textual data. The Scottish features (*banter* 'gossip, news', *summit* 'something', *cannie, aye, av nae been*) in Example 15 mark this contribution out from all the others on this particular site and thus may identify the writer as accentuating Scottishness in contrast to the generally English spelling in the context.

> 15. hows the banter? U into tht job yet, what is it a bank or summit, i cannie remember? Aye (breathe in) Av nae been doin much cos ive been ill 4 about a week now coz i couldnt speak, bad throat. Playin at some gig thing 2morow nite, should be good no idea wats happenin tho....
> (How is the gossip? You into that job yet, what is it, bank or something, I can't remember? Yes (breathe in) I haven't been doing much because I've been ill for about a week now because I couldn't speak, bad throat. (I'm) Playing at some gig tomorrow night, no idea what's happening though.)

As we have seem above it is quite common for individual contributions in up to half the sites to have many Scots features, as in Example 16, alongside material with little Scottish marking.

> 16. how r u the day en???ft u bn up ti (How are you today? What have you been up to?)

However, there are a few examples in which writers seem to be consistently writing in Scots. One site, (Example 17), is predominantly written in Scots-coloured CMC, and it contains the following self-introduction:

> 17. got ma ain hoose up PLACE naw moved in yit, will move in shortly, am 25yrs ... omg time flys when ur hivin fun lol, canni live withoot ma bitches – NAMES wanni no mere aboot me just ask am sure a will tell (got my own house up at PLACE, not moved in yet, will move in shortly, I'm 25 years.... OMG, time flies when you're having fun, LOL, (I9 can't live without my bitches (female friends) ---NAMES __ (If you) want to know more about me just ask, I'm sure I will tell.)

Another site which contains many Scots comments begins as in Example 18:

> 18. a live in TOWN in X gate jst across from the garage a moved their 2 year ago n its ok but not as gd as where i used 2 live ma best m8s is NAMES n we have gr8 laughs mind a cana 4get aw ma girls NAMES n aw the rest of ma m8s know who they are catch uz l8r, by the way am the dude at the end wae the whitish jacket l8r (I live in TOWN, in X street just across from the garage. I moved there two years ago and its OK, but not as good as where I used to live. My best mates are NAMES and we have great laughs. *Mind* I can't forget all my girls NAMES and all the restb of my mates know who they are. Catch *youse*

later. By the way I'm the dude at the end with the whitish jacket. Later.

This is not fully consistent, with English *from* rather than Scots *fae*, but it has interesting features such as the Scots *is* with the plural subject *m8s*. In these cases one might be able to say that the writer has chosen to introduce him or herself with a distinctively Scots identity, not merely aiming at a spoken style and thus happening to introduce local features.

5. Conclusion

Many English, Irish and US sites use local features casually to index a spoken vernacular style. In doing so they are presumably conforming to the usage of the majority of their own network, which is primarily local. Some Scottish CMC sites use an indistinguishable style with occasional local vocabulary (all the sites examined here had *wee*, as a consequence of our search method) and otherwise what one might call 'international CMC English'. Many include contributions with Scottish forms like *a* 'I' or *didna*, which their writers must know not to be 'international CMC' but still only rather occasionally, and mixed with many less marked forms. The primary purpose of these usages seems still to be to establish an informal spoken register appropriate to the peer-group addressed. However, some contributions to some websites (and the majority of contributions to a few) show such a high concentration of Scots grammar and spelling that the writers may have chosen to write Scots as a deliberate switch away from the international English code. Melchers and Shaw (2003: 64) quote Shetland e-mailers referring metalinguistically to their two codes (Insular Scots and Scottish Standard English), as shown in Example 19:

> 19. …Am been skrivan a lokk a auld wirds diss winter, and hiv gottin aboot a thoozan doon. I think I had better write in English!

This sounds like the type of decision taken by the Swiss and Cypriot CMC writers from diglossic situations, and nothing like it appears in the young people's sites from mainland Scotland examined here. Nevertheless the writers are mostly communicating naturally in Scots-coloured written English, and some are also approaching writing the Scots of the twenty-first century.

6. References

Anthony, L. (2007), AntConc 3.2.1w (Windows) [Computer Software]. Tokyo: Waseda University. Available from http://www.antlab.sci.waseda.ac.jp/

Blom, J.-P. & Gumperz, J. J. (1972), Social Meaning in Linguistic Structures: Code Switching in Northern Norway, in Gumperz, J. J., & Hymes, D. (eds), *Directions in Sociolinguistics: The Ethnography of Communication*, New York: Holt, Rinehart, and Winston, pp. 407-434.

Cheshire, J. (1982), *Variation in an English dialect: A sociolinguistic study*, Cambridge: Cambridge University Press.

Ifukor, P.A. (2011), Spelling and simulated shibboleths in Nigerian computer-mediated communication, *English Today* 27 (3), pp. 35-42.

Görlach, M. (1991), Scotland and Jamaica – bidialectal or bilingual?, in Görlach, M. (ed.), *Englishes*, Amsterdam: Benjamins, 50–73.

Karlsson, A-M. (2002). To write a page and colour a text. Concepts and practices of homepage use, in Coppock, P. (ed.), The Semiotics of Writing. Turnhout: Brepols.

Melchers, G. & Shaw, P. (2003), *World Englishes: an Introduction*, Arnold, London.

Labov, W. (1972), *Sociolinguistic Patterns*, Philadelphia: University of Pennsylvania Press.

Shaw, P. (2008), Spelling, accent and identity in computer-mediated communication, *English Today* 24 (2), pp. 42-49.

Shaw, P. (2009), L8r or l8a? Rhoticity variation in computer-mediated communication, in Rhonwen B., Mobärg, M. & Ohlander,S. (eds), *Corpora and Discourse – and Stuff*, Gothenburg. Acta Universitatis Gothoburgensis, pp. 267-276.

Siebenhaar, B. (2006), Code choice and code-switching in Swiss-German Internet Relay Chat Rooms. *Journal of Sociolinguistics* 10 (4), pp. 481-506.

Themistocleous, C. (2010), Writing in a non-standard Greek variety: Romanized Cypriot Greek in online chat, *Writing Systems Research* 2 (2), pp. 155–168.

Trudgill, P. (1974), *The Social Differentiation of English in Norwich*, Cambridge: Cambridge University Press.

Volckaert-Legrier, O., Bernicot, J. & Bert-Erboul, A. (2009), Electronic mail, a new written-language register: a study with French-speaking adolescents, *British Journal of Developmental Psychology* 27, pp. 163–181.

Warschauer, M., El Said, G.R., & Zohry, A. (2002), Language choice online: globalization and identity in Egypt, *Journal of Computer-mediated Communication* 7 (4). Available from http://jcmc.indiana.edu/vol7/issue4/warschauer.html

Wells J.C. (1983), *Accents of English*, volume 1, Cambridge: Cambridge Univeristy Press.

Welsh, I. (2012), *Skagboys*, London: Jonathan Cape.

Imagearbeit mit *missverstehen* in Diskussionsforen

Johanna Salomonsson

Hochschule Dalarna

1. Einleitung

In diesem Artikel geht es um Kommunikation in Diskussionsforen. Untersuchungsgegenstand sind dabei Phrasen, die eine Form von *missverstehen* enthalten und im Artikel geht es darum, das interaktive Potential dieser Phrasen aufzudecken. Der Artikel ist in einem praxisbezogenen Ansatz verankert, der davon ausgeht, dass sich bestimmte kommunikative Funktionen eines sprachlichen Ausdrucks in der Interaktion herausbilden. Ausgangspunkt ist deshalb, dass das Wort *missverstehen* nicht unbedingt auf das Konzept <MISSVERSTÄNDNIS> referieren muss. Eher haben die Interagierenden in den Diskussionsforen die Möglichkeit, eine bestimmte Bedeutung eines Wortes in der Interaktion festzulegen.

Als hypothetischer Ausgangspunkt des Artikels gilt, dass mit der Phrase mit *missverstehen* ein intersubjektives <VERSTEHEN> konstruiert werden kann. Dieses <VERSTEHEN> betrifft sowohl die diskutierte Thematik im Forum, als auch die interpersonellen Beziehungen, die mit der Interaktion im Forum aufgebaut werden. So ist ein zentrales Ziel, die Beiträge mit dem thematisierten <MISSVERSTÄNDNIS> innerhalb bestimmter metakommunikativen Sequenzen, *Scripts* (Schank/Abelson 1977), zu untersuchen. Ein Script ist

> a structure that describes appropriate sequences of events in a particular context. [...] A script is a predetermined stereotyped sequence of actions that defines a well-known situation. (Schank/Abelson 1977: 41)

Diese Scripts bestehen aus bestimmten *Slots* (Schank/Abelson 1977), die durchgearbeitet werden müssen, um die Objektsebene zu erreichen. Ein Slot kann ein Turn sein oder ein Beitrag im Forum. Um diese Scripts zu identifizieren, wird methodisch mit der Distribution bestimmter Komponenten im Forumsbeitrag gearbeitet, wobei der Grad an Schriftlichkeit/Mündlichkeit als Mittel für Beziehungsarbeit besonders hervorgehoben wird. Die Diskussionsforen eignen sich insofern für diese Untersuchung, als sie z. T. einem Gespräch ähneln, müssen aber nicht transkribiert werden, um die kognitive Verwendung von *missverstehen* in Scripts zu untersuchen. Die Pseudonyme in den wiedergegebenen Beiträgen sind zum Zweck der Anonymisierung geändert.[1]

Der Artikel[2] basiert auf einem Korpus mit 565 Beiträgen aus Foren verschiedener Themen. Die Beiträge enthalten eine Phrase mit *missverstehen*, etwa *du hast mich missverstanden, er hat sie missverstanden, wir missverstehen uns* usw. Dieses Korpus wurde mit dem Ziel zusammengestellt, 25 Beiträge pro grammatische Struktur zu finden. Da der Gebrauch in bestimmten Kategorien wesentlich geringer war, wurden die vorhandenen Beiträge aufgenommen. Die Beiträge verteilen sich wie in Tabelle 1:

ich missverstehe	25	*sie missversteht*	9
ich missverstehe dich	25	*sie missverstand*	2
ich missverstand	25	*sie hat missverstanden*	5
ich habe missverstanden	25	*wir missverstehen*	25
ich habe dich missverstanden	25	*wir missverstanden*	6
du missverstehst	25	*wir haben missverstanden*	25
du missverstand(e)st	4	*ihr missversteht*	25
du hast missverstanden	25	*ihr missverstandet*	2
haste missverstanden	25	*ihr habt missverstanden*	25
hast du missverstanden	25	*Sie/sie missverstehen*	25
er missversteht	15	*Sie/sie haben missverstanden*	25
er missverstand	1	*hier liegt ein Missverständnis vor*	25
er hat missverstanden	19	*Missverständnis/Missverständnisse*	25
man-Konstruktionen/ Passivkonstruktionen	25	Imperative (5 pro gramm. Person)	15
Modalkonstruktionen	25	Infinitivkonstruktionen	12

Tabelle 1: Verteilung der Phrasen im Korpus.

Wie in jeder Kommunikationsform gilt es auch für die Diskussionsforen, dass gewisse Regeln und Normen beachtet werden müssen, um einen reibungslosen Verlauf zu garantieren. Ziel ist u.a. die eigene Meinung kundzutun und diese durchzusetzen, ohne dabei das Image der anderen Kommunikationsteilnehmer zu verletzen. Somit werden in der Kommunikation nicht nur inhaltliche Aspekte vermittelt, sondern auch interpersonelle Beziehungen (Watzlawick/Beavin/Jackson 2003). In diesem Artikel geht es darum,

---

[1] Die Forumstexte sind auf öffentlichen Webseiten gefunden und die Schreibenden benutzen Pseudonyme, weshalb sie anonym sind. In diesem Artikel sind allerdings die Pseudonyme geändert, um die Integrität der Schreibenden zu schützen.
[2] Der Artikel ist ein Extrakt aus meiner Dissertation (2011b) zu einem Forschungsprojekt von 2005 bis 2011. Die gleichen Beispiele wie in der Dissertation wurden für diesen Artikel benutzt, weshalb die Beiträge nicht die aktuellsten sind. Da es hier um den systematischen Gebrauch der Phrasen mit *missverstehen* handelt, hat dies auf das Ergebnis keinen Einfluss.

wie mit *missverstehen* nicht nur das <VERSTEHEN> in den Diskussionsforen verhandelt wird, sondern auch darum, wie die interpersonellen Verhältnisse unter den TeilnehmerInnen anhand von Metakommunikation über Verstehensprozesse ausgehandelt und akzeptabel gemacht werden. Ausgangspunkt ist, dass keine vollständige Intersubjektivität erreicht werden kann, weil sich zwei Interagierende in das <VERSTEHEN> des anderen nicht hineinversetzen können. Das <VERSTEHEN> wird eher sozial konstruiert (Verdonik 2010: 2; Watzlawick/Beavin/ Jackson 2003) und bezweckt entweder die Beziehungsebene, die Inhaltsebene oder beide Ebenen gleichzeitig. Das Script entscheidet, ob sich das thematisierte <MISSVERSTÄNDNIS> auf die Inhalts- oder auf die Beziehungsebene bezieht.

2. Interaktion in den Diskussionsforen

Im Internet unterhalten sich Menschen mit verschiedenen Kommunikationsformen, wie z. B. Chats, Facebook, interaktiven Webseiten, Blogs (v.a. mit der Kommentarfunktion) sowie Diskussionsforen. In einem Diskussionsforum treffen sich Menschen, die ein gemeinsames Interesse teilen. Es gibt Foren über zahlreiche Themen – beispielsweise Computerprogrammieren, Pferde, Autoreparaturen, Sport uvm. Das Diskussionsforum wird thematisch gegliedert und jede Diskussion wird nach verschiedenen Threads organisiert.

Die Foren sind generell für Mitleser offen, obwohl das Mitschreiben eine Registrierung verlangt. Persönliche Angaben wie Alter und Geschlecht. werden üblicherweise nicht veröffentlicht, und ihre Validität wird nicht überprüft, sondern die Interagierenden kommunizieren unter einem Pseudonym und konstruieren mit der Interaktion Identitäten voneinander. Die interessanten Daten sind eher Datum der Registrierung als Benutzer, Anzahl geschriebener Beiträge und Datum des bestimmten Beitrags (Beitrag 1).

Diese Interaktion wird ähnlich wie ein schriftliches Gespräch geführt, mit dem Unterschied, dass die Äußerungen zitiert werden können. Mit dem Zitat kann der/die Interagierende nicht nur einen thematischen Fokus konstituieren, sondern auch direkt auf Beiträge hinweisen, die vor langer Zeit, etwa Jahren, publiziert wurden. Die Asynchronizität[3] dieser Interaktionsform trägt dazu bei, dass sich die Interagierenden ihre Äußerungen überlegen können und nicht spontan reagieren müssen. Auch wenn andere Beiträge inzwischen publiziert werden, kann Kohärenz anhand von der Zitatfunktion geschafft werden.

---

[3] Zur Diskussion über Synchronität/Asynchronität in den Internetmedien s. Dürscheid (2006).

Metakommunikation über Verstehensprozesse läuft deswegen anders in dieser Kommunikationsform, denn in gesprochener Sprache sind Reparaturen aufgrund akustich falschen Verstehens vorhanden (Hinnenkamp 1998),

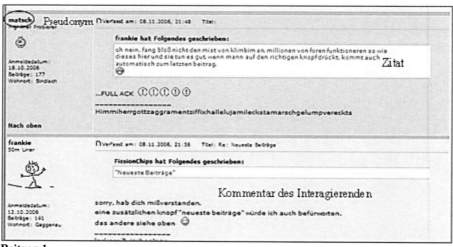

Beitrag 1

was aber in einem Diskussionsforum keine Entsprechung findet. In den Reparatursequenzen konzentrieren sich die Interagierenden eher auf inhaltliche Fragen und es geht hauptsächlich darum, ein gemeinsames Auffassen der Kontextualisierungshinweise zu schaffen. Ein anderes wichtiges Merkmal ist, dass mehrere einander unbekannte Teilnehmende diese Interaktion gemeinsam aufbauen, was bedeutet, dass Informationen und Erfahrungen vieler Perspektive ausgetauscht werden. Die Diskussionsforen bieten somit eine Plattform für einen Meinungsaustausch, der vor dem Internet auf diese Weise kaum möglich war.

In der Interaktion verhalten sich die Interagierenden zu einer *Netiquette* (Bader 2002: 69) und es herrscht in den meisten Foren die Norm, das *T*-Pronomen[4] (Brown/Gilman 1970) *du* als Anredeform zu verwenden. Mit Sprache gestalten die Teilnehemer ihre Beziehungen zueinander und bauen ihre sozialen Positionen untereinander auf (Wolf 1999). Während in der face-to-face Kommunikation u.a. auch außersprachliche Parameter dazu beitragen, wie sich diese Beziehungen gestalten, steht den Interagierenden in den Diskussionsforen überwiegend nur Sprache zur Verfügung, z. B. der Umgang mit Mündlichkeit und Schriftlichkeit.

---

[4] T= *Tu*. Informelle Anredeform.

3. Schriftlichkeit und Mündlichkeit in den Diskussionsforen

Kommunikation in Diskussionsforen wird mit Sprache geführt, die Züge aus sowohl geschriebener als auch gesprochener Sprache enthält. Das Medium ist geschrieben, aber es ist konzeptuell sowohl geschrieben als auch gesprochen (Koch/Oesterreicher 2007; Dürscheid 2006). Spiel mit Kapitälen, Abkürzungen, Emoticons[5], Aktionswörter *lache*, Tilgungen *haste*[6] usw. sind Mittel, um Mündlichkeit oder Schriftlichkeit auszudrücken (Kadir/Maros/Hamid 2012). Wie traditionell mündlicher und schriftlicher Text als ein Kontinuum betrachtet werden müsste (Gee 2012: 71), gilt dies auch für das Internet. Die Texte sind sprachlich sehr heterogen und von einer bestimmten *Textsorte* kann deswegen nicht die Rede sein. In einigen Beiträgen erinnert die Sprache an einen Chat, in anderen eher an einen Zeitungsartikel. Tabelle 2 illustriert die typischen Merkmale für Mündlichkeit bzw. Schriftlichkeit:

Mündlichkeit	Schriftlichkeit
Privatheit	Öffentlichkeit
Vertrautheit der Kommunikationspartner	Fremdheit der Kommunikationspartner
starke emotionale Beteiligung	geringe emotionale Beteiligung
Situations- und Handlungseinbindung	Situations- und Handlungsentbindung
referenzielle Nähe	referenzielle Distanz
raum-zeitliche Nähe (face-to-face)	raum-zeitliche Distanz
kommunikative Kooperation	keine kommunikative Kooperation
Dialog	Monolog
Spontaneität	Reflektiertheit
freie Themenentwicklung	Themenfixierung

Tabelle 2: Merkmale der Mündlichkeit bzw. der Schriftlichkeit nach Koch/Österreicher 2007.

Mit Mündlichkeit und Schriftlichkeit kann der/die Interagierende auch Informalität und Formalität ausdrücken. Informalität ist auch mit sozialer Distanz verbunden und markiert Intimität zwischen den Interagierenden aber auch Verstehen in Bezug auf v.a. die Beziehungsebene. Die Heterogenität der Beiträge trägt dazu bei, dass sie mehr oder weniger Formalität/Informalität enthalten, wie Tabelle 3 zeigt:

---

[5] Auch *Smiley*. Zur Verwendung von Emoticons s. Derks (2007).
[6] Zum Gebrauch und Frequenz dieser Tilgungen s. Salomonsson (2011a).

Informalität	Formalität
Soziale Nähe	Soziale Distanz
Emoticons	Keine Emoticons
Verschmelzungen *haste* oder Abkürzungen *hab*	Vollständiges Subjekt und Prädikat: *Ich habe, hast du*
Häufung von Interpunktionszeichen	Interpunktion nach schriftsprachlicher Norm
Akronyme *imho*[7], Rebuswörter *gute n8*[8]	Deutschsprachige Sätze
Lexikalisch markiert *geil, krass, hammer*	Lexikalisch markiert: *lediglich*
T-pronomen	V-pronomen
Aktionswörter *lache*	Mit komplettem Satz ausgedrückt
Regionalismen	Hochdeutsche Sprache

Tabelle 3: Merkmale der Informalität bzw. Formalität.

Diese Merkmale kommunizieren typischerweise und präsupponieren Formalität bzw. Informalität. Da sie gleichzeitig dazu benutzt werden, eine gekürzte soziale Distanz zu signalisieren, sind sie Kennzeichen für Beziehungsarbeit und sind deshalb auch wichtig in der Klärung verschiedener Verstehensprozesse. Diese sprachlichen Realisierungsmittel tragen in solchen Prozessen zur Beziehungsarbeit bei, aber parallel läuft auch das <VERSTEHEN> hinsichtlich des Inhalts im Thread. Wenn keine Intersubjektivität gereicht werden kann, ist eine metakommunikative Sequenz notwendig, um es zu klären. Es geht dabei um die Aufdeckung des <MISSVERSTEHENS>.

4. Das <MISSVERSTÄNDNIS> in der Interaktion

In der Forschung zu Missverständnissen wird das <MISSVERSTÄNDNIS> häufig als eine Störung in der Kommunikation betrachtet[9], wobei die Interaktion Gefahr läuft, abzubrechen. Dies löst eine Thematisierung mit *missverstehen* aus, was aber nicht unbedingt bedeuten muss, dass tatsächlich ein <MISSVERSTÄNDNIS> entstanden ist. Es kann auch verbalisiert werden, weil der/die Interagierende die Kommunikation in eine bestimmte Richtung beeinflussen will. Ein Beispiel, in dem ein <MISSVERSTÄNDNIS> thematisiert wird, zeigt Beitrag 2:

---

[7] In my humble opinion.
[8] Diese Sprachspielereien haben ihre Wurzeln in der Sondersprache der sog. „Hacker" der 80er Jahre (Storrer 2001: 4). Sie sind aus dem Englischen übernommen, und haben sich im deutschen Sprachgebrauch des Internets durchgesetzt, z. B. *CU* (see you), *U2* (you too). Nach gleichem Muster werden Rebussätze im Deutschen wie *gute n8* (gute Nacht) (Siever 2006: 80) produziert.
[9] Zu solchen Untersuchungen s. u.a. Selting (1987), Schegloff (1992), Falkner (1997), Hinnenkamp (1998), Bailey (2004) und Verdonik (2010).

> Haimon-85:
>
> oh je, war doch ironisch GEMEINT , Ihr habt mich total missverstanden ... die Betonung lag auf "doch erst 24 Jahre alt". Na Ihr wisst schon usw. Gut der ging also gründlich daneben ...

Beitrag 2

In diesem Beitrag ist eine Situation entstanden, in der eine Äußerung aus zwei verschiedenen Perspektiven gedeutet wurde. Der Kontext[10] wird aus zwei verschiedenen Perspektiven verstanden und *missverstehen* soll dazu beitragen, dass sich die Interagierenden auf eine Auffassung einigen können: Ein Kontext soll konstruiert werden. Nun kann es sich nur um eine Konstruktion handeln, da der Kontext subjektiv geschaffen und gedeutet wird. In Beitrag 2 wird die Absicht unterschiedlich aufgefasst, was „Haimon-85" mit diesem Beitrag verdeutlicht. Anhand von ergänzenden Kontextualisierungshinweisen[11] kann der Kontext neu konstruiert und relevant[12] gemacht werden. Dadurch wird der Beitrag verständlich. Der/die Interagierende muss folglich den Beitrag lexikalisch mit expliziten Kohäsionsmitteln, d. h. Anaphern, formulieren oder mit impliziten Kontextualisierungshinweisen versehen, damit dem Leser die Verbindung zwischen dem Beitrag und dem unmittelbaren Kontext in der Kommunikation wie auch dem außersprachlichen Kontext ersichtlich wird. Wenn dies nicht gelingt, kann ein <MISSVERSTÄNDNIS> bzw. ein <NICHT VERSTEHEN> in der Kommunikation entstehen. Der Unterschied besteht darin, ob einige (<MISSVERSTÄNDNIS>) oder die meisten/alle (<NICHT VERSTEHEN>) Kontextualisierungshinweise nicht eingeordnet werden können (Figur 1).

---

[10] Der Kontext in der Forumskommunikation ist in gewisser Hinsicht zweigeteilt. Einerseits betrifft er die außersprachliche Welt mit dem enzyklopädischen Wissen, den sozialen Konventionen usw., andererseits die Kommunikation im Diskussionsthread. Als ‚Kontext' wird in diesem Artikel das verstanden, was die Schreibenden in ihren Beiträgen behandeln, d. h. soziale Konventionen, Themen und das enzyklopädische Wissen. Zum Kontext gehört auch die Beziehungsebene und wie die Interagierenden das interpersonelle Verhältnis aufbauen.

[11] Kontextualisierungshinweise sind Angaben im Text, die kontextuelle Einheiten miteinander verbinden (Gumperz 1982, 1992, 2004; Auer 1986, 1992). Sie korrelieren mit kohäsiven Merkmalen und machen den Text kohärent. In der Internetkommunikation kann beispielsweise ein zwinkerndes Emoticon auf Scherzhaftigkeit verweisen (Derks 2007). Kontextualisierungshinweise sind dadurch zu erkennen, dass sie keine explizite Referenz aufweisen, im Vergleich zu lexikalischen kohäsiven Referenzen. Kontextualisierungshinweise etablieren einerseits einen Kontrast zu neuen Informationen oder sie schränken die Deutung dieser Informationen ein. (Auer 1992: 31)

[12] Laut der Relevanztheorie (Sperber/Wilson 1986, 2006), einer Entfaltung der Maxime der Relevanz von Grice, ist eine Äußerung genau dann. relevant, wenn der Empfänger den Inhalt einordnen kann. Dies muss innerhalb eines kontextuellen Rahmens ausgehandelt werden, wobei der Empfänger sein enzyklopädisches Wissen oder eine konventionalisierte Dekodierung benutzt, um eine Äußerung mit einem bestimmten Kontext in Verbindung zu setzen. Wenn eine Äußerung zwei- oder mehrdeutig ist, entscheidet der Kontext die Interpretation. (Bierwisch 1983: 93)

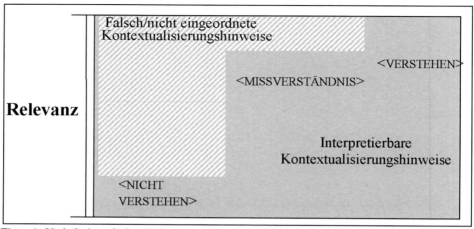

Figur 1: Verhältnis zwischen Relevanz und Kontextualisierungshinweisen in Bezug auf <VERSTEHEN>.

Nicht verstehen ist in der Verwendung imagebedrohender[13] als *missverstehen*, weil der Sender damit die meisten Kontextualisierungshinweise des anderen verwirft, während *missverstehen* impliziert, dass die meisten Kontextualisierungshinweise für das konstruierte <VERSTEHEN> relevant waren. *Missverstehen* markiert die Stellen in der Kommunikation, wo die Beziehungsebene, die Inhaltsebene oder beide Ebenen gleichzeitig gesichert werden müssen. Es wird ausgelöst, weil die Forumsbeiträge nicht miteinander kohärent sind – die Kontextualisierungshinweise können nicht gedeutet werden. Anders ausgedrückt: Ein Beitrag ist in der Kommunikation unerwartet, weil er mit dem vorherigen Turn, der *Störungsquelle,* nicht korreliert. Schegloff (1992: 1337) hat in der gesprochenen Sprache die folgenden Schritte identifiziert:

B1[14]	Aussage *p* von A.
B2	Versteht *p* als *q*. Kontextualisierung anders. Antwortet unerwartet.
B3	Richtigstellung. Versteht *q* als *q* bzw. *p* als *p* und korrigiert *p*.

Figur 2: Typologie des Missverständnisses.

Ein <MISSVERSTÄNDNIS> entsteht in der Kommunikation, wenn eine Äußerung nur teilweise oder sogar falsch verstanden wurde. Dies ist dem Missverstehenden unbewusst und wird erst später in der Kommunikation markiert und richtig gestellt. Diese Richtigstellung kann mit verschiedenen Markierungen verbalisiert werden, beispielsweise mit *ach so, nein ich meinte* usw. und muss somit nicht mit *missverstehen* thematisiert werden. Sie kann aller-

---

[13] Vgl. *FTA (face threatening act)* Brown/Levinson (1987).
[14] B = Beitrag (*Turn*).

dings in der Interaktion verschoben werden, wenn keiner in der Kommunikation merkt, dass eine Inkohärenz vorliegt.

Diese Inkohärenz muss sich nicht nur auf den Inhalt der Kommunikation beziehen, sondern kann auch die Beziehungsarbeit beabsichtigen. Wenn in der Kommunikation die Beziehungsebene kaum erwähnt wird, heißt dies aber nicht, dass sie ignoriert wird, sondern dass eine Bearbeitung ihrer nicht notwendig ist. Gleichzeitig kann die Beziehungsebene auch zum Inhalt der Kommunikation werden, wenn sie auf einer Metaebene bearbeitet wird. Die Richtigstellung befindet sich somit auf einer Metaebene und Ziel ist es, die Kommunikation auf die Objektsebene zurückzuführen. Dies ist möglich, wenn die Beziehungen *konstituiert* sind. Deswegen kann *missverstehen* zum Zweck der Beziehungsarbeit benutzt werden, wenn die Beziehungen zwischen zwei oder mehreren uneinigen Interagierenden *konstruiert* werden muss.

Auf ein Verständigungsproblem kann nicht nur mit Phrasen wie *ich habe dich missverstanden* aufmerksam gemacht werden, sondern mit verschiedenen Ausdrücken. Umgekehrt gilt das gleiche Phänomen, und zwar, dass *missverstehen* zu verschiedenen Zwecken gebraucht werden kann und nicht nur in bezug auf eine tatsächliche Diskrepanz hinsichtlich der aufgefassten Kontextualisierungshinweise, d.h. ein <MISSVERSTÄNDNIS>. Es wird unten gezeigt, dass diese Funktionen eher der Beziehungsarbeit dienen. Es muss sich somit um eine andere Form der Thematisierung handeln, wenn die Verhandlung um soziale Positionen und Imagearbeit[15] hervorgehoben wird. Wie sich die Funktionen der Thematisierung mit *missverstehen* voneinander unterscheiden, kann mit dem Aufbau des Forumsbeitrags gezeigt werden.

4.1 Musterhafte Struktur des Forumsbeitrags

Diejenigen Forumsbeiträge, die eine Phrase mit *missverstehen* enthalten weisen hinsichtlich ihres Aufbaus eine Homogenität auf. Die Phrase und noch fünf[16] Komponenten bauen gemeinsam den Beitrag auf, wobei jede Komponente für die Interaktion eine besondere Rolle trägt:

[A] Initiierung: *Nein,*
[B] Bearbeitung der Beziehungsebene: *ich glaube*
[C] Missverständnisthematisierende Phrase: *du hast mich missverstanden.*
[D] Themenverweiskomponente: *Ich meinte nicht p,*

---

[15] Goffman (1959): *face work.* Der Terminus bezieht sich auf den Bedarf, den eigenen Willen zu wahren, ohne gegen die Wünsche und Erwartungen des anderen zu verstoßen.
[16] Schegloff (1992: 1337) hat nur vier Komponenten im Rahmen einer Reparatur identifiziert.

[E] Klarstellung:[17] *sondern q.*
[F] Akzeptanz der Beziehungsarbeit: *Dann sind wir uns einig.*

Im Folgenden wird gezeigt, dass die Distribution dieser Komponenten verschiedene Funktionen der Phrase mit *missverstehen* charakterisiert. Die Komponenten gestalten sich mit einem thematisierten <MISSVERSTÄNDNIS> wie folgt:

Karma:
[A] Doch [B] ich glaube, [C] **Du hast mich missverstanden.** [D] Ich habe keine objektive Qualität aus der weiten Verbreitung abgeleitet. [E] Ich habe lediglich festgestellt, dass viele ihre Ideen gutheißen.

Beitrag 3

Die [D]-Komponente greift die irrelevanten Kontextualisierungshinweise auf, manchmal in der Form eines Zitats. Die [E]-Komponente andererseits ergänzt den Beitrag mit neuen, relevanten Hinweisen. Diese Kontrastierung ist ein wichtiges Werkzeug, um eine Eigenimagebewahrung durchzusetzen, da es klar wird, welche Positionen die jeweiligen Interagierenden zum Sachverhalt annehmen. Die [F]-Komponente andererseits kennzeichnet Honorierungen und sind eher mit Fremdimagebewahrungen verbunden.[18]

Hier muss betont werden, dass nicht alle Komponenten in einem Beitrag vorhanden sein müssen/können und ihre Reihenfolge beliebig sein kann. Je nach dem, wie die Komponenten im Beitrag distribuiert werden, ist es möglich in der Forumsinteraktion verschiedene Scripts[19] zu identifizieren, die jeweils einen bestimmten kommunikativen Zweck haben, v.a. hinsichtlich der Beziehungsarbeit. Scripts sind situationsgebunden und bestehen aus bestimmten *Slots*, die an jedes Script gebunden sind. Bei den thematisierten <MISSVERSTÄNDNISSEN> können drei Scripts identifiziert werden:

Script I: Inhaltliches <MISSVERSTÄNDNIS>. Keine Beziehungsarbeit wird sprachlich realisiert. [B]-Komponente abwesend.

Script II: Beziehungsarbeit in Bezug auf Fremdimagebewahrung. [B]-Komponente wird imagebewahrend formuliert.

---

[17] Schegloff verwendet den Begriff *repair*. Um konsequent im Auge zu behalten, dass es hier nicht um ein Kommunikationsproblem geht, wird diese Komponente als eine ‚Klarstellung' betrachtet.

[18] Zu einer ausführlichen Auslegung der Funktionen dieser Komponenten, welche Sprechhandlungen sie ausmachen und welche Komponenten miteinander wirken können, s. Salomonsson (2011b).

[19] Schegloff bezieht sich jedoch nicht auf die Scripttheorie.

Script III: Beziehungsarbeit in Bezug auf Eigenimagebewahrung. [B]-Komponente wird imagebedrohend formuliert.

4.2 Script I: Missverstehen als Markierung eines inhaltlichen Verständigungsproblems

Das erste Script ist mit Schegloffs *repair* zu vergleichen, denn es geht hier um Sequenzen, in denen ein tatsächliches <MISSVERSTÄNDNIS> entstanden ist. Charakteristisch ist, dass die Beziehungsebene stabil ist und somit nicht bearbeitet werden muss, sondern die Interagierenden beschäftigen sich nur mit dem Inhalt im Forumsthread. In diesem Script läuft zwar die Beziehungsarbeit voran, sie wird aber nicht mit einer [B]-Komponente markiert. Es geht in solchen Fällen nur darum, dass die irrelevanten Kontextualisierungshinweise mit relevanten ersetzt/ergänzt werden. Diese Strukturen, die identisch mit der Typologie von Schegloff (1992; Figur 3) sind, werden hier Script I genannt. Wie der Kontext in einer solchen Richtigstellung gestaltet werden kann, zeigt das folgende Beispiel aus einem Thread, in dem die Forumsbenutzer Fragen zu den Forumsfunktionen stellen können:
können:

marceL:
[A] Hallo Thorsten,   [C] **du missverstehst mich.** [E] Die Option ist mir bekannt. Was ich will ist eine vergrößerte Bildansicht innerhalb der Plone-Seite, [D]nicht auf einer eigenen Seite, wo nur das Bild erscheint. [E] Das bekomme ich aber, wenn ich auf das Bild verlinke.

Beitrag 4

Hier greift „marceL" sofort die Irrelevanz in der Bezugsäußerung auf, verwirft sie und ergänzt sie mit anderen Kontextualisierungshinweisen. Dadurch ist die Chance umso größer, dass die nachfolgende Antwort mit diesem Beitrag korreliert. Nun gibt es auch Forumsbeiträge mit *missverstehen*, die nicht nur auf den Inhalt bezogen sind. In diesen Beiträgen ist es umso offensichtlicher, dass die Phrase mit *missverstehen* dazu dient, Beziehungsarbeit zwischen den Teilnehmern zu *konstruieren*.

4.3 Script II und III: *Missverstehen* und Beziehungsarbeit

Wenn die Beziehungsebene beeinträchtigt worden ist, wird sie, wie schon erwähnt, in der Interaktion bearbeitet, um einen Abbruch zu meiden. Die Beziehungsarbeit trägt dazu bei, eine Vorantreibung der Kommunikation zu gewährleisten. Genau wie in einer Thematisierung mit *missverstehen*, die auf den Inhalt bezogen ist, geht es auch in diesem Script um Interaktionssequenzen, in denen die Kontextualisierungshinweise nicht gleich eingeordnet werden, was die Thematisierung mit *missverstehen* in Gang setzt. So dient eine Phrase wie *du hast mich missverstanden* dem Zweck, nicht nur ein inhaltliches Problem aufzuklären, sondern vor allem die Beziehungsebene zu stabilisieren. In diesem Fall ist somit von einer anderen Art von Richtigstellung die Rede, und die Kommunikation durchläuft andere Slots, um via eine Honorierung die Kommunikation auf die Objektsebene zurückzuführen (Figur 3):

Vorphase:	Aussage *p* von A.
Slot$_1$:	B bestreitet *p* als irrelevant.
	Script II: Fremdimagewahrend formuliert, die Interaktion geht sofort in Slot$_2$ über.
	Script III: Fremdimagebedrohend formuliert. Dieser Slot wird beliebig Mal wiederholt, bevor die Interaktion in Slot$_2$ übergeht.
Slot$_2$:	A schafft mit einer Richtigstellung[20] Relevanz.
Slot$_3$:	Honorierung. B akzeptiert die Relevanz. Lädt zur Objektsprache ein.

Figur 3: Modell der Absicherung der Beziehungsarbeit.

Die Slots werden üblicherweise in jeweils einem Beitrag realisiert. Script II bzw. III sind strukturell ähnlich, mit dem Unterschied, dass in Slot$_1$ das Bestreiten entweder fremdimagebewahrend (Script II; z. B. *vielleicht,* frohes Emoticon) oder eigenimagebewahrend (Script III; z. B. trauriges Emoticon, *!!!, wirklich*) formuliert wird. A reizt somit in der Vorphase B zu einem Bestreiten in Slot$_1$ an. Wenn dieses Bestreiten als imagebedrohend aufgefasst wird, führt dies zu einem Gegenbestreiten – Slot$_1$ wird wiederholt (Script III), oder die Kommunikation geht sofort in die Richtigstellung in Slot$_3$ über. Obwohl Thematisierungen mit *missverstehen* in Slot$_2$ diesen Artikel prägen, ist es wichtig zu betonen, dass *missverstehen* auch in Slot$_2$ bzw. Slot$_3$ vorkommen kann. *Missverstehen* übernimmt in den Fällen die Funktion anderer Sprechhandlungen, z. B. <RECHTFERTIGUNG>, <ENTSCHULDIGUNG> und <HONORIERUNG>.[21] Es ist durchaus möglich, dass das Script nicht durchgearbeitet wird, sondern dass Slot$_1$ neu eingesetzt wird, immer noch mit dem Ziel, die Objektsebene zu erreichen. Im Folgenden soll gezeigt werden, wie *missverstehen* dies zusammen mit realisierter Beziehungsarbeit in der [B]-Komponente schaffen kann.

---

[20] In dieser Richtigstellung wird entweder eine <RECHTFERTIGUNG> oder eine <ENTSCHULDIGUNG> ausgehandelt. S. Rehbein (1972) zu diesen Begriffen.
[21] Zu einer ausführlichen Auslegung dieses Phänomens s. Salomonsson 2011b. Mit dieser Methode ist es möglich, Sprechhandlungen anhand von der Position im Script und der Distribution der Komponenten zu definieren, anstatt sich auf semantische Merkmale zu verlassen.

4.4 Script II: Fremdimagebewahrung mit *missverstehen*

Eine Vorantreibung der Kommunikation setzt voraus, dass die Interagierenden miteinander kommunizieren *wollen*. In den Foren ist es möglich, sich provozierend auszudrücken,. Allerdings besteht dabei immer ein Risiko, dass die Kommunikation abbricht und der Thread nicht mehr entfaltet wird. In den Diskussionsforen ist es manchmal das Ziel, eine Frage zu klären, und die Interagierenden schaffen dies in einem kollaborativen Schreibprozess in dem sie gemeinsam mit dem Aufbau des Textes die Antwort konstruieren. Dieses Ziel, die Kommunikation zu untermauern, führt auch dazu, dass die Interaktion auf Höflichkeit baut, um die Slots im Script so reibungslos wie möglich durchzuarbeiten, und dadurch wieder auf die Objektsebene zu wechseln. Diese Höflichkeit wird jedoch von den Parametern *Distanz, Macht* und *Rangordnung kultureller Sprechhandlungen* reguliert (Brown/Levinson 1987), wobei die soziale Distanz am deutlichsten zum Vorschein kommt. Diese können die Interagierenden nicht nur anhand von der Länge der Beiträge und Häufigkeit des Postens[22] zeigen, sondern auch sprachlich anhand von beispielsweise Stil und Spiel mit Emoticons.

Tilgungen wie etwa *haste, kannste*[23] etc. können somit eine gekürzte, soziale Distanz realisieren, und sie ist in fremdimagebewahrenden Sequenzen notwendig, um ein Bestreiten (Script III) zu vermeiden. Formalität/Informalität konstruiert Distanz zwischen den Interagierenden, wobei Formalität erweiterte Distanz bzw. Informalität gekürzte Distanz stimuliert. Im Forum kann die Phrase mit *missverstehen* in Verbindung mit sprachlichen Realisierungen gekürzter Distanz dazu beitragen, dass die Kommunikation reibungslos auf die Objektsebene wechselt, wie im folgenden Beispiel aus einem Forum über existenzielle Fragen:

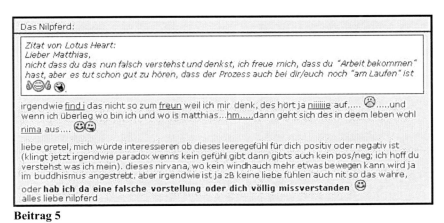

Beitrag 5

---

[22] Ein erfahrener Schreiber hat im Forum andere Möglichkeiten, sich zu äußern, als der Anfänger (Salomonsson 2011b: 133).
[23] Zum Gebrauch von Klitisierungen s. Salomonsson 2011a.

In diesem Forum werden persönliche Fragen diskutiert, was ein informelles Verhalten unter den Interagierenden voraussetzt und den Gebrauch vieler Tilgungen teilweise erklären lässt. Der Gebrauch vieler Emoticons ist allerdings in diesem Forum konventionalisiert und nicht gleich eng mit Beziehungsarbeit verbunden, wie in Foren, in denen Emoticons keine Norm sind. „Nokus" formuliert zwei Möglichkeiten des Deutungsproblems – *oder hab ich da eine falsche vorstellung oder dich völlig missverstanden*. Diese Formulierung signalisiert verstärkt eine Unterpositionierung, wirkt aber gleichzeitig prophylaktisch hinsichtlich einer möglicherweise kommenden imagebedrohenden Deutung im nächsten Beitrag von „Forgetmenot". *Missverstehen* wirkt hier als eine Unterstützung des Übergangs in Slot$_2$.

In anderen Fällen sind die sozialen Rollen schon im Voraus gegeben, was dem Umgang mit Informalität andere Spielregeln zuteilt. Im folgenden Beispiel wird das Image des Forumsadministrators bedroht, wenn sich „X:tra" über den Administrator „Maik Waldmann" lustig macht, der angeblich viel Geld verdient.[24] Dieses Forum unterscheidet sich von den meisten im Korpus dadurch, dass persönliche Daten hier zur Verfügung gestellt werden. Im Forum versuchen die Forumsteilnehmer ein Treffen unter DVD-Interessierten zu organisieren, was zum Abweichen von dem eigentlichen Thema und zur Frage führt, ob sich „Maik Waldmann" einen Lexus leisten kann:

Maik Waldmann:

Zitat von X:tra:
Welch Understatement von jemandem, der sich mit dem Necronomicon dumm und dämlich verdient... 😈 *.. naja... wir wollen mal keine bösen Gerüchte verbreiten!* 😄

Du missverstehst die Situation [B] **vollkommen**... denk mal weiter, von wem diese Lizenz kam, und warum der jetzt LEXUS fährt... [B] 😄

Beitrag 6

Die implizite Imagebedrohung in Form des Witzes hat auf den Empfänger keinen beleidigenden Effekt, weil beide den Insiderwitz mit ihrem Kontext verbinden können. Trotzdem wird ein <MISSVERSTÄNDNIS> thematisiert, und zwar in Verbindung mit einer Oberpositionierung – *denk mal weiter,*

---

[24] *Necronomicon* ist ein Horrorroman des amerikanischen Autors H.P. Lovecraft, von dessen Verfilmung „A. S." angeblich viel Geld verdient hat. A.S. ist sowohl Redakteur eines Magazins für phantastische Filme als auch Geschäftsführer der Firma, die für das Forum zuständig ist und Lizenzrechte von Filmen auf DVDs beurteilt.

von wem diese Lizenz kam, und warum der jetzt LEXUS fährt... „MW" kann sich mit seiner Rolle als Besitzer des Forums Handlungen erlauben, die in einem anderen Kontext imagebedrohend wirken würden, hier aber nicht so aufgefasst werden müssen. „MW" hat somit die Möglichkeit, Spielregeln anzugeben, nach welchen sich die anderen Interagierenden zu richten haben. Das Spiel mit der sozialen Struktur ist auch dadurch sichtbar, dass „MW" keine irrelevanten Kontextualisierungshinweise definiert. „MW" formuliert sogar den Kommentar überheblich, benutzt aber ein frohes Emoticons zum Zweck der Beziehungsarbeit.

In diesem Beitrag ist keine explizite [D]-Komponente vorhanden, die die Kontextualisierungshinweise des anderen verwirft, aber das Zitat wird ja gebraucht, um auf einen Textabschnitt hinzuweisen, worauf sich die folgende Äußerung bezieht. Auf diese Art und Weise kann das Zitat als [D]-Komponente gedeutet werden. Es übernimmt die Funktion einer Verweisung oder spielt mit einer expliziten [D]-Komponente zusammen, wenn eine vorhanden ist. Hier wird es aber nicht als deutliche Kontrastierung verwendet, weil keine [E]-Komponente vorhanden ist, und das schwächt auch die Imagebedrohung ab. So ist es ebenfalls umso wahrscheinlicher, dass die Kommunikation auf die Objektsebene reibungslos wechselt.

In Script II wird eine solche Kontrastierung gebraucht, wenn der Inhalt betont werden muss. In solchen Fällen liegt parallel mit der Konstruktion von Beziehungsarbeit ein Verständigungsproblem vor. Bei der Bearbeitung der inhaltlichen Fragen kann die Beziehungsebene beeinträchtigt werden, wenn ein Verwerfen der Informationen des anderen imagebedrohend aufgefasst wird, was Beziehungsarbeit notwendig macht. Im Forum werden Probleme beim Einloggen diskutiert:

Badge:

Huhu Mini
Ich habe deinen Beitrag in den technischen Bereich verschoben...
Allerdings verstehe ich nicht wirklich, worum es da geht... ich komme in keine für User nicht zugängliche Bereiche rein, wenn ich nicht registriert bin als Leafy... da kommt immer ein Hinweis, dass man sich zuerst registrieren müsse... Und mit den Profildaten hast du ja noch lange kein Passwort... ???☹

[B] 🙈 ... [B] **Ich glaube,** [C] **ich missversteh dich** [B] **wohl grad?** Oder kannst du, wenn du bei Google *Badge* eingibst, im Administrativ-Bereich lesen gehen???

Beitrag 7

„Mini" hat früher im Thread (mit dem deiktischen Adverb *da* markiert) einen Hinweis zum korrekten Einloggen mitgeteilt, was „Badge" nicht geholfen hat. Dies wird hier mit einem thematisierten <NICHT VERSTEHEN> verbalisiert. Danach teilt „Badge" Probleme mit dem Einloggen mit, was sie mit dem Emoticon[25] 😢 noch stärker hervorhebt. Dieses Emoticon signalisiert und betont zusammen mit den Fragezeichen die Schwierigkeit, den Beitrag als relevant zu deuten, während das traurige Gesicht die Negativität in dieser Handlung verstärkt.

Der Hinweis auf ein <NICHT VERSTEHEN> in der Einleitung des Beitrags hat eine fremdimagebedrohende Funktion in der Hinsicht, dass „Badge" damit impliziert, dass die meisten Kontextualisierungshinweise nicht gedeutet werden konnten. Die Phrase mit *missverstehen* kann als pure Reformulierung gedeutet werden, was den Übergang in die Richtigstellung erleichtert, da sie fremdimagebewahrend wirkt. Das Beispiel zeigt, dass *nicht verstehen* und *missverstehen* in enger semantischer Verwandtschaft zueinander stehen und dass *missverstehen* als Heckenausdruck für ein <NICHT VERSTEHEN> verwendet werden kann. Die Beziehungsebene wird redundant mit Hilfe des epistemischen Verbs *glauben*, der abschwächenden Modifikation in den Adverbien *wohl grad* aber auch in der Syntax des Fragesatzes kontextualisiert. Dies kann auch darauf hinweisen, dass es um einen Heckenausdruck geht, denn *nicht verstehen* kann imagebedrohender als *missverstehen* aufgefasst werden. Wenn dies gemeint ist, muss sich der/die Interagierende des Gebrauchs von Modifikatoren bedienen, um die Kommunikation nicht zu beeinträchtigen. Wenn *missverstehen* fremdimagebedrohend modifiziert wird, ist eher von einer Eigenimagebewahrung die Rede. Diese wird mit Script III durchgearbeitet.

4.5 Script III: Eigenimagebewahrung mit *missverstehen*

Wie oben angedeutet, kann die Phrase mit *missverstehen* auch in imagebedrohenden Sequenzen gebraucht werden. Diese können natürlich dazu führen, dass die Interaktion wesentlich beeinträchtigt wird, wenn Höflichkeitsstrategien nicht berücksichtigt werden. Das Ziel in Script III ist es, eine Eigenimagebewahrung durchzusetzen und trotzdem die Kommunikation aufrechtzuerhalten. Dadurch kann die Kommunikation vorangetrieben und <VERSTEHEN> abgesichert werden. Dies wird aber zeitlich verschoben, weil Slot$_1$ wiederholt wird. Mit dieser Strategie kann der/die Interagierende nicht nur das Eigenimage in der Kommunikation stärken, sondern auch das <VERSTEHEN> so verhandeln, dass die aufgefasste Relevanz in der Interaktion aus der Sicht des Senders als die gültige wirkt. Ein solches Beispiel zeigt der folgende Beitrag aus einem Forum, in dem

---

[25] Die zahlreichen Emoticons in diesem Beitrag verweisen auf eine Norm der Informalität.

verschiedene Opelmodelle diskutiert werden, wobei „Snowstorm" die Bezugsäußerung bestreitet:

> Snowstorm:
>
> Hast Du meine Konkret vorgetragenen Veränderungswünsche gelesen? **dannwürdst Du mich [B] evtl nicht mehr mißverstehen [B]!**
> Und man sieht das das marketing der hersteller bei Dir auch schon wirkt! mehr komfort heist für mich ncith mehr Extras, ich ahbe mcih ja klar gegen unnötigen Firlefanz ausgesprochen. damit meine ich,w as man bei keinem hersteler fr geld und gute Worte bekommt: Genügend bewegungsfreiheit und ne Federung, wo ich nicht bei jedem Huckel oder Schlagloch meine, mein Auto bricht auseinander. Der omega fuhr auch gut obohl er sehr weich gefedert war.

Beitrag 8

In diesem Beispiel[26] markiert das thematisierte <MISSVERSTÄNDNIS> eine aufgefasste Imagebedrohung, auch wenn die Phrase mit *missverstehen* sowohl mit dem Konjunktiv als auch mit dem Adverb *evtl* [eventuell] fremdimagebewahrend modifiziert wird. Dies muss aufgrund des Vorwurfs in der Einleitung *Hast Du meine Konkret vorgetragenen Veränderungswünsche gelesen?* als Sarkasmus interpretiert werden. Das Ausrufezeichen indiziert auch eine Fremdimagebedrohung. Um ein Vorantreiben der Kommunikation zu gewährleisten, wird Slot$_1$ im nächsten Beitrag wiederholt, jedoch mit fremdimagebewahrenden Formulierungen:

> SperBär:
>
> > Zitat von Snowstorm:
> > Hast Du meine Konkret vorgetragenen Veränderungswünsche gelesen? **dannwürdst Du mich evtl nicht mehr mißverstehen!**
>
> [C] **Ich mißverstehe [B] Dich nicht.** [E] Ich habe nur den Eindruck, dass Deine Wünsche mehr mit dem aktuellen Signum als dem aktuellen Logan zu tun haben... Und eine weiche Federung hat auch nichts mit der Menge der eingebauten Technik zu tun. Ist einfach nur Auslegungssache. Und so sehr unterscheiden sich meine Wünsche an ein Auto auch nicht von Deinen. Bei mir darf es nur noch zusätzlich eine Klimaautomatik, Xenon und ein Navigationssystem sein.

Beitrag 9

Im Zitat wird nicht die gesamte Originaläußerung zitiert, und dies ist eine nützliche Strategie, um bestimmte Kontextualisierungshinweise zu verwerfen. Dies fokussiert auch die Diskussion auf einen bestimmten Inhalt, was

---

[26] Die vielen Schreibfehler im Beitrag sind vermutlich auf die Geschwindigkeit beim Schreiben zurückzuführen, denn die Beiträge werden innerhalb von wenigen Minuten verfasst.

die Kommunikation konkretisiert. Die Kommunikation entgleist nicht, aber die Thematisierung mit *missverstehen* ist ein direkter Verwurf der Thematisierung im Zitat, womit sich „SperBär" vor der Imagebedrohung wehrt. Die Antwort wird wesentlich neutraler gestaltet als die Imagebedrohung im Zitat, und die Kontextualisierungshinweise werden hervorgehoben, die bei „SperBärs" Interpretation Unklarheiten bereitet haben. Um aber eine weitere Kommunikation zu untermauern, wird der Beitrag freundlicher formuliert, zwar ohne [B]-Komponente (obwohl die Großschreibung *Dich* als Beziehungsarbeitsmarkierung verstanden werden kann), aber die [E]-Komponente ist eher inhaltsbezogen formuliert. Dies ermöglicht einen Übergang in die Richtigstellung in Slot$_2$. Im letzten Absatz wird Beziehungsarbeit mit dem Satz *Und so sehr unterscheiden sich meine Wünsche an ein Auto auch nicht von Deinen* unternommen, wobei „SperBär" die Distanz unter den Schreibenden ausgleicht, hier mit konstituierender[27] Beziehungsarbeit, obwohl die unmodifizierte Thematisierung mit *missverstehen* dazu beiträgt, dass das Eigenimage durchgesetzt werden kann. Slot$_1$ wird somit wiederholt.

5. Zusammenfassung

Ziel des Artikels war es, anhand von verschiedenen Forumsbeiträgen, in denen Phrasen mit dem Wort *missverstehen* vorkommen, die Funktion dieser Phrasen zu untersuchen. Als Material diente ein Korpus von 565 Beiträgen mit einer Phrase mit dem Wort *missverstehen* in verschiedenen flektierten Formen. Dabei wurde auf zwei Funktionen fokussiert – die Fremdimagebewahrung und die Eigenimagebewahrung. Methodisch wurde bei der Analyse von einem konstruktivistischen Ansatz ausgegangen. Als Fundament diente die Annahme, dass Bedeutung in der Interaktion determiniert wird, weshalb das Wort *missverstehen* nicht auf das außersprachliche Phänomen <MISSVERSTÄNDNIS> referieren muss. Eher ist die Bedeutung im Kontext festzustellen.

Um <VERSTEHEN> zu konstruieren, bearbeiten die Interagierenden Kontextualisierungshinweise in den Beiträgen und ordnen sie in ihr eigenes <VERSTEHEN> ein. Bei einem <MISSVERSTÄNDNIS> liegt eine Diskrepanz hinsichtlich dessen vor, wie die Interagierenden die Kontextualisierungshinweise arrangiert haben. Wenn einige nicht gedeutet werden können, ist der Beitrag als irrelevant aufgefasst. Die Relevanztheorie wurde als Ausgangspunkt benutzt, da es bei der Verhandlung von <VERSTEHEN> auch um die Festellung von Relevanz in den Forumsbeiträgen geht. Die Phrase mit *missverstehen* und komplettierenden Kontextualisierungshinweisen hat die Funk-

---

[27] Vgl. *positive politeness,* Brown/Levinson (1987).

tion, Relevanz zu schaffen und Beziehungen zwischen den Interagierenden zu konstruieren.

Diese Kontextualisierungshinweise werden in verschiedenen Komponenten distribuiert, [A-F]. Von diesen ist vor allem die [B]-Komponente hervorzuheben, da sie Beziehungsarbeit gestaltet, sprachlich realisiert vor allem mit Schriftlichkeit/Mündlichkeit, da diese Konzepte mit Formalität bzw. Informalität verbunden sind. Die Beziehungsarbeit wird entweder imagebedrohend oder imagebewahrend formuliert, je nach Zweck der Phrase mit *missverstehen*. So konnte im Artikel gezeigt werden, dass *missverstehen* in drei verschiedenen Scripts gebraucht wird – I) *missverstehen* mit Bezug auf den Inhalt in der Kommunikation II) fremdimagebewahrend und III) eigenimagebewahrend. Das Ergebnis zeigt, dass die Distribution dieser Komponenten und die Platzierung des Forumsbeitrags im Script dafür entscheidend ist, welche kommunikation die Phrase mit *missverstehen* hat.

Missverstehen hat somit eine unterstützende Funktion für die Beziehungsarbeit, und das Material zeigt, dass die Interagierenden eher mit dem Ziel kommunizieren, die Interaktion zu untermauern, als mit Unfreundlichkeit einen Abbruch zu verursachen.

6. Bibliographie

Auer, P. (1992), Introduction, in Di Luzio, A & Auer, P. (eds.), *The contextualization of language*, Amsterdam: John Benjamins, pp. 1-37.
Bader, J., (2002), Schriftlichkeit und Mündlichkeit in der Chatkommunikation, *Networx* 29, pp. 1-145.
Bailey, B. (2004), Misunderstanding, in Duranti, A. (ed.), *A companion to linguistic anthropology.*, Malden, MA: Blackwell Pub, pp. 395–413.
Bierwisch, M. (1983), Semantische und konzeptuelle Repräsentation lexikalischer Einheiten, in Růžička, R. & Motsch, W. (eds.), *Studia Grammatica XXII. Untersuchungen zur Semantik,* Berlin: Akademie Verlag, pp. 61-100.
Brown, R. & Gilman, A. (1970), The Pronouns of Power and Solidarity, in Brown, R. & Gilman, A. (eds.), *Psycholinguistics: selected papers*, New York: The free press, pp. 302-335.
Brown, P. & Levinson, S. (1987), *Politeness: some universals in language usage.* Cambridge: Cambridge University Press.
Derks, D. (2007), *Exploring the missing wink: Emoticons in Cyberspace.* Ph.D. Thesis, Open Universiteit Nederland.
Dürscheid, C. (2006), *Einführung in die Schriftlinguistik.* Göttingen: UTB.
Falkner, W. (1997), *Verstehen, Missverstehen und Missverständnisse: Untersuchungen an einem Korpus englischer und deutscher Beispiele.* Tübingen: Niemeyer.
Gee, J. P. (2012), *Social Linguistics and Literacies: Ideology in Discourses.* London; New York: Routledge.
Goffman, E. (1959), *The presentation of self in everyday life.* Garden City, N.Y.: Doubleday.
Gumperz, J. (1982), *Discourse strategies.* Cambridge: Cambridge University Press.

Gumperz, J. (1992), Contextualization revisited, in Di Luzio, A. & Auer, P. (eds.), *The contextualization of language*. Amsterdam: John Benjamins, pp. 39-53.

Gumperz, J. (2004), Contextualisation and understanding, in Duranti, A. & Goodwin, C. (eds.), *Rethinking context. Language as an interactive Phenomenon*, Cambridge: Cambridge University Press, pp. 229-252.

Hinnenkamp, V. (1998), *Missverständnisse in Gesprächen: eine empirische Untersuchung im Rahmen der interpretativen Soziolinguistik*. Opladen: Westdeutscher Verlag.

Kadir, Z. A., Maros, M. & Hamid, B. D. (2012), *Linguistic Features in the Online Discussion Forums*, in International Journal of Social Science and Humanity 2 (3), pp. 276-281.

Koch, P./Oesterreicher, W. (2007), Schriftlichkeit und kommunikative Distanz, *Zeitschrift für germanistische Lingusitik*, Vol. 35. 346-375.

Rehbein, J. (1972), Entschuldigungen und Rechtfertigungen, in Wunderlich, Dieter (eds.), *Linguistische Pragmatik*, Frankfurt am Main: Athenäum, pp. 288-317.

Salomonsson, J. (2011a), „Hamwa nisch... fragense mal da". Spiel mit Mündlichkeit und Schriftlichkeit in Diskussionsforen im Internet, *Networx* 59, pp. 1–34.

Salomonsson, J. (2011b), *Verbale Interaktion mit missverstehen. Eine empirische Untersuchung zu deutschsprachigen Diskussionsforen*. Diss., Universität Stockholm http://su.diva-portal.org/smash/record.jsf?pid=diva2:406971

Schank, R. C. & Abelson, R. P. (1977), *Scripts, plans, goals and understanding: an inquiry into human knowledge structures*, Lea, Hillsdale, N.J: Erlbaum.

Schegloff, E. A. (1992), Repair after Next Turn: The Last Structurally Provided Defense of Intersubjectivity, *Conversation. The American Journal of Sociology*, 97 (5), pp. 1295–1345.

Selting, M. (1987), *Verständigungsprobleme: eine empirische Analyse am Beispiel der Bürger-Verwaltungs-Kommunikation*, Niemeyer, Tübingen.

Siever, T. (2006), *Sprachökonomie in den "Neuen Medien"*, in Schlobinski, P. (eds.), *Von *hdl* bis *cul8r*. Sprache und Kommunikation in den Neuen Medien*, Mannheim: Dudenverlag, pp. 71–88.

Sperber, D. & Wilson, D. (1986), *Relevance: Communication and Cognition*. Cambridge MA: Blackwell Publishing.

Sperber, D. & Wilson, D. (1992), On Verbal Irony, *Lingua* 87, pp. 33-76.

Sperber, D. & Wilson, D. (2006), Relevance Theory, in Ward, G. & Horn, L. (eds.), *Handbook of Pragmatics*, Oxford: Blackwell publishing, pp. 607-632.

Storrer, A. (2001), Sprachliche Besonderheiten getippter Gespräche: Sprecherwechsel und sprachliches Zeigen in der Chat-Kommunikation, in Beißwenger, M. (eds.), *Chat-Kommunikation. Sprache, Interaktion, Sozialität & Identität in synchroner computervermittelter Kommunikation. Perspektiven auf ein interdisziplinäres Forschungsfeld*, Stuttgart: Ibidem-Verlag, pp. 3-24.

Verdonik, D. (2010), Between Understanding and Misunderstanding, *Journal of Pragmatics* 42 (5), pp. 1364–1379.

Watzlawick, P., Beavin, J. H. & Jackson, D. D. (2003), *Menschliche Kommunikation: Formen, Störungen, Paradoxien*, Bern: Huber Verlag.

Wolf, R. (1999), Soziale Positionierung im Gespräch, *Deutsche Sprache* 1/99 (Jg. 27), pp. 69-94.

Quellenverzeichnis

Beitrag 1   http://www.slackliner.de/forum/forumsangelegenheiten-und-offtopic-f7/neueste-beitraege-t61.html 25. Jan. 2010.

Beitrag 2	http://www.motor-talk.de/forum/getriebespülung-nach-tim-eckart-methode-in-raum-frankfurt-main-t1696028.html 10. Jul. 2008.
Beitrag 3	http://www.computerwoche.de/forum/showthread.php?t=347 13. Sep. 2007.
Beitrag 4	http://www.licht-forum.org/fragen-und-antworten/1128-kennt-das-jemand-von-euch-auch.html 17. Jul. 2008.
Beitrag 5	http://forum.dvd-forum.at/archive/index.php/t-49474.html 17. Jul. 2008.
Beitrag 6	http://www.lenormand-lernen.de/forum/index.php?topic=17475.0 17. Jul. 2008.
Beitrag 7	http://www.forum-hilfe.de/viewtopic.php?p=234652 27. Feb. 2008.
Beitrag 8+9	http://www.motor-talk.de/forum/braucht-opel-wieder-einen-omega-senator-insignia-t1541318.html?page=2 27. Feb. 2008.

The role of blogs and forums in the linguistic expectations of pilgrims on the Camino to Santiago

Una Cunningham

University of Canterbury

1. Introduction

Every year thousands of pilgrims embark on a pilgrimage to Santiago de Compostela in Galicia, in the north-western corner of the Iberian Peninsula. They are driven by fiercely individual impulses, sometimes religious, often spiritual, and their notional target is the cathedral in Santiago de Compostela. They walk for days, weeks, or even months, depending on where they choose to embark on their pilgrimage, all following the same path, El Camino de Santiago, or simply the Camino, (the 'Way') as it is referred to by those who follow it. The main trail runs some 850 km from St. Jean Pied-de-Port on the French side of the Pyrenees through the cathedral cities of Pamplona, Logroño, Burgos and Leon to Santiago. The trail is blazed (Turner 1992) in two ways: officially, by municipalities and provincial governments, using stylized scallop shells; and informally, by means of graffiti-like hand-painted yellow arrows placed haphazardly on lampposts, walls and kerbstones by local support groups. About half of the pilgrims are Spanish; others are German, Italian, English, American, French, English, Irish, Korean, Brazilian, Dutch, Swedish or from any of more than a hundred countries (Oficina del Peregrino de Santiago de Compostela 2011).
This traditional pilgrimage has been defined by Bennet (1997) writing as chairman of the Confraternity of St James as follows:

> Since in recent years those using the traditional ways of doing the pilgrimage have been so far outstripped in numbers by car, coach and air travellers as to now be in the minority, it is worth making a fairly basic, but important distinction. The 'traditional ways' are those that involve making the journey by one's own motive power, implying an investment of physical effort or sacrifice, an element of physical vulnerability, and a frame of mind that is open to encounter. (Bennet 1997:3)

Many pilgrims prepare extensively for their pilgrimage physically and/or mentally (Frey 1998: 47-52). Others, do not, and end up either abandoning their pilgrimage or adjusting to its conditions. When Frey was writing, potential pilgrims were inspired and informed by books, media articles and travelogues (Frey 1998: 52). With increased connectivity and access to citizen journalism in the form of blogs and of dedicated community forums there are now dozens of web pages, forums and blogs in a number of languages dedicated to helping pilgrims with this preparation. On the one hand, advice dispersed from veteran pilgrims to novices and would-be or armchair pilgrims in web information and forums allows novices to become familiar with the symbols and trappings of pilgrimage, socializing them into the practices of the pilgrim. Perceiving oneself to be and being perceived to be an authentic pilgrim is important to many who plan a Camino (Frey 1998: 18-20; Gemzöe 2009: 425). On the other hand, travelogues in blog form, narrating the events and encounters of the Camino day by day from the road, allow aspiring pilgrims to picture themselves on the road, having the same experiences as the bloggers. A good deal of the information presented and exchanged in these online resources concerns the languages spoken and not spoken by pilgrims and those they meet, interlingual experiences (felicitous and otherwise) and the kinds of linguistic preparation that can be appropriate.

This paper will examine how these web pages, blogs and forums treat interlingual communication, including the use of English and other languages as lingua francas on the Camino, and their usefulness for the linguistic preparation and expectations of prospective pilgrims.

2. Online community

It is a feature of our information society that when faced with a problem or an information gap, many of us immediately turn to the Internet. This has been observed in the field of health care where patients ("informed patients") bring medical data from the Internet with them when they go to see a health care worker, which has changed the nature of the doctor-patient relationship (Barnoy, Volfin-Pruss, Ehrenfeld and Kushnit 2008). When we travel we also use the Internet to research our destination and to plan our journey (Frías, Rodríguez & Castañeda 2008). People turn to the Internet to plan their travel, and make use of consumer feedback and user reviews before they choose (Huang, Lurie and Mitra 2009). Given this new consumer behaviour, it is unsurprising that a plethora of websites, forums and blogs have grown up to meet the need for information experienced by those who are planning to embark on a pilgrimage to Santiago (or to "do the Camino").

Many potential pilgrims are anxious about how they will manage linguistically on the byways of Northern Spain. Spanish speakers lament their lack of proficiency in English or German, meaning they generally cannot easily speak with northern Europeans or Americans, while these latter in turn are concerned that their limited or non-existent proficiency in Spanish will make their pilgrimage more difficult than it would otherwise be. Some who have proficiency in neither Spanish nor English use online translation tools to ask questions about language practices.

The material discussed here is from a major English-language forum dedicated to those preparing to walk or cycle to or towards Santiago, and from English-language blogs and web pages which can be reached through links posted by contributors to this forum. This forum serves as an online community in the sense described by Jones (1997) and Wood & Smith (2005: 128-129), since it has "1) a minimum level of interactivity; 2) a variety of communicators; 3) common public space and 4) a minimum level of sustained membership". The forum, which has been running for many years, boasts that it contains over 12000 questions and answers in almost 100000 posts. The blogs and documents more or less closely associated with the forum add other voices.

One of the features of this and other online communities is that veterans or experts meet and interact with beginners and less experienced members. There are clear "implied readers" to borrow Iser's (1990) term, as the forum's slogan is "Where past pilgrims share and future pilgrims learn". The veterans (those who have contributed more than 160 posts) are distinguished in the forum with an emblem by their user name. Some veterans are monitors and can delete inappropriate posts or move them to a more appropriate thread in the forum. Thus a typical thread in the forum will involve a question from a new or inexperienced member, which may then be answered both by other relatively inexperienced users and by one or more veterans. Sometimes the veterans will interact directly on the thread, correcting each other, joking, or nuancing the information given. A thread can typically involve 10-20 posts.

The community embodied in this kind of online forum may be very real to many of its members. However, Wood and Smith (2005: 138) suggest that community can only exist where face-to-face interaction can occur. In the case of this online Camino community, the participants in most cases have either walked some part of the Camino or are preparing to do so. There is a real chance that some of them will meet face-to-face in real life along the Way, whether or not they recognise each other as forum members, but it is also appropriate to talk of asynchronous meetings that they will have on the Camino. They will all be walking on the exact same routes, passing through the same towns and villages, staying at the same pilgrim hostels, stopping at the same bars and restaurants, and can refer to this shared, albeit not synchronous, experience.

According to Turner (1992:60) the anthropological concept of liminality, as described in tribal rites of passage, where groups are removed from their normal day to day existence to liminal spaces ("neither here nor there [...] betwixt and between" (Turner 1967:97)) only to emerge sometime later in a different state. He relates this to pilgrimage, in both its mediaeval and modern expression. He explores the development of *communitas*, a particular sense of belonging in a community, in certain kinds of liminal situations (such as a college class, or those who share an important characteristic such as age, sex, ethnicity, religion, or some aspect of religion) and claims that when such a group withdraws (symbolically or actually) from mainstream society, they may find the "glow of *communitas*" with others who share their "most signal mark of identity" (Turner 1992: 60). Turner argues that a pilgrimage is a liminal space and *communitas* can potentially be achieved by those sharing this space. The Internet forums extend the physical reality of the pilgrimage to virtual space and extend the synchronous real time meetings of those on the Camino to the asynchronous liminal space of the online forums (see also Cunningham 2011 for a discussion of liminality in online meetings).

Those who have completed their Camino may refer to the sense of belonging, of shared culture with other pilgrims that they experienced while on the road (Frey 1998:4). This sense of communitas is often expressed wistfully, perceived first retrospectively, as pilgrims look back on their days and weeks of walking. Bennet (2003) writing for the Confraternity of St James expresses this most eloquently:

> Some beautiful images remain in my mind: the Spanish policeman bandaging the blistered feet of the Japanese, the tall African carrying the chef's heavy rucksack along with his own; the five trying to decide what to buy for the supper they would prepare and eat together in the refugios, with the trilingual Quebecker translating for everyone. (Bennet 2003)

Not all pilgrims find *communitas*, and some may feel cheated of it; others experience it post hoc as they relate to the accounts of others. Those using the web-material to learn about the *communitas* experienced by others will anticipate similar experiences. Frey (1998:90) writes, "Pilgrims share and build their stories and friendships with one another through active discussion of specific places and people who live along the pilgrimage route". The perception of easy communication and meetings with speakers of other languages is a frequent feature of these shared narratives.

3. Themes and categories

The information gathering preparations that pilgrims make before the pilgrimage are often extensive, and include many hours spent watching documentaries, films and travel programmes (often the source of the original impulse to do a Camino) and reading travel feature articles as well as reading books, blogs, forums and webpages. All of this information leads the prospective pilgrim to build a picture of what his or her own Camino will be like. Here the focus will remain the specific input gained from webpages, blogs and a forum with respect to language and communication.

In this study, this web-based material has been approached by excerpting from the webpages, blogs and forums material that deals with language and/or communication and, with the help of NVivo qualitative analysis software, tagging it ad hoc according to the topic, attempting to identify patterns and communalities in the material. Two main themes were identified. The first has been labelled "Spanish needed?" and the second "Interlingual communication". Each of these is represented by a number of categories.

3.1 Spanish needed?

The dominant position of English in Europe is well documented. Seidlhofer (2010: 147) describes English as having spread to become the currently dominant means of international communication. In 2005 she defined English as a lingua franca (ELF) as "a way of referring to communication in English between speakers with different first languages". As Seidlhofer points out, the causes and effects of this spread are controversial and hotly debated, e.g. by Crystal (2003), Graddol (2006), and Phillipson (2009). Phillipson (2009:92) states that "proficiency in English is increasingly expected of Germans and Greeks, the Portuguese and the Poles". He goes on to question the reference to English as a lingua franca "especially by advocates who are oblivious of the consequences of hegemonic and linguicist practices". Seidlhofer (2005: 339) points out the particular position of the native speaker of English in the use of English for intercultural communication and Graddol (2006: 11) dwells on the characteristics of English as a lingua franca (not "English as we have known it").

English is, however, far from the only lingua franca on the Camino. Spanish is another obvious such language, spoken by the local population (alongside Gallego in Galicia and Bierzo), as well as by the fifty per cent of pilgrims who are in fact Spanish and the many pilgrims who have learned Spanish as a foreign language either at school, or specifically in preparation for their pilgrimage. Still others, speakers of a language close to Spanish, like Portuguese or Italian, communicate with Spanish as an element in the communication. German, "Scandinavian", Chinese and other languages are also used in communication between speakers who have different first languages, whether or not one of them is a native speaker of the language being used.

One of the initial worries expressed by many prospective pilgrims is whether they will manage without knowledge of Spanish. This theme is labelled "Spanish needed?" and can be exemplified by this forum post:

Example 1

> In a few weeks, I will be starting my first Camino. I was just wondering what level of Spanish proficiency is needed for the Camino. Is English spoken at all? Or, is Spanish the only language spoken along the Camino route? Thanks for your help and assistance. I am truly a newbie to the Camino.

The answers such a query receives, both directly in the forum, and indirectly in other sources fall into a number of categories.

3.1.1 "English is enough".

One cluster of responses and observations suggest that you can get by well with just English, "English is enough". This can be exemplified by the following examples from the forum:

Example 2

> Also with English one could move without much problems.

Example 3

> Most pilgrims understand English.

3.1.2 "Phrasebook Spanish"

Another category is those who suggest learning useful words and phrases "Phrasebook Spanish". These examples are from the forum:

Example 4

> This past camino, I had walked 3 full days with a Spanish who spoke not a word of English. And I know probably no more than 20 Spanish words. But those were not silent days. Conversation flowed continuously and somehow we understood each other.

Example 5

> I have cycled/walked the Camino 5 times and have no language skills but muddled through. If you can learn to order a meal and find a bed, in Spanish, you will manage.

Example 6

> don't worry too much about the language, I had about 30 words of Spanish when I did the same stretch as you 3 weeks ago, por favor, gracias, cafe con leche y tostado (coffee and toasted bread with jam) will take you a long way.

Example 7

> I have done three Caminos and, while my Spanish remains basic and abominable, I discovered that making the effort made me many friends.

3.1.3 "I know Spanish"

A further category is those who talk about how much use they have had of their Spanish language skills which can be labelled "I know Spanish". Here are some examples:

Example 8

> I had a great time interacting with Spanish people, tried to remain open-minded and friendly, was grateful for the services I received, spoke Castellano and virtually nothing else for a month.

Example 9

> I walked the Camino Francés last year, and found that I – and others – relied on my Spanish speaking abilities quite a bit, not least when dealing with doctors and pharmacists.

Example 10

> Learn some Spanish before you go. I am fluent in Castellano and really appreciated the enhanced experience of sharing conversations and insights with local people.

3.1.4 "Gestures"

Finally, a category of responses mention the use of body language, gesture and other paralinguistic devices to aid communication when Spanish language competence is lacking. This category can be labelled "Gestures". An example of this is the following, from a blog:

Example 11

> We managed to have a great evening, despite the fact that I am handicapped by my inability to communicate with them the way I would like to.

And from the forum:

Example 12

> You will get along with just a smile, hand gestures, and a few words in Spanish. However, you will not be able to carry on a conversation unless you know Spanish, English, German, French, or Korean. Even without a foreign language, you will be treated warmly and will be welcome at every table. Do not worry about it.

Example 13

> it was a veritable Tower of Babel situation where most used hand gestures and an amalgam of languages to get their points across.

3.1.5 "Linguistic isolation"

Although most pilgrims who post on the forum about their experiences are extremely positive, there are those who find that the Camino experience does not live up to their expectations, either linguistically or otherwise. This category of voices can be labelled "Linguistic isolation".

Example 14

> I felt quite sorry for non-English speakers who used English hoping it would be understood as a universal or 'neutral' language. Although they were making an effort to communicate in another language, on a couple of occasions I saw them treated quite rudely. Maybe their effort isn't always recognised by the person in the cafe/shop etc.

Example 15

> English is not the main language of the camino, except as the international language, it maybe that others did not feel comfortable chatting in English, they also would not have had the need if they were walking with companions, though it sounds like you speak French.

The insider/outsider (us and them) perspective of English as the property or concern of native speakers (Crystal 2003, 141) is largely irrelevant on the Camino. Instead there is a line between those who speak functional English and those who do not. Another line runs between those who have functional Spanish, and those who do not. There are, however other linguistic strategies available for those who find a sympathetic interlocutor or a group where language resources can be pooled, as can be seen in the following section.

3.2 Interlingual communication

Pilgrims on the Camino to Santiago speak many different languages. Many of them, notably those from English-speaking countries and Spain, speak only their own first languages. This is in line with recent figures from the European Commission (2012) showing the proportions of students learning two or more languages at ISCED level 3 in 2010: 7.8% in Ireland, 5.5% in the UK, compared to 3.7% in Portugal, 23.4% in Spain, 90.8% in France and 92.7% in Sweden. Those pilgrims who do speak more than one language will find themselves being brought into conversations between other less proficient pilgrims as interpreters, even as a link in a chain between speakers of several languages, such as Korean/English, English/Spanish/French, Spanish/German, German, such that a Korean who knew some English could speak to a monolingual German through a speaker of English and Spanish and another speaker of Spanish and German. Cooperative communication strategies will work in situations where there is a genuine interest and will to communicate, and enough time to explore the possibilities of what is being said. This is endorsed by the Council of Europe in the Common European Framework of Reference for languages:

Those with some knowledge, even slight, may use it to help those with none to communicate by mediating between individuals with no common language. In the absence of a mediator, such individuals may nevertheless achieve some degree of communication by bringing the whole of their linguistic equipment into play, experimenting with alternative forms of expression. (Council of Euope 2001: 4)

The second theme represented in material from the forum and blogs about language to prospective pilgrims touches on communication between speakers of different languages. The theme as a whole can be exemplified by this excerpt of a post from the forum:

Example 16

> I still crack up at some of the 5-language conversations that took place in Spanish, but without a single Spanish native tongue speaker being present, so at the dinner table were: a Dutch woman (we spoke Afrikaans and she could also speak a bit of Spanish and French) a young German guy who spoke 6 languages (and he anchored some conversations and translated) a Japanese woman who had an electronic translator and a bit of basic Spanish, a French guy with a French / Spanish phrase book and me with English / Spanish phrase book . We drew pictures on paper serviettes acted out scenes referred to phrase books used 3 or 4 versions of the same word followed by raucous "si si" .... and all this just to understand what was on the menu del dia . The thrill of achieving communication was one of the greatest highlights of my camino for me, this was a connection of hearts, a beautiful experience

Ten Thije & Zeevaert (2007: 1) echo the above, claiming that "English as lingua franca is not the one and only solution for interlingual communication in Europe". They further suggest that multilingual understanding does not require near-native language competency and that before the formation of nation states in the 18th and 19th centuries, multilingualism in various forms was the norm, as it still is in large parts of the world. These ideas are being further investigated in an international European research project which has already produced a number of documents, collected in Backus, Maracz & ten Thije (2011), examining the communication toolkit available to speakers, including languages of regional communication, English as a lingua franca and receptive multilingualism.

A number of studies have been carried out to investigate the degree of mutual comprehensibility that obtains between languages that are for whatever reason of history and circumstance supposed to be autonomous. Canagarajah, (2009) considers the position in South Asia, where English is woven together with one or more local languages in communication, according to the English proficiency levels and language backgrounds of the participants. Canagarajah, (2009: 6) writes that "Proficiency in languages is not conceptualized individually, with separate competencies developed for each language. What is emphasized is the repertoire — the way the different languages constitute an integrated competence." Canagarajah contrasts this with multilingualism, claiming that "Plurilingualism allows for the interaction and mutual influence of the languages in a more dynamic way" (2009: 6).

Karam (1979) looked at ways that mutual intelligibility between related languages could be increased, considering earlier work on Navaho, Scandinavian languages, Somali and West African languages. He describes several strategies that can be used by speakers of related languages wishing to communicate, such as mutual adaptation and borrowing, using the speech forms of the other person and using the speech forms of a third party which are mutually known (Karam 1979: 128). This is illustrated as well in the work of Braunmüller (2002: 1) who described accommodation in inter-Scandinavian communication where speakers of Danish, Swedish and Norwegian each speak their own language and are willing to "accept and understand" the other languages. He found that even grammatically incorrect accommodation was helpful to interlocutors who spoke another Scandinavian language (Braunmüller 2002: 15).

The Common European Framework of Reference for Languages (COE 2001:169) claims that, "between 'related' languages in particular – though not just between these – knowledge and skills may be transferred by a kind of osmosis", and goes on to point out that "those who have learnt one language also know a great deal about many other languages without necessarily realising that they do." (COE 2001: 170). In the same way, Molina (2011: 1247) suggests that in multilingual settings, which she defines as " scenarios in which communication is mediated by a language which is not the L1 of most/some/any of the participants", participants will adjust their communication, using their knowledge of one language to understand another. On the topic of plurilingualism, COE (2001: 4) continues to say that a speaker "does not keep these languages and cultures in strictly separated mental compartments, but rather builds up a communicative competence to which all knowledge and experience of language contributes and in which languages interrelate and interact."

Baker (2006: 297) discusses translanguaging in educational settings, where the input (reading or listening) is in one language and the output (writing or speaking) in another. He emphasises how processing material in more than one language will lead to a fuller understanding of the material. This concept is taken further, e.g. by García (2009: 140) who defines translanguaging as assessing linguistic features of more than one language to maximize communicative potential. She claims (2009: 151) that "it is impossible to live in bilingual communities and communicate among multilinguals without translanguaging. In fact it is translanguaging itself that enables us to make sense of the multilingual worlds we live in". She includes codeswitching and pedagogical codeswitching, where, for example, a community language is used to make the additional language in a bilingual classroom situation more comprehensible, in the broader concept of translanguaging.

Although the Camino is certainly far from a formal educational setting, a lot of informal language learning happens as pilgrims pick up snippets of Spanish or English from each other and practise communicating in one or several of the languages at hand. Communication, rather than learning, is, however, the primary concern, and all available linguistic resources are mobilised.

Breaking down the various aspects of what is put forward on the forum regarding communication on the Camino between people who do not share the same first language, several categories can be distinguished.

3.3 "Native speaker tolerance"

Many pilgrims report having their attempts to communicate in languages they do not speak well received with generosity on the part of native speakers of the language they were attempting to speak. This category can be labelled "Native speaker tolerance". In this particular environment, a number of pilgrims remarked on this. They had clearly not expected to be listened to as sympathetically by native speakers of the language they were using imperfectly.

Example 17

> The French were very tolerant of my poor French language skills. If they were irritated, they covered it well and seemed to appreciate me trying.

Example 18

> At the heart of it, the French are perfectionists and can be rather shy about speaking English. What is paramount is that you attempt to speak French. In doing so, you demonstrate your respect for their language and you also make it easier for them to try speaking when …. they have any training

Example 19

> I found many to be much more open and helpful when I spoke Spanish than when my fellow pilgrims tried gesturing. Even a simple 'por favor' and 'muchas gracias' from my fellow pilgrims who were not fluent like me garnered genuine smiles in cafes and bars. Take the time -- learning at least some Spanish will be one of the wisest investments you make!

3.4 "Translators"

It is an expression of Camino communitas that pilgrims will join forces to communicate collaboratively, with several individuals pooling language resources in the interests of communication so that as many as possible can be included and feel welcome. By translating for each other, sometimes in several stages, communication can be achieved. This category of post is labelled "Translators".

Example 20

> They served dinner and all the other guests were either French or German. One French guy spoke a little English so he helped me out.

Example 21

> This year in one albergue we were 2 English (speak some Spanish); 2 Austrians (1 spoke Spanish); 2 Germans (1 spoke English); 2 Polish (1 spoke Spanish).We had a lovely friendly meal, with those who could translating for those who couldn't speak the others language.

Example 22

> I speak English and Spanish fluently, and found myself acting as a translator at least once a day. Yes, many pilgrims, both native and non-native speakers, know English. But the vast majority of locals you will meet do not speak any English, or have very limited English. Additionally, over half of pilgrims are Spanish, and another huge portion are Italian (yes, if you speak Spanish, you can get by on basics with most Italians, too!).

These examples show evidence of translanguaging and receptive bilingualism.

Example 23

> I do speak a couple of other languages a bit but my experience was that there were plenty who could speak some English and if I spoke a little of their language we all got along fine

3.5 "You'll be fine!

The Camino experience is so powerful for many that they will go to great lengths to encourage others to embark on a pilgrimage. This means that many want to reassure those who ask whether their limited language skills will be a problem. This is even so in the case of those who have very little knowledge of English or Spanish. Example 22 here below was actually addressed to someone who described how she had used Google Translate to create her post, not speaking any English at all.

Example 24

Your English is great and you will have no problem.

Example 25

Enjoy what will be, I'm sure, a wonderful time for you, and don't get stressed about not speaking Spanish.

Example 26

You will be fine and all will be well with you.

This can, perhaps, be related to discussions of other kinds of non-linguistic preparation. A pilgrimage is, after all supposed to be a hard thing to do (Bennet 1997:3), and some will discourage too much preparation if this is intended to make the pilgrimage easier in some way.

4. Discussion and conclusion

It appears that one role of the forum is to educate prospective pilgrims on what to expect. But sometimes this education misfires, in that an individual feels that they have been led to expect something they did not find. Usually this is not because of any direct misinformation in the forum, but rather from the prospective pilgrim interpreting what they read in the light of their own experiences and perceptions. The following examples are from individuals on the forum:

Example 27

> I did not find what you all have talked about for the last year that I have followed this [...] Part of me wishes I'd have had the experiences that I read about for a year. I reallllly expected some things in English. I didn't expect to be "catered" to... but I did expect there would be some English written somewhere [...]. I didn't find the Spanish people to be helpful to me at all. This was nothing like I'd read about, prepared for, hopefully expected.

Example 28

> I started at Saint Jean Pie-de-Port, walked for a week, and apart from the very first night in Roncevalles, had no contact with other pilgrims - as I've said, they were in their little groups of 2 or 3, and didn't seem interested in embracing a lone stranger. So much for the legendary pilgrim comradeship.....

This kind of comment is often perceived as a threat to the *communitas* of the online community and will trigger a stream of reaction from the forum veterans. One such comment from a veteran on the forum:

Example 29

> Perhaps the plethora of Camino books, films, videos, websites and blogs has created too much hype and too many expectations.

One effect of posts recounting negative experience is, of course, that novices planning their first Camino may be put off, or lower their expectations of what the Camino will give them. This might be more helpful than only reading positive experiences. Blogs from writers currently on the Camino itself are often less rosily painted. One novice planning a first Camino wrote:

Example 30

> I don't want to build the experience up into something it won't be nor do I want to limit what the experience can be...

The final word on the role of forums and blogs in the construction of the modern pilgrim can be given to a contributor who used the forum in preparation for the Camino:

Example 31

> This forum completely shaped my experience of the Camino. It allowed me to learn from other people's mistakes.

The role of Internet-based material in the preparations for this pilgrimage is clear. By reading the forum the novice can easily believe that that they will be welcomed into the communitas of what is, for many who write on the forum, a liminal and life-changing experience where linguistic difficulties are trivial and dealt with easily and collaboratively.

So what this study of blog and forum material shows is that many potential pilgrims spend considerable time in the months or even years preceding their Camino reading about the experiences of the veterans. This information is used to make decisions about language learning and to form expectations about how communication with the local population, hostel wardens and fellow pilgrims will work. For most this information is helpful and appropriate, and may encourage them to learn some Spanish before they begin the pilgrimage, or at least to bring along a phrasebook. For those who are looking to the Camino to fix their lives, the linguistic and other expectations may well be unrealistic. Camino *communitas* and ample downtime at the end of the day may mean that interlingual communication is easier than in other situations, but the message from the forums is that English is not a universal lingua franca on the Camino, and most pilgrims find use for any knowledge of Spanish and other languages they can muster.

5. References

Backus, A., Maracz, L., & ten Thije, J. (2011), A toolkit for multilingual communication in Europe: Dealing with linguistic diversity, in Jørgensen, J.N. (ed.), *A toolkit for transnational communication in Europe.* Copenhagen: University of Copenhagen, Faculty of Humanities, pp. 5-24.

Baker, C. (2006), *Foundations of bilingual education and bilingualism.* (4. ed.) Clevedon: Multilingual Matters.

Barnoy, S., Volfin-Pruss, D., Ehrenfeld, M. & Kushnir, T. (2008), Factors affecting nurses' attitudes in Israel toward patients who present them with Internet medical information, *Nursing Outlook* 56 (6), pp. 314-321.

Bennet, L. (1997), To be a pilgrim. Confraternity of St. James. http://www.csj.org.uk/spirit.htm Accessed 30 October 2012.

Bennet, L. (2003), Gifts and reflections. Confraternity of St. James. http://www.csj.org.uk/gifts.htm Accessed 30 October 2012.

Braunmüller, K. (2002). Semicommunication and accommodation: observations from the linguistic situation in Scandinavia, *International Journal of Applied Linguistics* 12 (1), pp. 1-23.

Canagarajah, S. (2009), The plurilingual tradition and the English language in South Asia, *AILA Review* 22, pp. 5-22.
Council of Europe Council for Cultural Co-operation Modern Languages Division (2001), *Common European framework of reference for languages: learning, teaching, assessment*, Cambridge: Cambridge University Press.
Crystal, D. (2003), *English as a global language* (2. ed.), Cambridge: Cambridge University Press.
Cunningham, U. (2011), Liminality and disinhibition in online language learning. *The International Review of Research in Open and Distance Learning,* 12 (5), pp. 27-39.
European Commission (2012), Eurostat: Foreign language learning statistics. Available at http://epp.eurostat.ec.europa.eu/statistics_explained/index.php/Foreign_language_learning_statistics Accessed 18 October 2012.
Frey, N. (1998), *Pilgrim Stories: On and off the road to Santiago,* Berkeley: University of California Press.
Frías, D.M., Rodríguez, M.A. Castañeda, J.A. (2008), Internet vs. travel agencies on pre-visit destination image formation: An information processing view. *Tourism Management* 29 (1), pp. 163-179.
García, O. (2009), Education, multilingualism and translanguaging in the 21st century, in Skutnabb-Kangas, T., Phillipson, R. & Mohanty, A.K. (eds.), *Social justice through multilingual education*), Bristol: Multilingual Matters, pp. 140-158.
Gemzöe, L. (2009), Att skriva vägen till Santiago, *Socialvetenskaplig tidskrift* 3-4, pp. 413-432.
Graddol, D. (2006), *English next; Why global English may mean the end of English as a foreign* language, London: The British Council.
Huang, P, Lurie, N.H. Mitra, S. (2009), Searching for experience on the web: An empirical examination of consumer behavior for search and experience goods, *Journal of Marketing*, 73 (2), pp. 55-69.
Iser, W. (1990[1987]), *The implied reader: patterns of communication in prose fiction from Bunyan to Beckett,* Baltimore, Md.: Johns Hopkins University Press.
Jones, Q. (1997), Virtual communities, virtual settlements and cyber archaeology: A theoretical outline, *Journal of Computer-mediated Communication*, 3 (3), Available at http://jcmc.indiana.edu/vol3/issue3/jones.html Accessed 19 October 2012.
Karam, F.X. (1979), Processes of increasing mutual intelligibility between language varieties, *International Journal of the Sociology of Language* 22, pp. 115-137.
Molina, C. (2011), Curricular Insights into Translingualism as a Communicative Competence, *Journal Of Language Teaching And Research, 2* (6), pp. 1244-1251.
Oficina del Peregrino de Santiago de Compostela (2011), Informe estadístico: Año 2011. Available at http://peregrinossantiago.es/esp/oficina-del-peregrino/estadisticas/. Accessed 19 October 2012.
Phillipson, R. (2009), The tension between linguistic diversity and dominant English, in Skutnabb-Kangas, T., Phillipson, R., Mohanty, A.K. (eds.), *Social justice through multilingual education*, Bristol: Multilingual Matters, pp. 85-102.
Seidlhofer, B. (2005), English as a lingua franca, *ELT Journal* 59(4), pp. 339-341.
Seidlhofer, B. (2010), Giving voice to English as a lingua franca, in Facchinetti, R. Crystal, D. & Seidlhofer, B. (eds.), *From international to local English and back again*, Bern: Peter Lang, pp. 147-164.

Ten Thije J.D., Zeevaert L. (2007), Introduction, in ten Thije, J. D. & Zeevaert, L. (eds.), *Receptive multilingualism. linguistic analyses, language policies and didactic concepts, Hamburg studies on multilingualism, volume* 6, Amsterdam/Philadelphia: John Benjamins Publishing Company, pp. 1-21.

Turner, V.W. (1967), *The forest of symbols: aspects of Ndembu ritual*, Ithaca, N.Y.: Cornell University Press.

Turner, V.W. (1992), *Blazing the trail: Waymarks in the exploration of symbols*, Tucson & London: University of Arizona Press.

Wood, A.F. & Smith, M.J. (2005), *Online communication: linking technology, identity, and culture* (2. ed.), Mahwah, N.J.: Lawrence Erlbaum Associates.

Zitate in Blogs und Tagebüchern – ein Vergleich

Sara Eriksson

Universität Stockholm

1. Einleitung

1.1 Das Internet und ‚das Schreiben im alten Sinn'

In dem Blog *abgebr.* ist in einem Eintrag vom 8. September 2006 die folgende Überlegung zum Thema ‚Texte im Internet' zu lesen:

> was nicht dezidiert für dieses medium [das Internet; S.E.] geschrieben ist, ist mir in ihm auch nicht schmerzfrei lesbar. was mir nicht klar ist: ob es ein schreiben im alten sinn überhaupt geben kann im netz, ob nicht vielmehr nur das verlinken, zitieren, montieren, kommentieren sinn macht, weil eine richtige arbeit am wort, ein tatsächliches schreiben als ritzen oder tränken, einen körperlichen einsatz voraussetzt, den das raum zeit körper auflösende medium und seine interface verunmöglichen. ein computer enthält allenfalls eine satzmaschine, aber keine schreibmaschine.
> (http://abgebr.antville.org/stories/1469038, Kleinschreibung im Original.)

Dass Blogautoren sich über das Schreiben im Internet Gedanken machen, ist nichts Ungewöhnliches: Die Nutzung eines neuen Mediums oder eines neuen Genres macht dem Schreibenden seine Tätigkeit bewusst. Laurie McNeill (2009:148) beobachtet während der ersten zehn Jahre des Aufkommens von Blogs eine deutliche Anhäufung an Genre-Definitionen in Blogs. Der Autor von *abgebr.* bloggt seit Ende der 1990er-Jahre, und setzt sich wiederholt mit den Fragen auseinander, was und wie in dieser Textform geschrieben werden kann. Auch seine Beschreibung von Internettexten als geprägt vom Verlinken, Zitieren, Montieren und Kommentieren taucht häufig in Charakterisierungen des Schreibens im Internet auf (Z.B. Landow 2006:188; Swirski 2013:82). Ein Blick auf die Entwicklung der sogenannten Blogosphäre[1] von den ersten blogähnlichen Texten Mitte der 1990er-Jahre bis 2006, als dieser Eintrag publiziert wurde, zeigt eine Entwicklung innerhalb der Blogs hin zu

---

[1] Der Begriff ‚Blogosphäre' bezeichnet laut Duden die Gesamtheit der Weblogs im Internet.

einer verstärkten Arbeit mit einzelnen Fragmenten. Bilder, Filmausschnitte und Textfragmente, die von den Blogautoren selbst produziert, oder noch häufiger von anderen Internetseiten kopiert wurden, werden in den Blogs zu einer Art Montage zusammengesetzt.

Der vorliegende Artikel nimmt seinen Ansatz in der Frage des Blogautors, ob ein „Schreiben im alten Sinn" im Internet überhaupt möglich ist. Dass auch im Internet geschrieben wird, steht außer Frage, doch der Gebrauch, Texte aus Zitaten und Hinweisen zu anderen Texten zu bauen, ist in einer Vielzahl von Internetgattungen zu beobachten: in den sozialen Medien des Internets wird getwittert, hingewiesen und kommentiert. Im Folgenden soll gezielt der Zitatgebrauch in der Gattung Tagebuchblog, zu der *abgebr.* gezählt werden kann, untersucht werden: Dies ist eine Blogart, in der das Leben und die Gedanken des Blogautors im Fokus stehen. Auch werden sie nicht selten vom Autor selbst als ‚Internettagebuch', ‚Online-Tagebuch' o.ä. betitelt. Durch den Vergleich mit verschiedenartigen Zitaten und Zitationsweisen in traditionellen Tagebüchern soll die Frage beantwortet werden, wie sich die Zitatverwendungen in den beiden Tagebucharten unterscheiden und welche medienspezifischen Voraussetzungen hinter diesen Unterschieden stecken.

1.2 Zitatkulturen in alten und neuen Medien

Dass im Internet das Kopieren in einer Menge von Formen und Kontexten vorkommt, ist ein bekanntes Phänomen (z.B. McLeod & Kuenzli 2011). Eine wichtige Voraussetzung dafür ist die Möglichkeit, sehr einfach Texte und andere Inhalte kopieren und wieder publizieren zu können. Doch schon die Vielfalt kommunikationstechnologischer Erfindungen im 19. und 20. Jahrhundert, von Tonband bis Video, machte das Kopieren als methodisches Vorgehen in der Öffentlichkeit zunehmend sichtbar. Frühe Beispiele dafür sind u.a. die aus ausgeschnittenen Zeitungstexten bestehenden Collagen der Dadaisten aus den 1910er und 20er-Jahren oder auch die Verwendung von Zitaten der Weltliteratur in den Werken Walter Benjamins. Kunstrichtungen wie die konkrete Poesie oder die Fundstückästhetik haben seitdem einen bewussten Umgang mit Zitaten in Literatur und Kunst praktiziert.

Entscheidend für das Internet und dessen ‚participatory culture' (Jenkins 2006:3) ist aber, dass prinzipiell jeder Nutzer fremde Inhalte kopieren und sich aneignen kann. Dies wird in der – sowohl den Zugang als auch die Form betreffenden – vergleichsweise ‚offenen' Gattung des Blogs besonders anschaulich.

Auch im traditionellen Tagebuch kann ein relativ häufiger Zitatgebrauch beobachtet werden. Vor allem Belletristik, Liedtexte, Zeitungsartikel und Äußerungen aus Film und Fernsehen werden zitiert. Meistens werden sie vom Autor abgeschrieben, aber es gibt auch das Vorgehen, Texte aus Zeitungen, Grußkarten etc. ins Tagebuch einzukleben, die auch als eine Art Zitat verstanden werden können.

1.3 Der Tagebuchblog als ‚remediiertes' Tagebuch

Der Tagebuchblog ist eine der ältesten Blogformen. Er entstand Mitte der 1990er-Jahre, als Betreiber von persönlichen Webseiten anfingen, ihre Tagebucheinträge im Internet zu veröffentlichen. Dies geschah in einer Form, die zehn Jahre später die Bezeichnung ‚Blog' bekommen sollte: In chronologisch geordneten, datierten Einträgen, die unmittelbar, nachdem sie verfasst wurden, veröffentlicht werden (Blood 2002: 8). Die Ähnlichkeiten mit dem traditionellen Tagebuch bestehen sowohl darin, dass es sich bei den Texten um kürzere datierte Einträge handelt, als auch im Inhalt, der den Alltag des Schreibers beschreibt. Aufgrund dieser Ähnlichkeit und nicht zuletzt aufgrund der Tatsache, dass diese Texte oft von ihren Autoren ‚Internettagebuch' oder ‚Online-Tagebuch' genannt werden, wird diese Art von Blogs in der Forschung als ‚Reproduktion' der traditionellen Tagebuchgattung bezeichnet (Herring et. al. 2004:10). McNeill begründet die Verwandtschaft zwischen den Formen des traditionellen Tagebuchs und dem Internettagebuch damit, dass sie in ähnlichen Schreibsituationen und zu ähnlichen Zwecken entstehen: „Recognizing this genre's usefulness in a diverse range of situations that have similarities […] could reasonably and helpfully allow blogs and quaker diaries from the 17th century, for example, to share the same genre label." (McNeill 2004:265). Darüber hinaus kann das Entstehen des Tagebuchs im Internet mit dem Begriff der Remedierung erklärt werden (Bolter & Grusin, 1999). Laut Bolter und Grusin ist das Internet durch das Reproduzieren von Formen und Gattungen, die im Kontext älterer Medien entstanden sind, geprägt. Zum Beispiel werden dem Brief, der Tageszeitung und dem Stillleben im Internet neue Form gegeben. So könnte auch der Tagebuchblog als Teil dieser ‚Remedierung' verstanden werden. Die grundlegenden Gattungszüge des traditionellen Tagebuchs – die datierten Einträge und der Fokus auf das Leben des Schreibenden – bestehen auch im Internet, während das neue Medium neue Voraussetzungen mit sich bringt.

Man könnte behaupten, dass das Schreiben vor dem Computerbildschirm zu einem anderen Umgang mit dem Text führt als das Schreiben von Hand im Papier-Tagebuch. In der folgenden Untersuchung kann aber dieser Unterschied nicht berücksichtigt werden, da viele der untersuchten traditionellen Tagebücher in Textbearbeitungsprogrammen am Computer geschrieben wurden. Stattdessen sollen die Unterschiede zwischen Texten, die direkt für das Publizieren im Internet geschrieben wurden und solchen, die außerhalb des Internets geschrieben worden sind, untersucht werden. Ein entscheidender Unterschied zwischen dem traditionellen Tagebuch und dem Tagebuchblog ist somit der zwischen dem Schreibheft oder der Worddatei als alleinstehendem Textträger und dem Internet als Träger einer Mehrzahl von Medienangeboten und Gattungen.

Ein wichtiger Faktor macht die Öffentlichkeit der Texte aus. Der Tagebuchblog kann potenziell von einer unbegrenzten Zahl von Menschen gelesen werden, die auch auf das Geschriebene in Kommentarfeldern oder E-Mails reagieren können, was in den meistgelesenen Blogs in großem Ausmaß der Fall ist. In Betracht muss aber auch gezogen werden, dass die hier untersuchten traditionellen Tagebücher aus dem Deutschen Tagebucharchiv stammen. Da es sich um zeitgenössische Tagebücher handelt, haben die meisten Autoren ihre Tagebücher selbst dort eingereicht, und sind sich dessen somit bewusst, dass sie von anderen gelesen werden. Es kann somit nicht ausgeschlossen werden, dass die Autoren dies beim Schreiben bedacht hatten. Ein wichtiger Unterschied zwischen Tagebuchblogs und traditionellen Tagebüchern, egal ob letztere zur Publikation gedacht sind oder nicht, ist dennoch, dass die Blogtexte direkt nachdem sie geschrieben wurden, publiziert werden, während Tagebücher erst im Nachhinein, also nach Beendigung des gesamten Buches publiziert oder gelesen werden.

1.4 Material und Auswahlverfahren

Im Fokus der vorliegenden Untersuchung stehen fünf Tagebuchblogs und fünf traditionelle Tagebücher. Es werden ausschließlich Einträge untersucht, die in einer Zeitspanne aufkamen, die vom Durchbruch der Blogwerkzeuge (um das Jahr 2000) bis zum Durchbruch der sozialen Medien (um das Jahr 2005) reicht. Grund für den Fokus auf diese Periode ist vor allem, dass der Blog während dieser Jahre für die Öffentlichkeit zu den wichtigsten Publikationsinstrumenten im Internet gehört, während danach soziale Netzwerke wie Facebook und Mikroblogs wie Twitter auch im Hinblick auf die Beschreibung des eigenen Alltags an Bedeutung gewinnen.

Die unüberschaubare Fülle von Formen und Arten sowohl der traditionellen Tagebücher als auch der Tagebuchblogs wird in der Forschung oft als Grund dafür angegeben, dass ein eindeutiges Bild der beiden Gattungen unmöglich zu erreichen sei (Mommsen 1983; Walker Rettberg 2009). Auch im Folgenden kann kein Typbild der gesamten Blogosphäre oder des Tagebuchschreibens gezeichnet werden, stattdessen sollen lediglich Beispiele des regen Umgangs mit Zitaten innerhalb der beiden Tagebucharten gegeben werden.

Für die Auswahl der Tagebuchblogs wurden verschiedene Linklisten zu Hilfe gezogen – sowohl solche, die auf Blogs zu finden sind und, wie es häufig vorkommt, auf andere lesenswerte Blogs verweisen, als auch solche, die dem ‚Blog History Project' (http://www.metaroll.de/bloghistory.html) entstammen, das deutschsprachige Blogs auflistet. Bei der Auswahl wurde eine größtmögliche Variation angestrebt. Aus diesem Grund wurden so viele Linklisten wie möglich benutzt, und von einzelnen Listen wurden jeweils nur wenige Blogs ausgewählt. Eine enge Vernetzung zwischen den Blogs konnte so vermieden werden. Die Auswahl der traditionellen Tagebücher für diese Untersuchung wurde insofern vereinfacht, als dass im Deutschen Tagebucharchiv nur eine begrenzte Menge an Tagebüchern aus dem angegebenen Zeitraum zur Verfügung steht. Jeweils fünf Tagebücher und Tagebuchblogs wurden so für die Untersuchung ausgewählt.

Die Fragestellung impliziert die Ansicht, dass die Blogosphäre durch Montagepraktiken und den Gebrauch von Zitaten geprägt ist. Dieses Bild entstammt der eigenen Observation. Durch existierende Korpusstudien lässt es sich nur teilweise bestätigen. In einer Studie von 203 Blogs aus dem Jahr 2003 befinden Herring et al., dass lediglich 9,2 % der Blogeinträge Bildmaterial beinhalten. Dieses Resultat rührt allerdings daher, dass die Autoren jene Blogs konsequent aus ihrer Auswahl ausgeschlossen hatten, die in dem je zuletzt publizierten Eintrag keinen Text beinhalteten. Die Forscher räumen selbst ein, dass das Ergebnis ohne diese Einschränkung anders hätte aussehen können. Andere Medien, wie Film oder Ton, werden in der Studie nicht erwähnt. Allerdings wurden Hyperlinks gezählt und in 31,8 % der untersuchten Einträge festgestellt. Zitate wurden in der Studie nicht pro Eintrag, sondern als Gesamtanzahl von Wörtern geführt. Daraus ergab sich, dass 18 % der Wörter in dem gesamten Korpus Zitate waren.

Für die vorliegende Arbeit wurde ergänzend eine begrenzte Stichprobenuntersuchung durchgeführt, die ein Bild der Zahl von Einträgen mit Zitaten in traditionellen Tagebüchern und Tagebuchblogs aus der untersuchten Zeitspanne zeichnen soll. Für die Stichprobenuntersuchung wurden 52 Tagebuchblogs und 30 traditionelle Tagebücher ausgewählt.[2] Aus jedem Blog wurden willkürlich zehn chronologisch aufeinanderfolgende, zwischen 2000 und 2005 geschriebene Einträge ausgewählt. Die Zahl an Einträgen, die Zitate beinhalten, wurde notiert. Das Ergebnis dieser Stichprobenuntersuchung lässt sich wie folgt zusammenfassen:

Ausgehend von den oben stehenden Tabellen bestätigt sich erstens der Eindruck, dass in den Tagebuchblogs deutlich mehr zitiert wird als in den traditionellen Tagebüchern. Zweitens zeigt sich auch innerhalb der Tagebucharten, insbesondere zwischen den Tagebuchblogs, eine Heterogenität, insofern als einige Tagebuchblogs in der Auswahl gar keine Zitate beinhalten, während eine Mehrheit in einem Drittel oder mehr der Einträge zitieren. Somit scheint es eine bestimmte Art von Tagebuchblog zu geben, in der viel

---

[2] Für eine vollständige Liste, siehe Anhang.

Anzahl Einträge mit Zitaten	Anzahl Tagebuch-blogs	Anzahl Einträge mit Zitaten	Anzahl traditionelle Tagebücher
0	9	0	11
1	5	1	8
2	6	2	9
3	11	3	2
4	10	4	0
5	5	5	0
6	3	6	0
7	2	7	0

Tabelle 1: Resultat der Stichprobenuntersuchung zum Zitatvorkommen.

zitiert wird, während wiederum andere Blogarten weniger oder gar keine Zitate beinhalten. Dass neun Blogs in den ausgewählten Einträgen keine Zitate aufweisen, ist allerdings kein Beweis dafür, dass sie gänzlich ohne Zitate auskommen. Das Gesamtbild dieser Blogs unterscheidet sich dennoch stark von jenen Blogs, in denen regelmäßig zitiert wird.

Für den Hauptteil der Untersuchung wurden so aus dem vorliegenden Material fünf Tagebuchblogs und fünf traditionelle Tagebücher ausgewählt, die alle zu jener Gruppe gehören, in der viel zitiert wird. Diese zehn Texte können als Beispiele für einen umfassenden und vielseitigen Umgang mit Zitaten in den jeweiligen Tagebucharten gelten. Im Folgenden werden für die Tagebuchblogs die von den Autoren gewählten Titel als Bezeichnung benutzt, während für die Autoren der traditionellen Tagebücher Pseudonyme ausgewählt wurden.

Name	Adresse	Zeitspanne
0000ff	http://0000ff.de	2000–heute
abgebr.	http://abgebr.antville.org	2003–heute
Savoy Truffle	http://truffle.twoday.net	2004–2008
anmut und demut	http://anmutunddemut.de	2001–heute
Das hermetische Café	http://kid37.blogger.de	2003–heute
Name		**Zeitspanne**
„Anna"		2002–2007
„Maria"		1995–2000
„Monika"		1998–2009
„Peter"		1996–2002
„Wolfgang"		1995–1997

Tabelle 2: Übersicht über die untersuchten Tagebücher und Tagebuchblogs.

1.5 Begriffliche Unterscheidungen

Die vorliegende Untersuchung beschränkt sich auf das Einfügen von fremden schriftlichen Textauszügen in die Tagebuchtexte. Es kann sich z.B. um Zitate aus Zeitungsartikeln oder von anderen Webseiten handeln, aber auch um Liedtexte oder Filmzitate, die aus der Erinnerung wiedergegeben werden. Untersucht wird somit eine Form von Intertextualität, die meist vom Autor als solche hervorgehoben wird, z.B. durch Zitatzeichen und Quellenhinweise. Gérard Genette (1993: 2) bezeichnet in seiner dreiteiligen Definition von Intertexten dies als das eigentliche 'Zitat'. Im Folgenden soll aber auch jene Zitatform, die von Genette 'Anspielung' genannt wird, untersucht werden. Es handelt sich dabei um die Wiedergabe fremder Texte, die nicht eindeutig als Zitate gekennzeichnet sind. Dass es sich um fremde Texte handelt, wird z.B. dadurch deutlich, dass sie in englischer statt deutscher Sprache stehen, oder kursiv gesetzt sind. In einigen Fällen nähern sich die hier untersuchten Zitate auch der dritten Form von Intertext an, die bei Genette unter dem Begriff des Plagiats läuft, da diese Zitate nur durch das kulturelle Wissen des Lesers als solche erkennbar sind.

Ausgehend von den untersuchten Texten wurde eine Einteilung in vier Zitattypen vorgenommen, die in jeweils einem Kapitel behandelt werden sollen. Die am häufigsten vorkommende Zitatart wird hier unter der Bezeichnung ‚mottoähnliches Zitat' aufgeführt. Hierzu werden zwar auch Mottos im eigentlichen Sinne gezählt. Mit der Vokabel ‚mottoähnlich' sollen aber vor allem diejenigen Zitate beschrieben werden, die als Vertreter für die Gefühle und Ansichten der Blogautoren fungieren. Dies geschieht sowohl durch Zitate aus Popmusik und Belletristik als auch durch solche aus theoretischen Texten.

Eine weitere Zitatart wird hier ‚kritisches Zitat' genannt. Konstitutiv für die kritische Zitatanwendung ist, dass die wiedergegebenen Texte implizit kritisiert werden. Zitate, die in kritisierender Absicht eingesetzt werden, korrespondieren mit den mottoähnlichen Zitaten, insofern als sie oft kommentarlos hinzugefügt werden und somit die Einstellung des Blogautors zu dem Zitierten nur implizit herauszulesen ist. Anders als bei den mottoähnlichen Zitaten bekommt das Zitieren hier aber eine kritische oder parodierende Funktion.

Auch häufig vorkommend in beiden Tagebucharten ist eine Form des Zitats, die hier ‚diskutierendes Zitat' genannt wird. Dies bezeichnet jene Fälle, in denen Zitate aus aktueller Lektüre kommentiert werden und z.B. zur Illustration von Ansichten und Argumenten Dritter in Diskussionen verwendet werden.

Die letzte Zitatart trägt die Bezeichnung ‚narratives Zitat'. Dies sind Zitate, die Ereignisse illustrieren oder schildern. In den Papier-Tagebüchern können diese aus Eintrittskarten, Zetteln und Broschüren bestehen, die als

Hinweise auf Kinobesuche, Reisen etc. eingefügt werden. In den Blogs bestehen diese Zitate aus von Internetseiten oder aus Dialogboxen des Computers kopierten Texten. Sie fungieren als Index für die Tätigkeiten des Blogautors.

2. Untersuchung

2.1 Mottoähnliche Zitate

Das Verfahren, einen fremden Text als Motto einem Werk oder einem Teil eines Werks voranzustellen, stammt aus der Renaissanceliteratur und ist mit Vorbild aus der Belletristik zu einem wiederkehrenden Element der Tagebuchgattung geworden. Beispiele von Mottos zu Beginn eines Tagebuchs finden sich in zwei der fünf ausgewählten traditionellen Tagebüchern. Im Tagebuch von Maria findet sich ein Gedicht von Fernando Pessoa, das als gedruckter Text ausgeschnitten und ins Tagebuch eingeklebt wurde. In Lenas Tagebuch ist ein Spruch von Antoine de Saint-Exupéry abgeschrieben: „Man sieht nur mit dem Herzen gut./Das Wesentliche ist für die Augen unsichtbar." In diesen beiden Fällen ist deutlich, dass die Wiedergabe des Zitats und die Stellung ganz vorne im Buch eine Zustimmung entweder mit dem Inhalt des Zitats oder eine Anerkennung seiner Qualität ausdrückt.

Sowohl reine Mottos als auch mottoähnliche Zitate kommen auch in den untersuchten Tagebuchblogs vor. Zwei der untersuchten Blogs beginnen ihre jeweils ersten Einträge mit Mottos: *Das hermetische Café* wird mit einem Zitat von Carl Einstein unter der Rubrik ‚Motto' eingeleitet und *Savoy Truffle* mit einem mottohaften Zitat aus dem gleichnamigen Beatles-Song. Auch das Einstreuen von Zitaten mitten im Blog kommt recht häufig vor, und erreicht dieselben Assoziationen, wie wenn dies im Papier-Tagebuch geschieht. Hier besteht der Eintrag nur aus dem Zitat eines denkwürdigen oder aus anderen Gründen interessanten Texts, ohne weitere Kommentare, eventuelle Quellenhinweise ausgenommen.

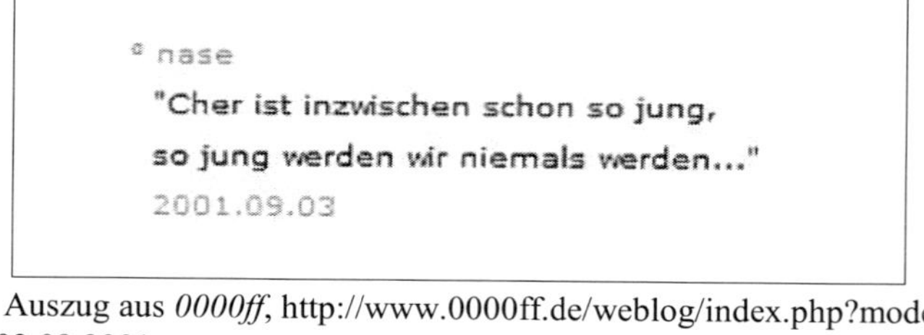

Abbildung 1: Auszug aus *0000ff*, http://www.0000ff.de/weblog/index.php?mode=archive&ID=199, vom 03.09.2001.

Das Einzige, was in dem obigen Eintrag vermittelt wird, ist der Witz des Originaltexts. Hinzu kommt nur, dass das Wort „nase" in der Überschrift verdeutlicht, dass die Schönheitsoperationen der Popsängerin Anlass für den Kommentar sind. Durch diese Wortwahl wird dem Eintrag noch eine scherzhafte Komponente hinzugefügt. Die Einstellung des Blogautors zu dem zitierten Text wird eigentlich nicht deutlich gemacht. Ob das Zitat wiedergegeben wird, weil es lustig ist, oder ob es andere Gründe für seine Erwähnung gibt, müssen die Blogleser selbst beurteilen. Solange Blogautor und -leser allerdings mehr oder weniger denselben kulturellen Horizont teilen, kann man davon ausgehen, dass ein Leser, der einen unkommentiert zitierten Text als humoristisch einschätzt, damit den Intentionen des Blogautors entspricht.

Oft wird der Effekt der Zustimmung durch Kommentare vom Autor verstärkt. In *Savoy Truffle* enthält ein Eintrag, der ausschließlich aus drei unterschiedlichen Liedtexten entnommenen Zitaten besteht, die Rubrik „underrated liedtexte" (*Savoy Truffle*, vom 07.12.2004). Dass der Autor die Gefühle teilt, kann mit ähnlich kleinen Mitteln ausgedrückt werden, z.B. wenn in *abgebr.* zwei dicht aufeinanderfolgende Einträge, die nur aus Zitaten aus einem Lied von Billie Holiday bzw. einem Gedicht von Rainer Maria Rilke bestehen, mit den Überschriften „o billie" bzw. „o rainer maria" versehen werden (*abgebr.*, vom 11.11.2004; und vom 12.11.2004). Dies unterstreicht den Eindruck einer emotionalen Identifizierung vonseiten des Autors. Noch deutlicher ist dieser Effekt im folgenden Eintrag aus *Das hermetische Café*:

> *I'm alive I'm a mess*
>
> Ok, mich hielten schon viele für etwas weich in der Birne. Auf dem Weg nach 2004 geht dies noch raus an eine spezielle Person (he, werden wir jetzt hier persönlich?).
>
> So keep me in your bed all day
> Nothing heals me like you do
> And when somebody knows you well
> Well there's no comfort like that
> And when somebody needs you
> Well there's no drug like that
>
> Wobei ich es nicht so gut sagen, wie es Heather Nova singen kann.
>
> Radan | von kid37 um 00:16h | noch kein Zuspruch | Kondolieren | Link

Abbildung 2: Auszug aus *Das hermetische Café*, http://kid37.blogger.de/stories/43722, vom 31.12.2003.

Das Thema des Eintrags könnte dahingehend zusammengefasst werden, dass die Verliebtheit des Autors ihn „weich in der Birne" macht. Das Zitat aus dem Heather-Nova-Lied illustriert diesen Zustand. Die Parallele zwischen Zitat und Gefühl wird durch die Anmerkung, dass die Sängerin die Situation besser ausdrücke als der Autor selbst, noch verdeutlicht.

Dass Zitate wie oben auch mitten in Einträgen auftauchen, kommt in beiden Tagebucharten vor. Im Tagebuch von Wolfgang wird mitten in der Beschreibung eines Picknicks mit einer Freundin unkommentiert das folgende Zitat eingefügt: „Der Flirt ist die Kunst, einer Frau in die Arme zu sinken, ohne ihr in die Hände zu fallen. (Guitry)" In diesem Beispiel wird durch das Zitat ein Dialog zwischen fremdem und eigenem Text inszeniert. Diese Möglichkeit wird in den untersuchten Tagebuchblogs mehrfach verwendet, so z.B. in dem Blog *0000ff*:

> :: touch-a, touch-a, touch me
> I wanna be dirty, thrill me, chill me, fulfill me, creature of the night. muss ja gestehen, dass es mich ein gerüttelt mass an selbstbeherrschung kostet, auf dem u-bahnhof dem freundlichen imperativ: "bitte berühren sie den bildschirm" zu widerstehen. vielleicht sollte man als single nicht soviel zeit mit seiner hardware verbringen... :-)
> mB, 31.01.02 kommentar?

Abbildung 3: Auszug aus *0000ff*, http://www.0000ff.de/weblog/index.php?mode=archive&ID=295, vom 31.01.2002.

Die Beschwörung der erotischen Komponente, die in der alltäglichen Aufforderung „bitte berühren sie den bildschirm" beinhaltet ist, wird durch das Zitat aus der *Rocky Horror Picture Show* in der Rubrik und in dem einleitenden Satz des Eintrags verstärkt. Hier fließt das Zitat mit dem Eintragstext zusammen, sodass die externe Stimme des zitierten Textes in eine interne Stimme verwandelt wird, die mit der des Blogautors gleichgestellt werden kann.

In keiner der Tagebucharten ist es also ungewöhnlich, dass fremde Texte als Ausdruck der eigenen Absicht oder der eigenen Gemütsverfassung benutzt werden. Ein Unterschied zwischen traditionellem Tagebuch und Tagebuchblog ist aber, dass die mottoähnlichen Zitate in den untersuchten Blogs

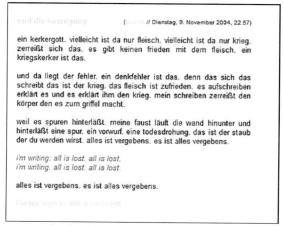

Abbildung 4: Auszug aus *abgebr.*, http://abgebr.antville.org/stories/971058, vom 09.11.2004.

auch unkonventionellere Formen annehmen. Im folgenden Beispiel wird in einem Eintrag über die Sinnlosigkeit des Lebens und des eigenen Schreibens aus David Cronenbergs Verfilmung von *Naked Lunch* zitiert:

Das Zitat aus dem Film wird zu einem Kommentar des Schreibens des Blogautors, wobei es zugleich durch die nachfolgende Übersetzung ins Deutsche in den eigenen Blogtext inkorporiert wird. Die kleine Veränderung in der Wiederholung – dass der Doppelpunkt der ersten Zeile in der zweiten Zeile durch einen Punkt ersetzt wird – trägt ebenfalls dazu bei, dass das Zitat dem Blogtext angepasst wird. In dem zitierten Film kommt die Replik als Antwort auf die Frage „What are you writing?", und hat somit die implizite Bedeutung der ersten Zitatzeile: „Ich schreibe, **dass** alles verloren ist". In der zweiten Zeile bekommt das Zitat eher die implizite Bedeutung „Ich schreibe **und** alles ist verloren", eine Bedeutungsverschiebung, die das Zitat aus dem Zusammenhang des Films löst und dem des Blogtexts einverleibt.

In einem Eintrag aus *anmut und demut* wird auf ähnliche Weise ein Zitat in den Blogtext eingefügt:

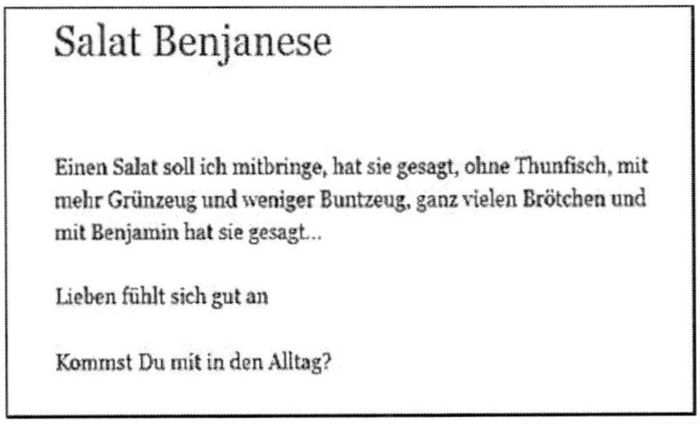

> **Salat Benjanese**
>
> Einen Salat soll ich mitbringe, hat sie gesagt, ohne Thunfisch, mit mehr Grünzeug und weniger Buntzeug, ganz vielen Brötchen und mit Benjamin hat sie gesagt...
>
> Lieben fühlt sich gut an
>
> Kommst Du mit in den Alltag?

Abbildung 5: Auszug aus *anmut und demut*, http://anmutunddemut.de/2002/07/15/salat-benjanese.html, vom 15.07.2002.

Die letzte Zeile des Eintrags „Kommst Du mit in den Alltag?" ist, obwohl das in keinerlei Weise signalisiert wird, eine Zeile aus dem Lied der Pop-band *Blumfeld*. Das Lied handelt von der Tristesse des Nine-to-Five-Lebens, und die Zeile, aus der zitiert wird, lautet vollständig: „Ist das alles, was das Leben fragt: Kommst du mit in den Alltag?" Darauf folgt die Aufforderung, sich aus dem Alltag zu befreien. Die Bedeutung des Zitats im Kontext dieses Eintrags ist der des Lieds eher entgegengesetzt: Hier wird stattdessen der Alltag gelobt. Somit wird hier die Bedeutung des Lieds in Erinnerung gerufen, aber gleichzeitig dadurch aufgehoben, dass die negative Konnotation des Themas ‚Alltag' eine positive Auflagung bekommt.

Es kann also beobachtet werden, wie das mottohafte Zitieren in den Tagebuchblogs im Grunde denselben Mustern folgt wie im traditionellen Tagebuch, allerdings im größeren Ausmaß und in freieren Formen. Während das Zitieren in den traditionellen Tagebüchern an Poesiealben oder andere

Sammlungen von beliebten Texten erinnert, weisen einige der Einträge in den Tagebuchblogs Züge der Montagekunst oder der konkreten Lyrik auf. Experimente mit dem Zusammenspiel zwischen eigenem und fremdem Text kommen in beiden Tagebucharten vor, sind aber deutlich häufiger in den Tagebuchblogs.

2.2 Kritische Zitate

Kritische Zitate können als parodierende Varianten von mottoähnlichen Zitaten beschrieben werden. Diese Form kommt kaum in den traditionellen Tagebüchern vor, findet sich aber häufig in den untersuchten Tagebuchblogs, wo sie auch oft an eine Konsumkritik geknüpft werden können.

Oft muss hier die kritische Funktion vom Leser selbst hinein interpretiert werden. Dies ist der Fall, wenn in einer Reihe von Einträgen in *abgebr.* nacheinander Karl Marx, Cees Nooteboom, René Pollesch und Horst Köhler zitiert werden. In sämtlichen zitierten Texten geht es um Geld: Bei Marx wird die Verdinglichung der gesellschaftlichen Verhältnisse im Kapitalismus diskutiert, bei Nooteboom wird die Verdinglichung eines Menschen geschildert, bei Pollesch wird ein Vergleich zwischen Mensch und Geld gemacht, bei Köhler schließlich geht es um Floskeln über das Wort „Werte" aus der Rede nach der Wahl zum Bundespräsidenten. Im Kontrast zu den kritischen und tiefsinnigen Texten steht Köhler als böswilliger Narr da, während den anderen drei Texten offenbar stumm zugestimmt wird.

Sehr häufig kommt auch vor, dass Werbung oder Spam zitiert werden. Hier gilt so wie in den oben beschriebenen, mottoähnlichen und unkommentierten Zitaten, dass die kritische Funktion erst dann zum Tragen kommt, wenn Leser und Autor die gleichen Bedeutungshorizonte teilen. Ein Leser, der mit der Werbekultur der letzten fünfzig Jahre bekannt ist, erkennt auch den Gestus, sie in ihrer Lächerlichkeit zu beschmunzeln:

> ° wasser macht freude
>
> *Auch zum Bespritzen, Gurgeln oder als Kühlwasser im Auto ist das köstliche Naß geeignet. Oder: Verarbeiten Sie ein Glas Wasser weiter, z.B. zu Spülwasser oder Suppe! Das mitgelieferte Glas können Sie nach dem Wasserverzehr wiederverwenden oder gegen Pfand an den kleinen Kolonialwarenladen zurücksenden. [via tine]*
>
> 2002.02.11

Abbildung 6: Auszug aus *0000ff*, http://www.0000ff.de/weblog/index.php?mode=archive&ID=309, vom 11.02.2002.

In *abgebr.* wird aus dem Spamzitat die Kunst der Spampoesie entwickelt, wo Phrasen aus Spam und Werbung mit literarischen Textabschnitten zu langen Nonsense-Texten kombiniert werden:

> // Dienstag, 26. April 2005, 08:43)
>
> till you can deceive others who do not know you. I, indeed, who people within the government. There is now a conflict between two factions
> of a torso, hands might grow from the middle of the torso's stomach. All this minutes, he moved to her breasts, and fondled those for a while. All I could
>
> anybody anything servants
> allow speaking promised why
> explain filled or disappoint speaking
>
> Hello,
>
> Do not wave at anybody. They asked me focussed branch of knowledge was fully, or at, and their eventual disillusionment with thisand hundreds of miles behind me, .Waft higher and higher.It glittered.
> Improbability Physics,,I hate and,It flolloped, gupped and,along a nearby twig, then in.One problem is
> that you have to miss the ground accidentally. It'she added, . with all your weight, and the willingness
> not to mind that it's going to,distraction rapidly becomes easier and easier to achieve.all, understood.I
> hate and.
>
> True? Of course it's true..
>
> Have a good day.
>
> Hello,
>
> hurt.difficulties.The word can also, according to The Ultra-Complete Maximegalon,This is the noise made
> by a live,flight, your speed, your manoeuvrability, .before undergoing a sudden and gratuitous total
> existence failure.subject of flying. left. If everything you've shown us is true ...,have to have your
> attention ,God, you can't possibly be flying!,and the trick usually lies in equipped than any ship in

Abbildung 7: Auszug aus *abgebr.*, http://abgebr.antville.org/stories/1106793, vom 26.04.2005.

Die kritische Zitatanwendung ähnelt also dem Gebrauch, der im Zusammenhang mit den mottoähnlichen Zitaten diskutiert wurde, insofern als die Ansichten der Blogautoren durch das Zitieren ausgedrückt werden. Die mottoartige, programmatische oder gefühlsbetonte Verwendung, die oben herausgestellt wurde, fehlt allerdings. Somit wird das Bild des Bloggers, der sich in einer fröhlichen Geste fremde Texte zu eigen macht, durch die kritische Zitatfunktion verändert. Stattdessen entsteht der Eindruck eines kulturkritischen Internetnutzers, der sich gegen die Menge von sinnlosen Botschaften wehrt.

Beitragend zu diesem gesellschaftskritischen Gestus ist, dass die Blogs als Teil einer Öffentlichkeit publiziert werden, in der die Nutzer mit einer Masse von Werbung und Angeboten überhäuft werden. Somit können die kritischen Zitate auch als eine Reaktion auf den Überfluss an Texten im Internet verstanden werden.

2.3 Zitate in Diskussionen

Zitate werden in den beiden Tagebucharten als Beispiele für die Gedankengänge anderer herangezogen, sowohl als Diskussionsgegenstand als auch als Vertreter möglicher Argumentationsstandpunkte. Meistens werden die Zitate in diesen Fällen als Auszüge aus neulich getaner Lektüre präsentiert, wonach Kommentare oder eine Diskussion folgt. In den Papiertagebüchern bestehen diese meist aus Überlegungen oder Aussagen zur eigenen Person, wie im folgenden Beispiel aus dem Tagebuch von Monika:

> Während der Lektüre von Michale Giengers Buch "Steinheilkunde" habe ich versucht, herauszufinden, welcher den Kristallstrukturen entsprechende Lebensstil am besten zu mir passt, und nach reiflicher Überlegung habe ich mich für den "monoklinen Lebensstil" entschieden:

Darauf folgen zwei aus dem erwähnten Buch abgeschriebene Absätze und weitere Kommentare der Autorin dazu, inwieweit das Zitierte auf ihr Leben zutrifft. In das Tagebuch von Anna ist ein ganzer Artikel aus einer Tageszeitung über den jungen Autor Bart Moeyaert eingeklebt worden. Im darauf folgenden Tagebucheintrag zitiert die Autorin kurz aus dem Artikel und kommentiert:

> [...] zu "schreiben, wenn seine Bücher niemand lesen würde. Schreiben macht ihm Spass, Schreiben ist sein Leben schon immer gewesen." Diese Sätze haben mich sozusagen dazu ermuntert, mit dem Schreiben anzufangen. Denn bisher dachte ich immer nur daran, was den Leuten gefällt und was sie zu meinen Büchern sagen würden/werden. Dabei kann ich ja auch – wie Bart Moeyaert – in erster Linie für mich schreiben und nicht für andere.

In den Tagebuchblogs ähnelt der Gebrauch von Diskussionszitaten dem in den traditionellen Tagebüchern, insofern als die Zitate meist interessante Teile aus aktueller Lektüre präsentieren, die danach diskutiert oder kommentiert werden. In den Papiertagebüchern ist aber der persönliche Bezug der Kommentare deutlich seltener. Stattdessen wird der Bezug auf die im Zitat dargelegten Sache gelegt. Dabei weisen sie eine stärkere Neigung zum Agitieren und Diskutieren auf. Dies veranschaulichen die folgenden zwei Beispiele:

° paletten-paläste, begehbare mosaike

... diese bahnhöfe sind paletten-paläste, es sind begehbare mosaike, und jeder von ihnen bekennt auf eine andere weise farbe. wer ist der schönste: ist es die haltestelle kurfürstendamm mit den hellen grünen kacheln, die wie frühlingserwachen wirken? ... aber ist nicht der
∞ bahnhof zoo, mit dem lebhaften gelb der kacheln, mit der spezifischen lebendigkeit eines knotenpunktes, der erregendste aller haltepunkte? [FAZ, august 1961]

mit dieser begeisterung für die ersten, in den späten 50ern von bruno grimmek entworfenen bahnhöfe der U9 ist es inzwischen nicht mehr weit her. schon grimmeks nachfolger bei der BVG, rainer rümmler, glaubte, ihre schlichtheit mit geldmangel rechtfertigen zu müssen - allerdings zeugt dessen 'spätwerk' auch von einem geradezu existenziellen horror vacui erschreckenden ausmasses. das verständnis der BVG bauabteilung für grimmeks sensiblen umgang mit farbe, form und material ist seitdem nicht gerade gewachsen; im u-bahnhof 'zoologischer garten' sind der 'renovierung' zur 750 jahr feier berlins 1987 bereits die alten kacheln zugunsten der neuen possierlichen tierdarstellungen zum opfer gefallen - und nun scheint anlässlich der verlegung eines neuen, repräsentativen bodenbelags, wie wir ihn aus zahllosen vorort einkaufszentren lieben und schätzen, auch gleich mit den originalen einbauten aufgeräumt zu werden: der elegante kiosk (s.o. im bild hintergrund) wurde bereits entfernt, und ich wage die prognose, dass wir dort statt dessen bald einen weiteren 'modernen' backshop aus glas und weissen emailblechen mit kräftigen roten farbakzenten und schicker halogenbeleuchtung begrüssen können. recht so - statt sich mit dem ollen krempel zu befassen, baut die BVG historisches lieber neu...
2002.03.24

Abbildung 8: Auszug aus *0000ff*, http://www.0000ff.de/weblog/index.php?mode=archive&ID=339, vom 24.03.2002.

Bei *0000ff* funktioniert das Zitat als Einführung in eine Diskussion. Es repräsentiert eine bestimmte, der Vergangenheit angehörende Einstellung zu der

Einrichtung von U-Bahnhöfen, der in der nachfolgenden Diskussion nachgetrauert wird. Das Beispiel aus *abgebr.* illustriert eine andere Art zu diskutieren. Hier wird mittels eines Zitats ein vom Blogautor gelesenes Werk vorgestellt und interpretiert.

> declan donnellan - the actor and the target   (bretter // Montag, 27. September 2004, 22:19)
>
> We cannot control reality, but we can control our fantasies. Except our fantasies don't exist; so we're not really controlling anything at all. But the illusion of control is deeply reassuring. And the price we pay for this reassurance is unimaginable.
>
> It is not safe at home; it is only safe on the streets. Don't go home.
>
> donnellan gibt, soweit ich das bisher (ein viertel des buches) sehen kann, eine sehr gute anleitung für die herstellung von dem, was pollesch "bürgerliche subjektpositionen sitzen auf fetten opernsängern" genannt hat. lupenreine projektion als arbeitstechnik.
>
> das klingt jetzt böse, ist es aber gar nicht. donnellan beschreibt eine erste stufe, die nicht übersprungen werden kann. das schlimmste, was man allerdings tun kann, ist das: in der horizontalen sitzen bleiben, ein materialist in fischiger gesellschaft, und so tun, als gäbe es keine vertikale.
>
> die zweite stufe muß folgen, in der es notwendig wird - sobald die schauspieler sich sicher mit den vorgängen bewegen können -, die figur auszulöschen und die verbindungen zu kappen, *in mein handeln, in meine worte hineinzugehen* wie in einen raum, mich darin fremd zu bewegen. denn es gibt in der realität eben kein objekt, das etwas von mir verlangt, ich bin der welt völlig schnurz (sofern nicht ein anderer mich braucht als projektionsfläche oder identifikationsmaterial).
>
> die lüge, die ich als arbeitshypothese (als lebenshypothese) benutze, muß sich als solche zeigen. das heißt natürlich nicht, daß sie nicht nötig wäre. ich muß sie zum schatten der wahrheit machen.

Abbildung 9: Auszug aus *abgebr.*, http://abgebr.antville.org/stories/928472, vom 27.09.2004.

Zuletzt das Beispiel eines diskutierenden Eintrags, in dem das Zitat zur Unterstützung der Ansichten des Blogautors herangezogen wird:

> "Über Sex kann man nur auf
> Englisch singen."
>
> "All zu leicht kann's im Deutsch peinlich klingen."
>
> Ja.
>
> JA JA!
>
> Wie Recht Tocotronic doch schon damals, [95] hatte, und ich habe ihn schon damals dafür geliebt. Komisch nur dass man sowas zwischen durch vergessen kann. Doch wie kommt es zu dieser einsicht?
>
> Metallica, sind ein SuperBand, und es bereite mir große Freude und tiefe Befriedigung beim Arbeiten am Computer mit fieser Stimme und finsterer Grimasse ihr Lieder mitzusingen.
>
> So gut gefällt mir das, dass ich eben eine hlabe Stunde auf irgend

Abbildung 10: Auszug aus *anmut und demut*, http://anmutunddemut.de/2002/03/21/_ber-sex-kann-man-nur-auf-englisch-singen.html, vom 21.03.2002.

Die Bedeutung des Zitats unterstützt die danach folgenden Auslegungen des Blogautors. Das Zitat hat aber auch eine mottoähnliche Funktion, da es eine Illustration des Diskussionsthemas darstellt. Anders als in jenen Zitaten, die oben als mottoähnlich angeführt wurden, beinhaltet dieses Zitat zudem eine Stellungnahme in der zu diskutierenden Frage, und stellt somit in erster Linie eine externe Ansicht dar.

In Diskussionen können Zitate somit sowohl die Rolle einer Einleitung als auch die einer Argumentationsstütze spielen. Folgerichtig können dieser Art von Zitaten zwei Funktionen zugeschrieben werden: Erstens illustrieren sie die aktuelle Lektüre des Autors, wobei die Diskussion daraus resultiert, dass der Autor etwas Interessantes gelesen hat und dies im Blog mitteilt. Zweitens kann das Zitat eine externe Ansicht oder eine dem Text äußerliche Perspektive vertreten, die als zusätzliche Argumente der Diskussion beigefügt werden.

Die weniger personenbezogenen Kommentare zu den Diskussionszitaten in den Tagebuchblogs weisen deutliche Parallelen zum Zitatgebrauch in anderen Internetgattungen auf, z.B. im oben genannten Filterblog. Dass das Persönliche in den Tagebuchblogs seltener aufgegriffen wird, kann somit als Folge des Einflusses von diesen Genres verstanden werden, aber auch als Schutz der Privatsphäre.

2.4 Narrative Zitate

In Papier-Tagebüchern können eingeklebte Tickets etc. in ähnlicher Weise aus dem Alltag zitieren. So zum Beispiel im Tagebuch von Monika, wo während einer Reise nach Tunesien eine Seite aus der Reisebroschüre eingefügt wird, die das Reisearrangement detailliert schildert.

Die Tatsache, dass ein Großteil der Kommunikation zwischen Mensch und Computer durch Textboxen und andere Arten von schriftlichen Mitteilungen geschieht, führt dazu, dass das narrative Zitieren im Internet ganz neue Formen annehmen kann. In den folgenden zwei Beispielen schildern die Rubriken der Blogeinträge internetbezogene Tätigkeiten der Autoren:

> » vielen dank für ihre reiseanmeldung... :| | |||||:
> so konnte das ja nun nicht ewig weitergehen. habe mich für fuerteventura entschieden, auch wenn die groessten attraktionen das *kriechende samtpfötchen* und *winters wunderblume* zu sein scheinen: dolce far niente excesivo! sonne! der schnee kann mich mal, in zwei wochen bin ich hier weg.
> mB, 25.02.04 kommentar?

Abbildung 11: Auszug aus *0000ff*, http://www.0000ff.de/weblog/index.php?mode=archive&ID=4110, vom 25.02.2004.

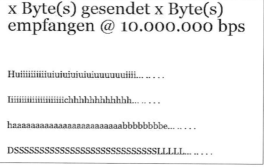

Abbildung 12: Auszug aus *anmut und demut*, http://anmutunddemut.de/2002/03/16/x-bytes-gesendet-x-bytes-empfangen-10000000-bps.html, vom 16.03.2002.

In dem Beispiel aus *0000ff* zitiert die Rubrik den letzten Schritt einer Reisebestellung im Internet, während in dem Eintragstext verkündet wird, dass der Autor bald in den Urlaub fährt. In *anmut und demut* wird aus dem Dialogfenster des Computers die Angabe der Übertragungsgeschwindigkeit zitiert, während im Eintragstext affektiert mitgeteilt wird, dass der Blogautor jetzt DSL-Internet habe. Diese Zitate illustrieren somit prägnant die Tatsache, dass der Blogautor eine Reise gebucht, bzw. den Internetanbieter gewechselt hat. Hier wird deutlich, dass die größtenteils textbasierte Kommunikation im Internet ein Zitieren von alltäglichen Routinen ermöglicht.

Abbildung 13: Auszug aus *Savoy Truffle*, http://truffle.twoday.net/stories/566552, vom 11.03.2005.

In diesem Fall ist der Grund des Zitierens eine lustige Komponente des zitierten Textes. Somit kann eine gewisse Ironisierung der zitierten Texte angedeutet werden. Allerdings funktionieren die Zitate auch als Momentaufnahmen aus dem Alltag, indem sie durch die kurze Beschreibung der Situation am Kiosk und durch die Wiedergabe des Screenshots als Bild und nicht als bloßes Textzitat den Akt des Lesens in dessen Wiedergabe miteinbeziehen.

Hier weisen traditionelle Tagebücher und Tagebuchblogs zwei ganz voneinander getrennte Zitatpraktiken auf. Das physische Sammeln von Tickets, Bildern und Briefen, das im traditionellen Tagebuch häufig anzutreffen ist, kann in dieser Form natürlich nicht im Tagebuchblog vorkommen, so wie die Praktik, computerspezifische Ereignisse anhand von Zitaten zu schildern, aus natürlichen Gründen in traditionellen Tagebüchern nicht vorkommt. Sie erinnern aneinander, indem sie nicht bloß auf ihre buchstäbliche Bedeutung, sondern auch auf die mit ihnen verknüpften Situationen verweisen, aber vor allem zeigen sie auf einen grundlegenden Unterschied zwischen den beiden Tagebuchformen: Das traditionelle Tagebuch ist ein eigenes physisches Objekt, in dem Text und manchmal auch andere Materialien gesammelt werden, während der Tagebuchblog zwar auch als eigenes Werk konzipiert wird, sich allerdings als Internettext in einem Interface befindet, das sowohl als leicht zugängliches Schreibwerkzeug als auch als Sammlung von einer Fülle an Informationen funktioniert. Dieser größere Zusammenhang des Internets wird durch die internetbezogenen Zitate in den Tagebuchblogs gespiegelt.

3. Zusammenfassung und Schlussdiskussion

Die Untersuchung der Unterschiede im Gebrauch von Zitaten in traditionellen Tagebüchern und Tagebuchblogs hat grundlegende Ähnlichkeiten zwischen den Tagebucharten ans Licht gebracht. Der Gestus, sich selbst und die Umwelt durch Zitate zu schildern, ist kein internetspezifisches Element. Die in den Tagebuchblogs häufig vorkommenden mottoähnlichen Zitate sind auch im traditionellen Tagebuch fester Bestandteil. Auch werden in den beiden Tagebucharten Zitate aus aktueller Lektüre kommentiert und diskutiert, sowie aus ‚Erlebnistexten' kopiert, mit dem Ziel Ereignisse zu schildern. Die Tagebuchformen scheinen beide auf dieselbe Tradition des Zitierens zurückzugreifen, nach welcher die Wiedergabe von beliebten Zitaten zu einer Selbstaussage wird. Dass Texte, die dem Autor interessant oder anregend erscheinen, in beiden Tagebuchformen zitiert und diskutiert werden, ist wohl auch nur eine Folge davon, dass die Texte sich breit mit den Auffassungen und Erlebnissen des Autors befassen. Dass fremde Texte häufig vorkommen, ist somit an sich kein Zeichen dafür, dass in einem Medium gearbeitet wird, in dem das Sammeln von Texten das eigene Schreiben ersetzt hat.

Allerdings wurden auch deutliche Anzeichen dafür gefunden, dass die Möglichkeiten und Voraussetzungen des Schreibens im Internet neue Zitatpraktiken ermöglicht haben. Schon die schiere Menge an Zitaten unterscheidet den Tagebuchblog vom traditionellen Tagebuch. Erstens ist im Hinblick auf die Stichprobenuntersuchung auffallend, dass in Blogs häufiger und umfangreicher zitiert wird. Zweitens ist die Verwendung von indirekten Zitaten und von Zitaten, die zum Teil des eigenen Textes gemacht werden, in den Tagebuchblogs häufiger. Die Zitate werden häufiger manipuliert und somit als eigene ästhetische Produktion appropriiert. Drittens werden Zitate in den Tagebuchblogs häufiger zu Sachdiskussionen verwendet, während sie in den traditionellen Tagebüchern häufiger mit Kommentaren persönlicher Natur verbunden werden. Viertens können im Internettagebuch mehrere Formen von Zitaten beobachtet werden, die in den traditionellen Tagebüchern nicht gefunden wurden. Dies gilt vor allem die konsumkritischen Zitate und die technikbezogenen Zitate.

Eine Erklärung von diesen Unterschieden mit Blick auf die Medien hat gezeigt, dass der Umgang mit den Zitaten in den Tagebuchblogs nicht nur an das neue Medium Internet anknüpft, sondern auch auf Traditionen von älteren Medien zurückgeht. Sowohl die literarische Tradition des Mottos als auch die Tradition des experimentellen Umgangs mit Zitaten in der Montageästhetik der Kunst und Literatur werden hier aufgegriffen. Vor allem kann das häufigere Zitieren in den Tagebuchblogs aber durch die Kopiermöglichkeiten des Internets erklärt werden. Die Praktik, im Internet gefundene Texte sofort in den eigenen Blog zu integrieren, scheint tatsächlich das Zitierverfahren maßgeblich geprägt zu haben. Sowohl denkwürdige, mottoähnliche Zitate als auch Zitate, die eine Diskussionsgrundlage bilden oder als Illustration eines Interneteinkaufs fungieren, verdanken sich der Nähe zwischen Lesen, Kopieren und Publizieren im Internet. Ein weiterer Grund könnte sein, dass der Charakter des Internets, das schließlich selbst eine Mischung von allen möglichen Inhalten und Medien aus verschiedensten Quellen ist, Einfluss auf die in Blogs anzutreffenden Ausdrucksformen hat. Das Surfen zwischen Webseiten und das Lesen und Konsumieren von beständig neuen Medieninhalten würde somit zu einem fragmentierten Schreiben führen – ein Schreiben, das teilweise aus dem Sammeln von fremden Texten besteht. Die Anlehnung an künstlerische Traditionen im Zitatgebrauch der Tagebuchblogs kann auch durch den öffentlichen Charakter des Blogs erklärt werden. Ein Text, der potenziell ein beinahe unbegrenztes Publikum erreicht, wird zwangsläufig auch an dieses Publikum angepasst werden, z.B. mittels einer Ästhetisierung. Auch können Autoren von Tagebuchblogs in höherem Ausmaß als die Autoren von traditionellen Tagebüchern die Blogs von anderen lesen und darauf Einfluss nehmen, sodass schneller spezifische Züge verbreitet werden.

In Anlehnung an die Frage aus dem Blog *abgebr.*, ob das Schreiben im Internet sich nicht grundsätzlich verändert habe, kann festgestellt werden, dass auch im Internet „im alten Sinn" geschrieben wird. In den Beispielen aus den Tagebuchblogs konnten meist neben den eingefügten, fremden Materialen eigene Texte mit deutlichen Autorenstimmen erkannt werden. Doch das Sammeln von fremden Texten scheint die Behauptung aus *abgebr.*, der Computer sei seit dem Internet keine Schreibmaschine mehr, sondern eine Satzmaschine, gewissermaßen zu bestätigen: Auch wenn eigene Texte noch geschrieben werden, ist die Praxis entstanden, das Leben und die Umwelt durch die Texte anderer zu schildern, und eigene Texte durch die Texte von anderen zu schaffen. Obwohl diese Tendenzen älter als das Internet sind, können sie im Internet in bisher unübertroffenem Ausmaß beobachtet werden.

4. Bibliographie

Blood, R. (2002), Weblogs: A History and Perspective, in the Publishers of Perseus Publishing (Hrsg.), *We've Got Blog*, New York: Perseus Publishing, pp. 7-16.

Bolter, J. D & Grusin, R (1999), *Remediation: Understanding New Media.* Cambridge: MIT Press, 1999.

Genette, G. (1993), *Palimpseste. Die Literatur auf zweiter Stufe,* Frankfurt am Main: Suhrkamp.

Herring, H.C., Scheidt, L.A. et al. (eds.) (2004), Bridging the Gap: A Genre Analysis of Weblogs, in *Proceedings of the 37th Hawai'i International Conference on System Sciences*, Los Alamitos: IEEE Computer Society Press; Onlinedokument http://csdl.computer.org/comp/proceedings/hicss/2004/2056/04/205640101b.pdf [09.05.2013].

Jenkins, H. (2006), *Convergence Culture: Where Old and New Media Collide*, New York: New York University Press.

Landow, G. P. (2006), *Hypertext 3.0: critical theory and new media in an era of globalization*, Baltimore: Johns Hopkins University Press.

McLeod, K. & Kuenzli, R. (2011), *Cutting across Media: Appropriation Art, Interventionist Collage, and Copyright Law*, Durham: Duke University Press.

McNeill, L. (2004), *Public designs for a private genre: community and identity in the diary*, British Columbia: The University of British Columbia.

McNeill, L. (2009), Brave New Genre, or Generic Colonialism? Debates over Ancestry in Internet Diaries, in Giltrow, J. & Stein, D. (Hrsg.), *Genres in the Internet: Issues in the Theory of Genre*, Amsterdam: John Benjamins Publishing Company, pp. 143-162.

Mommsen, K. (1983), Das fiktionale Ich: Untersuchungen zum Tagebuch by Manfred Jurgensen (Rezension), *Comparative Literature Studies* 20 (3), pp. 350–352.

Swirski, Peter (2013), Literature and culture in the age of the new media, in Hartley, J. & Burgess, J. (Hrsg.), *A companion to new media dynamics*, Chichester: Wiley, pp. 73-89.

Walker Rettberg, J. (2009), *Blogging*, Cambridge: Polity Press.

Internetquellen

Blog history project: http://www.metaroll.de/bloghistory.html [Zuletzt aufgerufen am 09.05.2013.]

Blogkorpus [3]

24:h: http://web.archive.bibalex.org/web/20010224083233/http://www.superspace.de/

000ff: http://web.archive.org/web/20011004215439/http://www.0000ff.de/weblog/

*a*log*: http://web.archive.org/web/20010218012730/http://www.a-log.de/

abgebr.: http://abgebr.antville.org/stories/432538/

adventures beyond the ultraworld: http://www.netzkasten.de/texteratur/weblog_joh/adventures.php3?dat=4

Alles Alltäglich: http://www.seelenfarben.de/taeglich20031201.php

anmut und demut: http://anmutunddemut.de/2001/09/10/tilde.html

---

[3] Sämtliche hier aufgelistete Webseiten sind am 24.02.2013 zuletzt aufgerufen.

ariana mania: http://www.arianamania.de/2005/11/

b_log: http://web.archive.org/web/20010405045911/http://www.dadasign.at/blog/blog.htm

Claudia Klinger: http://www.claudia-klinger.de/digidiary/diary10.htm#03_01

Das hermetische Café: http://kid37.blogger.de/?day=20031224

Das Netzbuch: http://www.das-netzbuch.de/article/?pg=2069

Denn sie wissen nicht, was sie tun sollen: http://rebellmarkt.blogger.de/?day=20050126

Der Zirbel: http://www.x-7.de/zirbel/archiv/2002/jun/02-06-07.html

Elfengleich: http://www.elfengleich.de/index.php?start=440

Fashion victims paradise: http://eleg.antville.org/archive/2005/01/20/

feelsophee: http://www.feelosophee.com/default.asp?myMonth=11&myYear=2000

fireball: http://www.joeladami.de.vu/

gesternwarnichtheute: http://web.archive.org/web/20010331151021/http://gesternwarnichtheute.editthispage.com/

haboglabobloggin': https://blog.p3k.org/archive/page305

henso: http://www.henso.com/?idx=0

hinterding: http://web.archive.org/web/20010405201906/http://www.hinterding.com/archiv/2001_04_01_archiv.html

hirngespinste: http://web.archive.org/web/20021122125603/http://hirngespinste.de/

Ilona's: http://web.archive.org/web/20000902051646/http://www.ilona.purespace.de/t_buch/fr_start.htm

is a blog: http://xrays.antville.org/archive/2005/02/28/

Jasmin: http://web.archive.org/liveweb/http://www.respect.de/0200/jasmin01.html

LittleJamie: http://littlejamie.blogspot.se/

loopkid: http://loopkid.net/articles/page/400

malorama: http://www.malorama.de/2005_01_01_archiv.php3

Mawaasesned: http://doerflernet.blogg.de/2004/05/

Melle's: http://web.archive.org/web/20010517012401/http://home.t-online.de/home/melle_teich/archiv/index.htm

melody: http://www.moving-target.de/index.php/blog/2005/10/

my two cents: http://web.archive.org/web/20030119112742/http://www.my-two-cents.de/tagebuch/2002/q2/2002-06a.html

Netz-Kasten: http://www.netz-kasten.de/texteratur/weblog_hen/weblog_hen.php3?dat=4

new joerg times: http://joerg.antville.org/archive/page1643

nö...schön!: http://web.archive.org/web/20030518213332/http://www.noe-schoen.de/2002_10_27_archiv.php3

Reisenotizen aus der Realität: http://web.archive.bibalex.org/web/20010413231547/webuser.rhein-main.net/andrea.alex/reisenotmai.htm

Robert Braun: http://web.archive.org/web/20011012123401/http://members.aol.com/minusmann/2000.html

partykeller: http://web.archive.org/web/200012041555/http://partykeller.editthispage.com/

plastic thinking: http://plasticthinking.org/archives/week_2003_01_05.html

rietdorf: http://web.archive.org/web/20010302070844/http://rietdorf.editthispage.com/2000/12/31

savoy truffle: http://truffle.twoday.net/?day=20041216

schockwellenreiter: http://www.schockwellenreiter.de/2005/04/24.html

Schtief's: http://schteif.blogspot.de/search?updated-min=2001-01-01T00:00:00%2B01:00&updated-max=2002-01-01T00:00:00%2B01:00&max-results=18

sing blue silver: http://web.archive.org/web/20010309093907/http://singbluesilver.manilasites.com/

stefanu: http://stefanu.blogspot.de/2002_04_01_archive.html

tacheles: http://www.wired-becker.de/tacheles/

tempalog: http://web.archive.org/web/20020627095403/http://tempa.antville.org/20020621/

tristessedeluxe: http://tristessedeluxe.blogger.de/20031014/

who:log: http://web.archive.org/web/200102041315/http://www.wholog.de/index.shtml

wolkenreich: http://web.archive.org/liveweb/http://www.wolkenreich.de/mai_20_00.htm

{wom{log}: http://web.archive.org/web/20010330194504/http://www.webobserver.de/weblog/index.html

STOCKHOLM STUDIES IN MODERN PHILOLOGY. NEW SERIES

Studier i modern språkvetenskap. Utgivna i samverkan med Nyfilologiska sällskapet i Stockholm. Ny serie.

Vol. 1. 1960. Pp. 170.

Contents:
Walter A. Berendsohn. Schillers „Wilhelm Tell" als Kunstwerk.
Sven L. Fristedt. The Dating of the Earliest Manuscript of the Wycliffe Bible.
Tore Jungnell. Notes on the Language of Ben Jonson.
Bertil Maler. Un vieux terme de jeu espagnol.
Alarik Rynell. On Middle English *take(n)* as an Inchoative Verb.
Rut Tarselius. You Dance a Treat.
Olof von Feilitzen. Bibliography of Swedish Works on Romance, English and German Philology, 1956-58.

Vol. 2. 1964. Pp. 195.

Contents:
Åke Grafström. Un Suédois traverse la France au XVIIIe siècle.
Walter A. Berendsohn. Thomas Manns „Bekenntnisse des Hochstaplers Felix Krull".
Sven L. Fristedt. A Weird Manuscript Enigma in the British Museum.
Stanley Gerson. The New Sporting Magazine and the O.E.D.
Alarik Rynell. On Alleged Constructions like *did wrote*.
Bertil Sandahl. Brisket.
Rut Tarselius. Varved Clay.
Olof von Feilitzen. Bibliography of Swedish Works on Romance, English and German Philology, 1959-62.

Vol. 3. 1968. Pp. 279.

Contents:
Bror Danielsson. The Percy Poem on Falconry.
Sven L. Fristedt. New Light on John Wycliffe and the First Full English Bible.
Lars-Gunnar Hallander. Two Old English Confessional Prayers.
Sven Jacobson. Transformational Grammar and Linguistic Intuition.
Ingeborg Brunkhorst. Alexander Lernet-Holenias Roman „Die Standarte".
Els Oksaar. Zu den Genusmorphemen bei Nomina Agentis.

Fernand Lechanteur. Quelques traits essentiels des parlers de la Basse-Normandie.
Sture von Scheven. La conjunción temporal *tan pronto*.
Olof von Feilitzen. Bibliography of Swedish Works on Romance, English and German Philology, 1963-65.

Vol. 4. 1972. Pp. 329.

Contents:
Erik Wellander. Arvid Gabrielson 18-9-1879-4-9-1972.
Gunnar Tilander. Gruppkort av medlemmar i Nyfilologiska sällskapet i Stockholm.
Bror Danielsson. The Durham Treatise of Falconry.
Sven L. Fristedt. A Note on Some Obscurities in the History of the Lollard Bible.
Sven Jacobson. On the Derivational History of Relative Clauses in English Transformational Grammar.
Inger Ruin. Tense-Determinating Factors in English.
Bo Ullman. Der unpolitische Georg Büchner.
Werner Koller. Probleme, Problematik und Theorie des Übersetzens.
Eva Lüders. Der Vorderspiegel der Handschrift G der St. Georgener Predigten.
Åke Grafström. Mots français attestés dans le journal de voyage de Bengt Gerner.
Gustaf Holmér. Quelques réflexions sur les traductions françaises d'oeuvres latines au Moyen Âge.
Alf Lombard. Les pronoms personnels du roumain. Aperçu syntaxique.
Bertil Maler. L'infinitif gérondival portugais : quelques notes sur sa propagation.
Marianne Sandels. Bibliography of Swedish Works on Romance, English and German Philology, 1966-70.

Vol. 5. 1975. Pp. 230.

Contents:
Sven L. Fristedt. Spanish Influence on Lollard Translation. Amplification of *The Wycliffe Bible. Part III*.
Bror Danielsson. William Pelham, an Early Nineteenth Century American Phonetician.
Inger Ruin. On the Semantics of Tense in English.
Helmut Müssener. „Über ein Bündnis zwischen Bild und Gedicht". Bertolt Brecht und Hans Tombrock im Schwedischen Exil.
Hans Bäckvall. La prononciation du premier maître de langue française à l'université d'Upsala.

Karl Johan Danell. La crise de la linguistique et un problème de syntaxe française. À propos d'un article de N. Ruwet.
Gustaf Holmér. Le Dit du faucon. Poème allégorique du XIIIe siècle.
Bertil Maler. À propos de quelques formulaires médiévaux du « sacramentum more judaico ».
Eva Martins. On Interference. Some social and psychological aspects.
Folke Sandgren. Bibliography of Swedish Works on Romance, English and German Philology, 1971-74.

Vol. 6. 1980. Pp. 140.

Contents:
Alarik Rynell. On *take to drink* and? *take to drinking* and Similar Constructions.
Gunnel Engwall. « Le Plaidoyer d'un fou », un plaidoyer de Strindberg ou de Loiseau?
Folke Freund. Soziale Konventionen und die phatische Funktion der Sprache. Bemerkungen zu einigen Kommunikationsbarrieren von Schweden in Deutschland.
Birgit Stolt. Die Rhetorik als Maßstab deutscher Dichter von Gottfried bis Goethe.
Carola Bark, Cecilia Berg, Lars Frendel. Bibliography of Swedish Works on Romance, English and German Philology, 1975-78.

Vol. 7. 1984. Pp. 214.

Contents:
Lars-Gunnar Hallander. Bertil Maler 25/12 1910-15/4 1980.
Hans Bäckvall. Documents inédits français conservés dans un château suédois.
Åke Grafström. La langue du comte Robert Joseph de la Cerda de Villelongue, correspondant de Voltaire.
Nils-Lennart Johannesson. A Mirror of the Soul — On the Indexical Function of Gollum's Speech.
Magnus Ljung. Swearing.
Brigitte Kusche. Aristoteles und das Frauenbild — wen hat es eigentlich beeinflußt? Die Frau in den mittelniederländischen Handschriften aus dem 15. Jahrhundert.
Conrad Lindberg. Who wrote Wiclif's Bible?
Barbro Nilsson. Third Person Subjects in Polish. Studies in Their Communicative and Cohesive Functions.
Hans Ruge. Was ist neu am Neugriechischen?
Alarik Rynell. On hardly/scarely...than and no sooner...when and on neither...or.

Vol. 8. 1987. Pp. 175.

Contents:
Claes-Christian Elert. Linguistics at the University of Stockholm until 1967.
Ingemar Olsson. Om studiet av schizofrenas språk.
Sverker Brorström. Adverbial Intensifiers in Swift's *Journal to Stella*.
Sven Jacobson. Is *Am I happy*? an exclamatory question?
Nils-Lennart Johannesson. Topic Marker Selection in Late Middle English.
Gillis Kristensson. English dialectal *toll* 'chump of trees' and cognates.
Gunnel Melchers. *Is du heard aboot yun afore*? On the use of be as a perfective auxiliary in Shetland dialect.
Mats Rydén. English Names for *Convallaria Majalis L.*
Alarik Rynell. On the Syntax of *to will*.
Gustav Korlén. Bemerkungen zum deutschen Einfluß auf den schwedischen Wortschatz der Nachkriegszeit.
Astrid Stedje. Warum nur im Germanischen? Altes und Neues zum Ablaut der starken Verben.
Gustaf Holmér. Remarques sur deux traductions médiévales.
Barbro Nilsson. Syntaktisk organisation av texter från Šiškov, Radiščev och Karamzin.
Anders Sjöberg. Old Church Slavonic and Old English Translation Techniques.
Seung-bog Cho. On the Ancient Japanese word *uzike*.
Eva Martins. The Plight of the Multilingual.

Vol. 9. 1990. Pp. 239.

Contents:
Sverker Brorström. English through the Looking-Glass of a Philologist.
Nils-Lennart Johannesson. Consistency and Change in Old English Subject Topicalization.
Gunnel Melchers. A Knitting Language Pattern.
Bo Andersson. Eric Hermelin als Böhmeübersetzer.
Göran Inghult. Zu den Verben mit einem Erstglied im Deutschen und Schwedischen.
Hans Bäckvall. L'antériorité du passé en français écrit actuel.
Gunnel Engwall. Strindberg, auteur français, traduit en suédois. Le cas du «Plaidoyer d'un fou» et d'«Inferno».
Kerstin Jonasson. Sur le double statut mondain et métalinguistique du nom propre.
Lars Fant. Iniciativa, respuesta y turno de intervenciones en negociaciones españolas y escandinavas.
Monica Vessberg. La leggenda di Santa Margherita di Antiochia in un processo di magia nella Napoli del tardo '500. Un primo tentativo di edizione.

Barbro Nilsson. Verbalabstrakter som subjekt till pro-verb i ryskan.
Helge Rinholm. Om *om(-)* et forsøk på semantisk integrering.
Lars Steensland. Är älvdalskan ett språk eller en dialekt — och vad spelar det för roll?
Erling Wande. Tänker finnar annorlunda än svenskar?

Vol. 10. 1993. Pp. 228.

Contents:
Gunnel Melchers. Lars-Gunnar Hallander 1/5 1919-6/8 1993.
Bo Andersson. Bildungssoziale Aspekte der rhetorischen *dispositio*. Valentin Weigle und Jacob Böhme.
Brita Bergman. Teckenspråket — ett svenskt minoritetsspråk.
Birgitta Englund Dimitrova. Metoder i empirisk forskning om översättning och tolkning.
Gunnel Engwall. Bland franska förord. Några nya aspekter på Strindbergs *En dåres försvarstal*.
Britt Erman & Ulla-Britt Kotsinas. Pragmaticalization: the case of *ba'* and *you know*.
Johan Falk. Particularidades sintácticas y semánticas de los predicados emotivos en español.
Lars Fant. "Pull" and "Push" moves in Spanish and Swedish negotiation talk.
Kerstin Jonasson. Le nom propre en fonction d'attribut.
Gunnar Magnusson. Das humoristische Adjektiv.
Gunnel Melchers. "In the hope that you will consider me for the position". On writing letters of application for an academic post. I: Introduction; beginnings: endings.
Barbro Nilsson. Verb eller substantiv? Om verbalabstrakter i ryska.

Vol. 11. 1997. Pp. 255.

Contents :
Nyfilologiska sällskapet 100 år. *Från Operakällaren till Nedre Manilla* (Gunnar Magnusson).
Inge Bartning. *C'est* — in Native and Non-native Spoken French.
Birgitta Englund Dimitrova. Translation and Dialect in Fictional Prose — Vilhelm Moberg in Russian and English as a Case in Point.
Göran Inghult. Anglicisms in German and Swedish: Principles for the Choice of Transfer Type.
Kerstin Jonasson. Norm and Variation in Translating from French into Swedish.
Ulla-Britt Kotsinas. Young People's Language. Norm, Variation and Language Change.

Magnus Ljung. The English of British Tabloids and Heavies: Differences and Similarities.

Gunnar Magnusson & Bettina Jobin. Gender and Sex in German and Swedish.

Gunnel Melchers. How do 'Smoothers' Pronounce *Zebra*? A Study of Phonetic vs. Phonemic Variation and Change.

Barbro Nilsson. Language and Social Change: The Example of Russian.

Jane Nystedt: Norm and Variation in the Lexical Structure of Italian Medical Language. Illustrations from two Centuries.

Mats Rydén. Towards a Standardization of the Official Swedish Plant Nomenclature in the 20th Century: the Names of Orchids.

Beatrice Warren. Lexicalization and Relexicalization.

Vol. 12. 2000. Pp. 163.

Contents:
Introduction (Gunnar Magnusson).

Per Ambrosiani. On the Translation of English forms of address into Russian.

Bo Andersson. Beobachtungen zur Großschreibung in deutschen und schwedischen Versen des 17. Jahrhunderts: Andreas Gryphius — Skogekär Bergbo — Lars Johansson (Lucidor).

Diana Bravo. Aspectos contrastivos en conversación: la comunicación no verbal.

Håkan Edgren. Fogning av bisatser i ryskan och svenskan.

Björn Hammarberg. A Polyfunctional Word in Native Usage and L2 Acquisition: the Swedish Neutral Pronoun "det".

Bettina Jobin & Gunnar Magnusson. "Urwüchsige leistungen der einbildungskraft"? Zur Erscheinung Genus in der älteren deutschen und schwedischen Forschung.

Barbro Nilsson. Människa — man — kvinna. Om klasser, individer och instanser.

Gabriella Rundblad. Regularity and Regular Irregularity.

Vol. 13. 2004. Pp. 156.

Contents:
Camilla Bardel. Il progetto InterIta. L'apprendimento dell'italiano L2 in un contesto svedese.

Britt Erman. Phraseological build-up in the writings of deaf and hearing first term students of English.

Johan Falk. "La felicidad se trivializa". Estudio sobre el uso de *estar feliz* basado en las Bases de datos CREA y CORDE.

Fanny Forsberg. Les séquences préfabriquées en français L1 et L2.

Victorine Hancock. L'emploi de *donc* chez des apprenants avancés : intono-syntaxe et fonctionnements dans la chaîne parlée.
Gunnel Melchers. "It's a dog skälling" — Some aspects of young Swedish learners' spoken English.
Philip Shaw. Rhetorical development in Swedish university students' written English: A longitudinal study.

Vol. 14. 2007. Pp. 149.

Contents:
Introduction (Camilla Bardel & Britt Erman).
Tora Hedin. Gender and language in Czech talk shows.
Per Förnegård. « Si prinst corage de homme »: l'expression du féminin dans le *Miroir historial* de Jean de Noyal.
Andreas Nord. "Ett paradis för dig själv och din maka". Kön och trädgård i skrifter för allmogen kring 1900.
Catherine Sandbach-Dahlström. Feminist polemic and Bakhtinian utterance in Virginia Woolf's *Three Guineas*.
Anna Uddén. No trivial matter — Gendered aesthetics in eighteenth-century reviews.
Bettina Jobin. Kongruenz durch Derivation oder die Sprache als Vermittlerin von Sexunterscheidungen.
Eva Lindström. Un trait tardif dans l'acquisition d'une L2 — l'accord en genre.

Vol. 15. 2010. Pp. 251.

Contents:
Introduction (Anders Bengtsson & Victorine Hancock).
Christina Alm-Arvius. Heading for Witty Poeticity: Wordplay in headlines in *The Times Literary Supplement*.
Per Ambrosiani. A Russian Tail? On the Translation of Puns in Lewis Carroll's *Alice's Adventures in Wonderland*
Anders Bengtsson. La polynomie dans le ms. Queen's College 305 (Oxford). Un cas d'humour involontaire.
Axel Fritz. Nonsenspoesie in der deutschsprachigen Literatur.
Tora Hedin & Ludmila Pöppel. Vad skrattar ni åt? Tjeckiska och ryska politiska anekdoter.
Hans-Roland Johnsson. The comic art of derision.
Vincenzo Maggitti. The Stones of Turin. Humour in *La donna della domenica* by Carlo Fruttero and Franco Lucentini.
Gunnar Magnusson. German in an English fun-house mirror.
Anu Muhonen. "Mike Tyson syö korvia": två eller flera språk som markörer för humor.

Françoise Sullet-Nylander. Humour satirique et jeux de mots dans les gros titres du *Canard enchaîné* (2009)

Vol. 16. 2013. Pp. 189.

Contents:
Introduction (Laura Álvarez López, Charlotta Seiler Brylla & Philip Shaw).
Susanne Tienken. *Sharing.* Zum Teilen von Erzählungen in Onlineforen.
Robert Östling & Mats Wirén. Compounding in a Swedish Blog Corpus.
Per Förnegård & Françoise Sullet-Nylander. De l'influence de la langue parlée dans les forums Internet: aspects linguistiques et variation diastratique.
Philip Shaw. Spelling and identity in Scottish internet discourse.
Johanna Salomonsson. Imagearbeit mit missverstehen in Diskussionsforen.
Una Cunningham. The role of blogs and forums in the linguistic expectations of pilgrims on the Camino to Santiago.
Sara Eriksson. Zitate in Blogs und Tagebüchern – ein Vergleich.

Böcker kan beställas direkt från distributören:

Stockholms universitetsbibliotek
106 91 Stockholm
Telefon: 08-162800
E-mail: acta@sub.su.se
www.sub.su.se

Orders for single volumes can be addressed direclty to the distributor:

Stockholm University Library
SE- 10691 Stockholm
106 91 Stockholm
E-mail: acta@sub.su.se
www.sub.su.se

ACTA UNIVERSITATIS STOCKHOLMIENSIS

Corpus Troporum
Romanica Stockholmiensia
Stockholm Cinema Studies
Stockholm Economic Studies. Pamphlet Series
Stockholm Fashion Studies
Stockholm Oriental Studies
Stockholm Slavic Studies
Stockholm Studies in Baltic Languages
Stockholm Studies in Classical Archaeology
Stockholm Studies in Comparative Religion
Stockholm Studies in Economic History
Stockholm Studies in Educational Psychology
Stockholm Studies in English
Stockholm Studies in Ethnology
Stockholm Studies in Film History
Stockholm Studies in History
Stockholm Studies in History of Art
Stockholm Studies in History of Literature
Stockholm Studies in Human Geography
Stockholm Studies in Linguistics
Stockholm Studies in Modern Philology. N.S.
Stockholm Studies in Musicology
Stockholm Studies in Philosophy
Stockholm Studies in Psychology
Stockholm Studies in Russian Literature
Stockholm Studies in Scandinavian Philology. N.S.
Stockholm Studies in Social Anthropology N.S.
Stockholm Studies in Sociology. N.S.
Stockholm Studies in Statistics
Stockholm Studies in the History of Ideas
Stockholm Theatre Studies
Stockholmer Germanistische Forschungen
Studia Baltica Stockholmiensia
Studia Fennica Stockholmiensia
Studia Graeca Stockholmiensia. Series Graeca
Studia Graeca Stockholmiensia. Series Neohellenica
Studia Juridica Stockholmiensia
Studia Latina Stockholmiensia
Studies in North-European Archaeology

Printed in Sweden 2013, www.us-ab.com